NOW WHAT?

THE VOTERS HAVE SPOKEN

Essays on Life After Trump

NOW WHAT?

THE VOTERS HAVE SPOKEN

Essays on Life After Trump

EDITED BY STEVE KETTMANN
WELLSTONE BOOKS

WELLSTONE CENTER
in the Redwoods

SOQUEL, CA

STEVE KETTMANN is the co-founder,
with Sarah Ringler, of the Wellstone Center in the
Redwoods (www.wellstoneredwoods.org)—a Northern
California writers retreat center—and publisher of
Wellstone Books. A former staff reporter for *New York
Newsday* and the *San Francisco Chronicle*, as well as
Berlin correspondent for Wired.com and columnist for
the *Berliner Zeitung*, he has reported from more than
40 countries for publications including *The New York
Times*, the *Washington Monthly*, *The New Republic*,
NewYorker.com, Salon.com, *GQ* and *Parade Magazine*.
He conceived and edited *Game Time*, a collection of
New Yorker baseball writing by Roger Angell; authored
One Day at Fenway and *Baseball Maverick*; and has
co-authored more than 12 books, including six *New
York Times* bestsellers. He still hopes to run the Berlin
Marathon one more time, all the better to try to keep
up with his two young daughters, Coco and Anaïs.

INTRODUCTION

BY STEVE KETTMANN

It was one of many times that week when I thought the networks might call the 2020 election for Biden-Harris any minute and I didn't want to miss a thing. I'd carried the girls' little blonde-wood table and chairs into my work room, computer in the background tuned to election coverage as we sat down to dinner. We don't have a TV. For most of their lives, Coco and Anaïs had never seen us watching cable news on a computer. October 20 had been the first exception. Coco, six, came in at one point during the first Biden-Trump debate and sat on the sofa next to my computer. She gave the screen a few minutes of blank-faced scrutiny, more confused the longer she watched, then her face collapsed into a scowl. "I don't like this!" she wailed. "Why are they so *mad*?" I lay in bed with her that night for an hour before she had fully calmed down and could sleep. Now, two days after the election, the girls and I were discussing food preference. Or were we?

"I hate parsnip!" Coco, never halfway on anything, insisted.

Our conversation took a few twists and turns from there. Soon she was asking, "What is 'hate,' Daddy?"

It was a rhetorical question. Or a philosophical one. Coco knew what the word meant. She wanted to hear me expand on the idea, which I did, giving her a somewhat sanitized answer about hate meaning really not liking something a lot. A light went on in her eyes.

"Do you hate Trump?" she asked me suddenly.

I stared back at her. *Did* I hate Donald Trump? I had to give my daughter an honest answer.

"No, Coco," I said. "I don't hate Trump."

At times, yes, I wondered. I hated, really hated, so much of what

I

he said and did since he came down that escalator at Trump Tower. I once stood near Donald Trump on a short elevator ride at old Yankee Stadium in the late 1990s and saw him then, as I see him now, as a shell of bluster and bluff with sharp enough edges to try to prevent you from looking within to the hollow, pain-filled center. I don't hate the man. But I hate that his con, running for president as a publicity stunt, led to four of the worst years in the history of our country. I hate what his utter cynicism and naked racism did to bring out the worst in so many. I hate how his manipulation, shamelessness and craven bad faith challenged us to be better and do better, and so often, these terrible four years, we collectively came up short. As John Lewis once told me, removing Trump from office will be a "down payment" on our future, not more. Will Rayman, a 23-year-old who regrets not having voted for Hillary Clinton in 2016, writes from Estonia, where he's a professional basketball player: "The Biden-Harris victory is a step in the right direction, but in no way is it the end-all-be-all."

I think each of us has to look within and challenge ourselves to do better, be better, if we are truly going to move forward and find ways to connect with other Americans who might disagree on much but can agree on our common humanity. I hope the perspectives that follow can help kick-start that reckoning, a reckoning not only with the depths of depravity and corruption the Trump years unleashed and exposed, but also a reckoning with ourselves.

Leave it to Dave Chappelle, delivering a "Saturday Night Live" monologue the day the networks finally called it for Biden-Harris, to put the raw truth of the moment into perspective. "I would implore everybody who's celebrating today to remember it's good to be a humble winner," Chappelle said in closing. "Remember when I was here four years ago? Remember how bad that felt? Remember that half the country right now still feels that way." Then Chappelle showed his empathy for those Trump voters, talking about the life expectancy of white people actually declining, for the first time. He talked about heroin and suicide. "All these white people out there that feel that anguish, that pain, they're mad, 'cause they think nobody cares. And maybe they don't. Let me tell you something. I know how that feels," he continued. "But here's the difference between me and you. You guys hate each other for that. And I don't hate anybody. I just hate that feeling."

Among the most important things Joe Biden said during the campaign was to declare early on that he sees himself as a bridge, "nothing else"—a bridge to a new generation of leaders, a bridge to the future. The words were not the sort of clickbait incitement to light up social media, but they had the ring of truth. Eight months later, we could finally start to live out the reality of those words, with Senator Kamala Harris of California—*my* Senator—poised to be sworn in soon as vice president, and young people inspired to turn out and vote in record-setting numbers.

On the Friday morning after the election, Coco stirred early and came into my work room, where I'd been in the chair since 5 a.m. I had a lot of work to do, reaching out to people about this collection, but I welcomed her into my lap. She was happy, there in the chair with Dad. A few moments later came the news: Biden had moved into a lead against Trump in Pennsylvania. Our long, national nightmare was almost over. I smiled, and Coco smiled with me. It was a moment I'll never forget, and one I'll never stop working to honor, hoping that with imagination and courage and care, we can learn from the many mistakes of recent years and play our part, with Joe, in being a bridge to the future.

This collection started as an idea of my wife, Sarah Ringler, co-director of the small writers retreat center we run in Northern California. She suggested we put out a collection of essays through our Wellstone Books imprint on life in the pandemic, personal essays capturing what one typical day was like. Great idea. I wish we could have done it. Instead, we're publishing this quick-turnaround attempt to capture this unforgettable juncture, the week the American people voted out Donald Trump. Our working title going in was *The Morning After*, echoing a song some of you will remember from long ago, and many of the essays explore that feeling of arriving, finally, at the morning after, even if it was clear even then that the transition through to January was going to be weird and dangerous.

The essays convey how so many of us felt as the end of the Trump presidency neared, what we thought, what we saw and what we did. The hope is that in putting out these glimpses so quickly, giving them an immediacy unusual in book publishing, we can help in the mourning for all that has been lost, help in the healing (of ourselves and of our country), and help in the pained effort, like moving limbs that have gone numb from inactivity, to give new life to our democracy. We stared into the abyss, tottered on the edge, and a record-setting surge of voting and activism delivered us from the very real threat of plunging into autocracy. We have to celebrate that deliverance and remember it, like Luke blowing up the Death Star. We also have to keep searching for answers.

As Sophia Lear, a TV writer in L.A., puts it in her essay: "For one moment it smacked me in the face—I know nothing. I know nothing of what is happening in this country. Everything I thought I knew fell away—and I was left humbled and curious. We have to go in. There is something big we don't understand. And we need to go in. The liberal mistake is the certainty our story is true—that the others will come to see our story as theirs, too, and the rest are just beyond salvation. There is another story. I don't know what it is. I do not know where we go from here, because I have no idea where 'here' is. And that, perhaps, is a place to start."

I want to thank our amazing lineup of contributors for jumping at the chance to be included. I'm astonished and deeply encouraged by their leap of faith in agreeing to write about a week filled with so much uncertainty, let alone for a small regional publisher, and I'm in awe of the pain and beauty and truth that come through in their words. When my old friend Mark Ulriksen, a colleague going back to our days at *San Francisco Focus* magazine in the late 1980s, writes in his essay of his wife, Leslie, and him hearing the news—"Can you feel our exhale of relief? It feels hurricane strength" —he's speaking for so many of us. In Mark's case, he's also a brilliant artist whose *New Yorker* covers I usually want to frame and put on my wall. That's his stunning cover art. He cites David Remnick's observation that the objective of a *New Yorker* cover is to go just too far. That might be a good description of some of our essays as well.

Angela Wright Shannon writes of her absolute certainty that a woman as strong, as proud, as Black as Kamala Harris would never be elected vice president. "No way in hell she was going to be allowed within striking distance of the White House," she writes. "So at midday on Saturday, November 7, 2020, when major news networks began projecting the Biden-Harris ticket a winner, I cried those warm slow tears that start somewhere deep inside, tears that reside in a dream deferred."

I texted *Sacramento Bee* columnist Marcos Bretón that I was getting a little emotional reading the first few lines of his essay, just after he sent it—then read on and had tears streaming down my cheeks. "When

I had to break the news to my daughters the morning after Trump's unbelievable Electoral College win in 2016, I faced the hardest moment I had ever encountered as a father," Marcos writes. "'Daddy, you said he wouldn't win,' they said. 'Well, clearly daddy was wrong,' I replied."

I've written about three different Christopher Buckley novels for the *San Francisco Chronicle* over the years, and love his work. I'd waited—please, Christopher!—for a Buckley novel skewering the Trump presidency, and started devouring *Make Russia Great Again* the day in June 2020 it was delivered downstairs and Coco brought it to me with a big smile. I laugh just thinking about the book. The Buckley essay included here, forceful as much as funny, hits like smelling salts, a bold and brilliant salvo. He compares Trump and Hitler by the second sentence and is only getting started.

"Face it, folks (as Mr. Trump would say), we now live in an America where peaceful protestors in Lafayette Square, the nation's front yard, are gassed and shot with rubber bullets *by military police* to clear the caudillo's way for a farcical presidential photo op," Christopher writes. "The Republican Senate, with one exception, has become a sty of ovine, lickspittle quislings, degenerate descendants of such giants as Everett Dirksen, Barry Goldwater, Howard Baker and John McCain."

One of the tragedies of the Trump years was the sense almost of a mute button having been hit, or of a cacophony that drowned out the possibility of writers with distinctive voices rising to the moment. We needed a Hunter S. Thompson, who could have carved up a bland-faced bloated fanatic like Bill Barr with the painstaking thoroughness of Hannibal Lecter, his slashing wit amplified tenfold by the bold tendrils of Ralph Steadman's caricature. Call me a nut, but I really think if we'd had Molly Ivins tossing off her one-liners, full of Texas zing and political canniness, we'd have helped many Americans see through the Trump con much earlier. Or Murray Kempton, oh how we needed a Murray Kempton, the Pulitzer-Prize-winning columnist, who sat one cubicle over from me at *New York Newsday* for a few weeks in 1986, a man with a penetrating eye, an anguished-over moral imagination, and the prose to render indelibly the truths that for most of us exist at best in the amorphous fog of half-thought. Now, Election Day behind us, the cosmic static forever frying our circuits blessedly beginning to relent, writers are again finding the power in their voices. Again and again, reading the essays, I was struck at the sense of energy and power welling up, T-minus zero to ignition. Keith Olbermann's rocket ride of an essay, both brilliant and important, jumps out.

I also want to thank John Lewis. I understand it can feel easy to cite John Lewis as an inspiration. The urgency of virulent racism in this country, a festering and inflamed open sore, leaves little room for talk of progress or inspiration. The vision of Lewis and Dr. King, a vision of arriving one day at the Beloved Country, surely strikes some as a fairy tale. I choose to believe in Lewis and his vision nonetheless. I choose to believe in his strength of spirit, and his relentless optimism. I visited him in his office in March 2019 to talk about the heartbreak of Charlottesville, the weekend in August 2017 when President Trump came out as a full-fledged racist, and KKK leader David Duke applauded, the time of "very fine people on both sides."

I'll never forget what it felt like to have John Lewis turn to face me, and focus his attention—really, I now see, his *love*—fully on me. The biggest single challenge we face as a people cannot be boiled down into a policy point, it's this: To rediscover how to listen to each other, maybe not with the spiritual transcendence of a John Lewis, a man of faith and exceptional strength, but like we mean it. The biggest lie of the Trump years was not among the thousands of falsehoods spoken by the man himself, and his enablers, it was the obvious fantasy presented throughout the Trump presidency by major media outlets that Trump was a man acting in good faith. He was not. He was a pathological con man whose words were thrown out for effect. In consistently presenting those words—in repeatedly autocorrecting gibberish into more coherent thoughts—the combined effect was to turn actual good faith into a fool's mission. The work that looms before us now will come in listening to each other and in saying, at long last: Enough with parading all this bullshit around, dressed up as the truth, when of course we know better.

Even baseball has been dealing with a crisis of legitimacy as the human, spontaneous side of the sport has been squeezed out. The problem is not the efficacy of analytics, which is evident and obvious, the problem is arrogance and heartlessness—and an utter lack of curiosity and humility that have run rampant. The month before Joe Biden was elected president, running as the man with empathy, Houston Astros Manager Dusty Baker went out to the pitching mound during the American League Championship Series, ready to follow the script the front office had created for the game, and tell starting pitcher Zack Greinke he was headed for the showers. Instead, Baker pulled the ultimate old-school move: He looked into Greinke's eyes, took his measure of the man, and trusted his gut. He trusted in the common humanity that told Baker Greinke could get the job done, script be damned—and the move worked brilliantly. When it comes to how to tap into our common humanity to bridge what Angela Wright Shannon calls an "abyss" dividing the country, Baker tells us in his essay: "I don't know how we get people talking to each other. ... I honestly don't know if it's possible to step back from the brink."

We need more looking into each other's eyes with enough alertness and openness to see something there, not just a projection of our own big-brain certitudes. Joe Biden is a far more interesting figure than Donald Trump on every level, a man who has endured loss and pain and grown. The campaign was not that complicated: Joe Biden was running as himself, a man of genuine conviction, who cares about other people and wants to use government to make a difference. Donald Trump was performing, playing a part, doing a routine, part standup, part reality-TV losing-it-in-front-of-our-eyes spectacle, part tough-guy wannabe dictator. As Terry McAuliffe writes in his contribution to this collection, "For years he was a big Democratic donor." What changed? Trump, as he told many people, thought Republican voters were the easier mark.

Now what? How do we try to rebuild a society that helps people think for themselves a little more often? How do we encourage each other—and ourselves—to understand our neighbors a little better? We challenge ourselves more. We think less about what's comfortable and more about what's compelling. We spend less time on Twitter threads reacting to other Twitter threads and more on conversations with real people—and more on what sustains us, including books. As former *Times* chief book critic Michiko Kakutani put it in her glorious new book, *Ex Libris: 100 Books to Read and Reread*, "Reading matters more than ever."

"Books can jolt us out of old habits of mind and replace reflexive us-versus-them thinking with an appreciation of nuances and context," Kakutani told me in a recent interview for the *San Francisco Chronicle*. "Literature challenges political orthodoxies, religious dogma and conventional thinking, and it does what education and travel do: It exposes us to a multiplicity of viewpoints and voices. ... Empathy—the ability, as the saying goes, to walk in another's shoes—can help bridge divides, enable people to engage in conversation (as opposed to confrontation), and bring people from very different backgrounds together with a shared sense of purpose. As Pope Francis put it: Empathy can help bring about 'a true human dialogue in which words, ideas and questions arise from an experience of fraternity and shared humanity.'"

I roamed Europe at the turn of this century as a Wired News correspondent, writing about the new hope and possibility of the internet. I covered hacker conventions and eulogized founding fathers of the hacker ethos. I look on now with horror to see that online connectivity has turned into, above all, an instrument of mass control and manipulation, a breeding ground of toxicity and disease. The ongoing Russian hack of America was so successful, it covers its own tracks, and even opinion leaders fail to grasp how central it is to turning us into a country where the very nature of truth is constantly questioned. Reporters sprint to write stories about how Biden "lost" the Latin vote, all about a shift of a few percentage points, with zero interest in slowly emerging reports of a massive Spanish-language disinformation campaign that dwarfed all past efforts.

The one takeaway: We need to get better at talking to each other, at letting a variety of voices have their say, as this collection does. No, we have no hardcore Trump supporters. They'd parrot talking points and ask us to print obvious lies. Not going to happen. But this collection does offer an eclectic mix of viewpoints, a range of contributors checking in on where they are, and where we are, in November 2020. We hope that living out these pivotal months through their eyes will help all of us limber up and do better at thinking beyond narrow categories and limiting assumptions. Put another way: We hope that our reinvigorated imaginations, primed by all these takes, will help us all see that which we've missed, to hear that which we've muffled, and to feel what, in the numbness of the last years, we've not had the heart to feel. It won't all be pretty, it won't all be optimistic or hopeful, but the truth has its own way of registering, with a life of its own.

TABLE OF CONTENTS

TABLE OF CONTENTS (CONT.)

CHARLOTTE, NC

MARY C. CURTIS, a columnist at *Roll Call*, has worked at *The New York Times*, *The Baltimore Sun*, *The Charlotte Observer*, as national correspondent for *Politics Daily*, and is a senior facilitator with The OpEd Project. Her *CQ Roll Call* podcast, "Equal Time with Mary C. Curtis," examines policy and politics through the lens of social justice. Follow her on Twitter @mcurtisnc3

THE PROGRESS AND
THE STRUGGLE

BY MARY C. CURTIS

Watching Joe Biden and Kamala Harris thank poll workers on the day the networks finally called the election, I smiled and thought of my late mother, Evelyn Curtis. She was a bona fide GOP election official, tasked with making sure a representative from each party spent the big day surveying the scene, checking that all was legal and proper. Election Day was always special in our house.

From my mother, I learned the almost sacred ritual of going to the polls, of studying every candidate and bond issue, of thinking about the duty all Americans must fulfill. In our home, we knew the stories of heroes such as Medgar Evers, Fannie Lou Hamer and John Lewis, who bled to make it possible, and sometimes did not survive their efforts to protect something fundamental—the vote. How could any Black person dishonor that?

Yes, if you missed it, my parents were old-fashioned Republicans, as in party of Lincoln, at a time when a sturdy moderate contingent formed an important piece of the GOP base. Think Senator Edward Brooke of Massachusetts or Governor Nelson Rockefeller of New York, exemplars of that now rare middle-of-the road brand, many of whom represented states now colored blue on most electoral maps. My mom felt comfortable there, with her conservative economic views, Catholic values and socially liberal leanings.

She believed in a healthy two-party system and in maintaining faith in the integrity of the vote. So, when protesters crowded public servants counting ballots in 2020, in Detroit and Philadelphia and Maricopa County in Arizona, accusing them of fraudulent sleight-of-hand, I realized the toll of their long hours and meticulous work and the injustice of accusations from citizens they were trying to serve by doing democracy.

Can civics return as a staple in America's elementary school curriculum? Can schools make history come alive for students, distracted even before the days of virtual learning? Please?

The reason for Mom's political change of heart, her party's Southern strategy, broke her heart. The racial division stoked by Republicans, taking advantage of whites alienated by Democratic President Lyndon B. Johnson's signing of civil rights legislation, led the party on a path that raised up Donald Trump, his sycophants and supporters, who opportunistically and diabolically used fear of Black Lives Matter protesters and the specter of hordes of the "other" invading suburbs, apparently led by a marauding Cory Booker, as a last-ditch campaign message.

I could tell in our conversations back then that Mom felt saddened and betrayed and left with no political home, and, if she were alive, she would have been disappointed that fear has such staying power. The GOP tactic found fertile ground, in the country and in our hometown of Baltimore, where fellow Catholics jeered Lawrence Cardinal Shehan for speaking in favor of open-housing legislation in the 1960s (some of those providing the boos likely the parents of girls I would sit next to in religious school a decade later).

While Ronald Reagan lured Reagan Democrats with his message and persona, my mom and dad ran in the opposite direction, and bristled at the great communicator's tales of "welfare queens" and his choice of the Neshoba County Fair to herald "states' rights," so near the Mississippi site of the murders of the civil rights activists James Chaney, Michael Schwerner and Andrew Goodman.

Neither Mom nor a very young me had to look far to appreciate the bravery and resolve of those young fighters. Our home was the meeting place for young activists—who included my brothers Tony and Thomas and my sister Joan—planning frequent demonstrations for racial justice, much like the Black Lives Matter protesters of today.

While Mom would have been appalled at the evolution of a political party she never had the heart to completely abandon, she would have found kinship in the goals of the Movement for Black Lives, which has energized so many young people to vote and take part in a system that often finds new ways to disappoint. (Think of Florida's GOP-controlled legislature thwarting voters' will by putting up obstacle after obstacle for former felons who have served their time and only want to be a part of society by casting a ballot.) She might be out there with them, this woman who donned high heels and a Sunday best hat and, with her church group, traveled on a bus to join her three eldest children at the March on Washington in 1963.

My parents were proud of the young people then, when opening our home to interracial gatherings of freedom song-singing, sign-painting organizers, making the "good trouble" the late Congressman John Lewis hailed, was a controversial move, even in their own social circles. They stayed the course when they had the house deed ready to bail Tony out of jail—twice—after his arrests at diner sit-ins.

"They have courage," Dad would say, as the meetings ran into the night, with me hiding under the dining room table soaking in every bit of knowledge it took years to fully understand.

The morning (or was it evening) after, when a Biden-Harris victory was pretty much a done deal, I called my niece in Los Angeles, Cheryl L. Bedford, Joan's daughter, to get her thoughts on what to make of America's next move. We've grown even closer since Joan died several years ago, and I've joined the board of her own activist group, Women of Color Unite, a social action organization focusing on "fair access, fair treatment and fair pay for women of color in all aspects of the entertainment and media industries." Its extensive, searchable database of women of color is labeled "The JTC List," the initials a tribute to Joan.

Cheryl, in her unique way a fighter in the mold of my mother and her mother, said: "It's not going to be perfect, but it's going to be better." I believed this next-generation leader.

Is America so distracted that it's missing history worth celebrating? Lost in the noise of Election 2020 and the never-ending reality show named "Trump," at least at first, was the barrier-breaking achievement of the first female vice president, the first Black female vice president, the first Asian American female vice president. Finally after the election was called for Biden-Harris the Saturday after the election, attention turned to Kamala Harris, a person who will not be rendered "invisible" or judged using tired tropes and stereotypes, no matter the ramped-up efforts of critics.

"I just got finished crying," my big sister Janice, a griot, or storyteller, told me when I called. But she was ready to face the work ahead, to be clear-eyed about all that has been placed on Harris's shoulders.

In this election, Black women were praised for showing up in numbers and intensity to save Joe Biden, the election and the fate of the world (that last bit only a slight exaggeration). So many were eager to elevate Stacey Abrams to sainthood, for initiating one of the many grassroots groups to turn Georgia a shade of blue, I'm sure Pope Francis heard about it.

Of course, that's part of the problem. We don't want to be saviors or saints, just complex human beings who have something to say and deserve to be listened to as innovative and creative leaders. We are vulnerable, too, deserving of loving care.

My only living sister is a spiritual person, so we talked about the faith and strength Harris the pioneer will need. And she talked about Joe Biden's referencing the Catholic hymn: "And he will raise you up on eagle's wings, bear you on the breath of dawn. Make you to shine like the sun and hold you in the palm of his hand."

Her words to me before we ended our conversation—two Black women excited about the new role model in the White House, and scared too—quoted Biden's own closing message as president-elect: "Spread the faith."

Harris's first speech as vice president-elect was a powerful moment for me. "Protecting our democracy takes struggle," she said. "It takes sacrifice, but there is joy in it, and there is progress, because we, the people, have the power to build a better future."

The message resonated, and was familiar to me, someone who grew up witnessing the progress and the struggle, surrounded by people working from within the system, and others pushing against it. It was both an inside and outside game, often with contradictory rules, or no rules at all. But that's America.

I felt lucky to have had that real-life lesson, growing up surrounded by activism, realizing without ever hearing the words that saying you're not interested in politics is dangerous because, like it or not, politics is interested in you. While it took the election of a president who obliterated every democratic norm to wake up so many Americans to that simple fact, nothing that has happened in the last four years has surprised me.

That special kind of home-schooling was an education I took to heart early in life as I found my niche as witness, observer and, eventually, journalist. It allowed me to enjoy my front-row seat while maintaining a certain detachment. Getting too close could hurt, after all, another lesson I learned up close.

I've covered every presidential election since 2008, the year of Barack Obama, in a category all its own for the history made and resentments fueled, all of which led us to the four years that followed the first Black president's eight years in office.

In the days of Election 2020—momentous, historic and nerve-wracking—journalism was as much refuge as profession, even when divisive rhetoric fueled by leaders who should know better figuratively and literally reached my front door.

Mornings (and evenings) before, during and after, covering the developments, commenting online and in print, on television and radio and podcasts, kept me plenty busy. I appeared on so many local, national and even international shows, it was hard to keep them straight.

My message was consistent: America is a country divided, with more fault lines than anyone can count. The next president, who appears to be Joe Biden, and his history-making vice president, Kamala Harris, have won the big prize, and possibly the worst job in the world. But that, too, is America—messy and always a work in progress. You can't move forward without looking back. And in moments in between all the turmoil and rush of news, I was not too busy to reflect on what led me and the country I love to November 3, 2020, with so much on the line.

Remaining on the outside looking in during this election season was not an option, worrying about what comes next the question on an anxious country's mind. How do you transition from relief to optimism in a future the new president promises to unite against incredible odds facing him and his team when only half of the country seems willing to cooperate? Perhaps by reliving the examples of ancestors, who never wavered despite having much less encouragement and support, and so much less to be hopeful about. That was my plan, anyway.

One thing that everyone in my profession has to fight is the bubble, and the temptation to remain in it a little too long out of convenience or force of habit. The morning after a historic election, when promise overcame resignation and millions put their faith in a better tomorrow, was the time to take a walk and listen to what the world was saying.

My husband I decided the day after an exhausted country stayed up late to witness that history was the perfect time to hit the grocery store—well, after a gym visit allowed me a little self-care. Most of the people there were the store employees, essential workers our country has come to belatedly appreciate during a pandemic. True to form in America, most of them were black and brown. Behind their masks, we could see their smiles. Trust me.

I sat in that for a moment and reflected on my family and their contributions to our country's greatness, despite the difficult challenges ahead for America and the new team at the top: from Covid-19 to economic upheaval to racial inequities to a climate crisis and more. I was in this lovely, well-stocked store close to my home in a neighborhood that barred me with restrictive home covenants and threats of violence not that many years ago. I could not have married the husband at my side in states including the one where we live if not for the Supreme Court's Loving decision.

Our son, the committed progressive, already pushing for a policy shift that is more inclusive and more just, makes us proud. As a historian, he teaches me that with progress always comes pushback. But he and others like him, following the lead of so many brave Americans, including those in his own family, won't stop. That is how I came to hope the morning after.

And don't forget the joy, as Kamala Harris reminded everyone in that speech, and every time she smiles. In the store, everyone offered a good morning, and one, an older African-American gentleman who always stocks the vegetables just so, looked me in the eye and said: "It fills your heart, don't it?"

Pawleys Island, SC

CHRISTOPHER BUCKLEY worked as a merchant marine, graduated from Yale University with honors, and became managing editor of *Esquire* magazine at the age of 24. He served as chief speechwriter to Vice President George H.W. Bush from 1981 to 1982 and from 1989 to 2007 was editor in chief of *Forbes FYI* magazine. He is the author of 19 books, including a number of satirical novels about American politics, most recently *Make Russia Great Again*. His bestselling novel *Thank You For Smoking* was adapted into a successful movie in 2006. Other works include: *The White House Mess*, *Supreme Courtship*, and *Losing Mum and Pup*, a memoir about his parents, William F. Buckley Jr. and Patricia Taylor Buckley.

GOPDÄMMERUNG

BY CHRISTOPHER BUCKLEY

MONDAY, NOV. 9, 2020

I've tried these past four years to behave and avoid the H-word. But President Trump's deranged rant on Thursday night about how the election was being stolen from him was like watching one of the "Hitler Reacts To" parodies of the tantrum scene in the movie *Downfall*. Bruno Ganz, brilliantly playing the Führer, explodes when he's informed that one of his generals is unable to stop the Soviet Army's march on Berlin. The subtitles in the parodies have him fulminating about such earthshaking matters as the final episode of "Game of Thrones," the price of the PS5 digital edition of Xbox, and his staff's objection to his habit of ending sentences with a preposition. I just went to YouTube and whaddya know, there's already a new one: "Hitler is informed the presidential election winner is still unknown."

But seriously: In his final days on earth, prior to transitioning to Hades, Hitler was determined to bring all of Germany down with him. Had Albert Speer not disobeyed that order, nothing would have remained but scorched earth. His megalomania and narcissism dictated that he hadn't failed—Germany had failed him.

Mr. Trump's appalling display of denial and defiance in the White House briefing room was a transparent display of his attempt to bring down American democracy with him, by negating the most fundamental principle of American democracy, namely: every vote matters. (Not a bad hashtag, that—#everyvotematters.) Anderson Cooper of CNN likened Mr. Trump's performance to "an obese turtle on his back, flailing in the hot sun, realizing his time is over." SAD!

The morning of January 20, 2017, I remarked on NPR that "morning in America" can also be spelled with a "u." As I type, it appears that it is about to be morning in America again, minus that "u." But before we launch into "Happy Days Are Here Again" and "Ding-Dong! The Witch Is Dead" consider: 70 million of our fellow Americans voted to give four more years to a president who lied about, and then fatally botched, a pandemic that has killed 240,000 of us, and counting. A meme making the rounds this fall, ostensibly of German origin, warns: "Dear America, you are waking up, as Germany once did, to the awareness that one-third of your people would kill another third, while one-third watches."

In 1986 I published a novel, a parody White House memoir, that begins on inauguration day 1989 with the president-elect arriving at the White House to escort outgoing President Reagan to the Capitol for the ceremony. But Mr. Reagan won't leave. Not for reasons of obduracy or to thwart the democratic process. He's just gone a bit dotty. It's cold outside, he's still in his jammies, and he doesn't feel like leaving. Maybe tomorrow.

That turned out to be a risqué premise in 1986. It got the book attention. I remarked to an interviewer from *The Washington Post* that I worried I might have offended Mr. Reagan. Four days later the U.S. Postal Service—not yet ruled by a presidential donor-crony—delivered a handwritten note from the president saying he was delighted by his part in my novel. That's class. That was then.

When his successor, George H.W. Bush, conceded victory to Bill Clinton on Election Night 1992, he went briskly to the podium and said, "The people have spoken, and we respect the majesty of the American system." He then extended warm congratulations. In time, he and Clinton became Best Friends Forever. That, too, was then. Viewed through the swamp miasma of the last four years, Mr. Bush's character shimmers like a steeple rising above a mythical Brigadoon.

What now? From one quarter, sound and fury, the acrid stench of sour grapes and lawsuits, ending in fingernail marks on the Resolute Desk. The GOP, which now might as well stand for Gutless Opportunistic

Poltroonery, is trying to raise $60 million for a "legal defense" to overturn the results of "the stolen election." (Good luck with that.)

What else? Violence, possibly. The 13 members of the troglodyte right arrested for plotting to kidnap the governor of Michigan were responding to the dog whistle, doing their part to Make America Great Again. Goebbels, remember, urged Germans to "work toward the *Führer*," rather than wait for explicit instructions. His avatar Steve Bannon, taking time off from planning *his* legal defense for (allegedly) embezzling Mexican border wall funds, announced that he wanted a restoration of Tudor justice, with Dr. Fauci and the director of the FBI "beheaded." (I'm putting that in quotes so you won't think I'm making it up.) Donald Trump Jr. meanwhile is calling for "war." (Ibid.) Something went very wrong during Junior's potty training, though not nearly as wrong as Dad's, as First Niece Mary Trump has related.

Face it, folks (as Mr. Trump would say), we now live in an America where peaceful protesters in Lafayette Square, the nation's front yard, are gassed and shot with rubber bullets *by military police* to clear the caudillo's way for a farcical presidential photo op. The Republican Senate, with one exception, has become a sty of ovine, lickspittle quislings, degenerate descendants of such giants as Everett Dirksen, Barry Goldwater, Howard Baker and John McCain. One incoming Republican congressperson is an ardent believer in QAnon, a sodality of bedwetters who (actually) believe that Democrat leaders are Satan-worshiping, child-trafficking pedophiles. What a distance we've traveled since Cole Porter's "Now, heaven knows, anything goes." When I was a wee Republican lad in short pants, passing out Nixon bumper stickers, the lunatic fringe consisted of cuckoos of far paler plumage. The John Birchers (actually) believed that President Eisenhower was a communist agent. Russell Kirk put that one down with his imperishable quip that "Eisenhower isn't a communist. He's a golfer."

Back then, before the internet honeycombed the public square with silos and echo chambers, a well-turned *Oh, puh-leeze* on occasion had the power to put paid to a demagogue and his noxious-ism. The nail in Joe McCarthy's coffin was hammered in by Army chief counsel Joseph Welch when he confronted him across the hearing table with, "At long last, have you no sense of decency?" I've been hoping, these past four years, to hear someone quote that at the president. There's still time, between now and January 20, 2021.

In October 1999, I essayed a Donald Trump presidential inauguration speech for the op-ed page of *The Wall Street Journal*. It began, "This is a great day for me, personally." He went on to gripe about the shabbiness of the National Mall that spread westward before him. "You call this a mall?" It seemed funny at the time. Some months ago, Mr. Trump was at the opposite end of the Mall, sitting beneath Daniel Chester French's iconic statue, being interviewed on TV. He wasn't in the least reticent about comparing himself to Lincoln; indeed, spent much of the time grousing that he was getting scant credit for his Lincolnesque-ness. UNFAIR! His sense of grievance was resplendently on display in the briefing room Thursday night. Trump as Victim-in-Chief is one of his frequent incarnations. Watching, I thought: *Any minute now he's going to claim that someone shot him.*

Having scripted a Trump inaugural speech, I wondered what a concession speech might sound like.

Fake election, folks. You know it and I know it. A total disgrace. It's very sad. The saddest thing ever in history. The Biden crime family and the radical socialist—actually, let's call them what they really are—disgusting communists. Disgusting. They stole the election. Not from me. From you. That's right. But don't worry, folks. We're gonna get it back. Oh yeah. We are soo going to get back. I will rise again in four days. Was it four days? I think it was four days. Some say three. Whatever. But don't worry, folks. I'm not going anywhere.

Actually, sir, you might be. New York District Attorney Vance knows more than I do about those tax returns you've been promising to release, just as soon as they're "out of audit." I don't much like the idea of a former president of the United States going to jail. It smacks of what happens in sh*thole countries. But Mr. Trump has done much to make America into a sh*thole country in the eyes of the world.

No one, even among his most ardent detractors, has suggested he go to jail for presidential crimes. That's what we have impeachment for—or so we thought until the aforementioned GOP nullified that lofty idea. But America being a nation of equal justice under law, why should anyone be immune from prosecution for crimes committed *as a citizen*?

Magnanimous, these thoughts may not be, I stipulate. But there's a satisfying karmic aspect to color-coordinating Mr. Trump's attire with his hair and complexion. Criminality aside, ex-president Trump has a number of financial appointments in Samarra on his calendar. Deutsche Bank (Germany, again—*Ach du Liebe!*) may at long last be weary of extending credit. How that will play out is anyone's guess. As the saying goes, if you owe the bank a million dollars, you have a problem; if you owe the bank $421 million, the bank has a problem.

Meanwhile, the IRS may decide to disallow that $73 million tax refund. Please remit in enclosed envelope. Mr. Trump faces more palms than there are on the grounds of Mar-a-Lago, among them those of $1,200-an-hour lawyers. *The New Yorker* recently noted that when he left office, Bill Clinton's legal bills amounted to $10 million. It will be interesting—and I confess vastly entertaining—to watch this next chapter of "The Apprentice."

There's a word for this in—*Achtung!* wait for it—German: *Schadenfreude*: a mischievous delight in the misfortune of others. My friend Paul Slansky, a sharp and longtime observer of American politics, introduced me to another German term, apropos of Mr. Trump: *Backpfeifengesicht*. "A face crying out for a fist to be smashed into it." You can't beat German for compound nouns.

Harsh? You tell me: How much sympathy is owed to a leader who has evinced not one scintilla of genuine concern for the 240,000 Americans whose deaths took place on his watch? Who warred against science, and, at the end, against the doctors themselves? (See also: "I don't take responsibility at all.")

By contrast to Trump's snarls and raging, there was Vice President Biden speaking to us, urging patience and unity, pledging to work as hard for those who voted against him as he would for those who voted for him. A spa treatment for the soul of America.

After typing that sentence, I held my breath and went on CNN's website. Banner headline: BIDEN ON VERGE OF VICTORY. More concretely hope-inspiring was the smaller one below: AIRSPACE RESTRICTED OVER BIDEN'S HOME AND EXTRA SECRET SERVICE AGENTS DEPLOYED. I thought: *It's happening. It's actually, finally happening.* As a great Republican president said: "My fellow Americans, our long national nightmare is over."

San Francisco, Ca

Artist and illustrator **MARK ULRIKSEN** has been
a regular *New Yorker* magazine cover artist for over 25
years. He's covered The Masters and British Open for
Golf Digest, painted murals for the Chicago Bears and
written and illustrated the book *Dogs Rule Nonchalantly*.
His past work for Wellstone Books includes the covers
of *Kiss the Sky* by Dusty Baker, *Shop Around* by Bruce
Jenkins and *Holy Toledo* by Ken Korach.

GENERALISSIMO

BY MARK ULRIKSEN

Today is literally the morning after, November 8, 2020. Yesterday was the date that will live in infamy for our family, the day that hope and joy returned to our family and hopefully our nation, if not the world.

My wife, our two daughters, my mom and I have waited three years, nine months, fourteen days and an agonizing election week for the hopeful demise of our own Valdemort—the personification of greed, grievance, division and hatred—to be vanquished from our land. That day finally arrived yesterday.

After both my wife, Leslie, and I couldn't sleep following Tuesday's election, stomachs churning at the thought of a 2016 redux of that shocking election result, I vowed to stop watching the "map show" on TV or my laptop. The outcome would not be affected by my obsessing over the result. Life needed to return to some semblance of normal, except of course that nothing is normal in 2020.

When Leslie shouted something like "He won!" a little after 8:30 Saturday morning I knew for once that "he" was not our 45th president. For four years one of us would invariably start our day off with some manner of cursing along the lines of "now what the %^$%#* has he done?!!" It was always in reference to the current president and his latest assault on our collective integrity, humanity, governance.

We are so looking forward to starting the days ahead without clenched teeth, high blood pressure or churning stomachs.

Can you feel our exhale of relief? It feels hurricane strength.

As a *New Yorker* magazine cover artist, I have had reams of material to work with over the past four years. When I first began contributing covers in 1994 the art director Françoise Mouly told me to look at my life and comment on it visually. As a result, my "beat" has been my interests and passions—dogs, baseball, movies, NYC, contemporary mores, current events. As the magazine's editor, David Remnick, has said, the objective of a *New Yorker* cover is to go just too far.

I'm a news junkie, maybe to the detriment of my health. I read *The New York Times, Washington Post, Guardian,* Axios and my local *San Francisco Chronicle* daily, along with helpings of Politico, the BBC, NPR and the PBS NewsHour. My day feels incomplete without them. At every turn I'm constantly attuned to news, imagery or metaphors that whisper to me: "That could make for a *New Yorker* cover."

I submitted the image on the opposite page, "Generalissimo," to the magazine in 2017, shortly into the first year of Trump's presidency. I could see that this narcissist couldn't care less about what happens to our country or the Republican Party under his helm. A Civil War battlefield littered with the remains from his cruel reign meant nothing to the man in charge. It's going to always be about him and as long as he could claim victory each and every time a new norm was shattered, a new wedge driven between "we the people," a new juvenile nickname created, he was as happy and clueless as I portrayed him. Sitting on a horse backwards, revealing its ass, was none too subtle, but I did try to make the Confederate flag he's waving understated. The word I hid in the tree trunk on the left was my final dig at this heinous human, my own hat tip to the great caricaturist Al Hirschfeld, who hid his daughter Nina's name in his work. I didn't hide a name, rather I hid my opinion of Trump's character.

Even though the magazine didn't accept this submission (and all *New Yorker* covers are submissions, not assignments) I was determined to get my utter disgust for this charlatan out of my system, thus the finished painting you see here. My submissions are always quick pencil drawings that if accepted next get refined and then painted for publication. I painted this even though the magazine had passed on publishing it. Call it a labor of loathing.

The image on the cover of this book is also a rejected *New Yorker*

"Generalissimo" by Mark Ulriksen. © Ulriksen

cover submission. In my field one has to accept failure, sort of like a baseball batter making an out seven out of 10 times; that makes him a star. The mere fact of landing a cover negates all the disappointment when one is inevitably rejected. Submitting a cover is a little like dating:

You wonder if you'll ever hear back from the object of your attention.

Among the many ideas I've submitted over the past four years about the Trump administration only one has landed, a Halloween cover entitled "Boo!" where all the kids in their scary masks run from the kid with *the* scariest mask, that of Trump.

Originally, I submitted this idea in

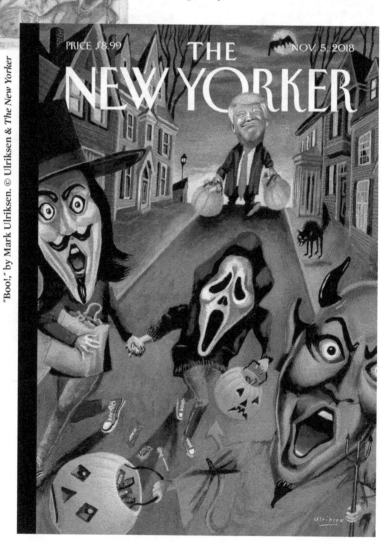

GENERALISSIMO • MARK ULRIKSEN

2016 prior to that election when I figured half the nation was scared to death of Trump while the other half was equally terrified of Hillary Clinton.

But my timing was off, the magazine already had a Halloween cover slated to run. Two years later it made sense to resubmit this one, albeit without Hillary, who was no longer a candidate and thus not a threat to those who opposed her, unless some folks were still concerned about "those missing emails." I'm glad we've moved on from that canard.

Today I'm feeling glad all over. Glad and grateful that American democracy continues on, tarnished but no longer teetering on the brink of authoritarianism. Can we all exhale now and instead of fighting each other, which doesn't do anyone any good anywhere (save for craven politicians), fight together against the many problems confronting us all? That's a cover I'm looking forward to working on.

CHARLOTTE, NC

ANGELA WRIGHT SHANNON is a freelance
writer, editor and actor. She was formerly a reporter
and editor at *The Charlotte Observer*, managing editor
for *The Winston-Salem Chronicle* weekly newspaper,
and a regular panelist on "North Carolina This Week"
on North Carolina Public Television. She has managed
communications for Mecklenburg County (N.C.), the
U.S. Equal Employment Opportunity Commission
and the U. S. Agency for International Development.
She has served on the staff of the late Congressman
Charlie Rose (D-NC), the National Republican
Congressional Campaign Committee and the Republican
National Committee. She received two White House
appointments in the Reagan administration (USAID and
EEOC), and has the distinction of being the "uncalled
witness" in the Anita Hill/Clarence Thomas hearings.

FOR ME, IT'S ALL ABOUT KAMALA

BY ANGELA WRIGHT SHANNON

I didn't believe that White America would be willing to put a woman of color a heartbeat away from the presidency. Not the White America that had chosen Donald Trump as president just four years earlier, triggering the most emboldened white supremacists we've seen in half a century. And not the woman that Senator Kamala Harris had proven to be: bold, confident, willing to "get into good trouble."

She is the woman many professional Black women don't allow themselves to be for fear of being labeled: difficult, angry, too aggressive, too confrontational. Many accused her of being too ambitious during her presidential campaign, as if ambition should have its limits, as if a woman who aspires to be president should do so timidly. Every Black woman who has ever been denied a promotion or a raise, despite being the hardest working and the best qualified, understood the basis of those accusations.

Senator Harris fought hard for the presidential nomination; I must confess that after her jab at Biden during the debate on school busing, I too wondered about her ability to be a loyal No. 2. But I quickly realized that she was the perfect choice. Her confidence, her fire, is exactly what we need to help restore confidence in our democracy. We need gallantry. Kamala Harris can speak truth to power because she exudes power. Her exacting prosecutorial skills were on public display during the Kavanaugh and Comey hearings. On top of that, she is undeniably beautiful and unabashedly Black, a proud graduate of an HBCU who dances in the street and professes a love for hip-hop and rap, specifically Tupac, Snoop Dogg and Cardi B. No way in hell she was going to be allowed within striking distance of the White House.

So at midday on Saturday, November 7, 2020, when major news networks began projecting the Biden-Harris ticket a winner, I cried those warm slow tears that start somewhere deep inside, tears that reside in a dream deferred. The last time I felt such an explosive release was in 2008 when Barack Obama won the presidency. I cried and danced most of the day, celebrating not so much the Biden-Harris win as Trump's loss, the end of a literal four-year reign of terror. My playlist included "Happy," by Pharrell Williams, "We are the Champions," by Queen and "Hit the Road Jack," by Ray Charles.

The gravity of Kamala Harris's win soon became the dominant narrative about the election results. She is the first woman vice president, first Black vice president, first Asian American, first child of immigrants, first graduate of an HBCU. With her win she casts bright rays of hope in so many different directions; young girls and women from points around the globe now see their own potential in her—something she readily acknowledges. When she danced onto the stage in Wilmington, Delaware, to deliver her victory speech and introduce President-elect Joe Biden, everything was intentional, from the white pantsuit she wore in homage to the women's suffrage movement to the music she chose for her entrance: "Work That" by Mary J. Blige.

"...There's so many of you girls, I hear you been runnin'
From the beautiful queen that you can be becomin'
You can look in my palm and see the storm comin'
Read the book of my life and see I've overcome it
Just because the length of your hair ain't long
And they often criticize you for your skin tone
Go on and hold your head high, 'cause you a pretty woman
Get your runway stride honed and keep it goin'...
...Feelin' great because the light's on me
Celebratin' the things that everyone told me

Would never happen
But God has put his hands on me
And ain't a man alive could ever take it from me..."

Kamala Harris knows her worth and understands her value, especially to young women of color. She won for Shirley Chisholm, Geraldine Ferraro and Hillary Clinton. Her win is also redemption for the hundreds of thousands of women who protested the election and inauguration of self-proclaimed sexual molester Donald Trump.

I had praised and pilloried Joe Biden for promising to put a woman on the ticket. At the time it seemed like a knee-jerk response, a promise made on the run. After all, if Hillary Clinton couldn't win, what woman could? Willing to concede that—as a white man with extensive political experience including the vice presidency—Biden was likely our best bet for defeating Trump, part of me feared that he had tanked his chances with an off-the-wall commitment that overestimated the benevolence of American voters. I worried we would end up suffering through another four years of Trump's megalomania. Biden had made an honorable choice, but was it the right choice?

I have firsthand experience with Joe Biden's attempts to do the honorable thing. It can lead to less than honorable outcomes, like it did in 1991 when he presided over the Clarence Thomas Supreme Court confirmation hearings after Thomas had been accused of sexual harassment by law professor Anita Hill. I had known Clarence Thomas for years. We were founding members of the Black Republican Congressional Staff Association, and I had worked for him as his director of public relations when he was chairman of the Equal Employment Opportunity Commission. I had experienced the behavior of which Professor Hill spoke and I was willing to testify. Biden probably thought he was doing the honorable thing when he told Clarence Thomas at the start of the hearings that "the benefit of the doubt" accrued to him. He may have thought he was doing the honorable thing when he allowed his fellow Judiciary Committee members, specifically Orrin Hatch, Alan Simpson and the late Arlen Specter, to ridicule and debase Professor Hill, allowing her character to become the central issue rather than that of Clarence Thomas, the man who sought a lifelong job interpreting and applying constitutional law to the populace.

Biden may have thought he was doing the honorable thing when he had a letter couriered to my lawyers' office in the wee hours of the morning, after I had spent two days in Washington anxiously waiting to corroborate Professor Hill's testimony, suggesting that due to "the lateness of the hour" they thought it best to just insert my statement into the record, instead of allowing me to testify. With that action, and his negligence to call several other women who were prepared to testify against Thomas, Biden sealed the narrative of Professor Hill as a woman scorned and a political pawn, and he facilitated the ascension of a bitter and totally undeserving Clarence Thomas to the Supreme Court.

Despite his bungling of the Hill/Thomas debacle, most people would probably agree that Biden is a well-intentioned, empathetic and decent man. He has borne unfathomable losses and stood with dignity and renewed commitment to public service, despite it all. He has attempted to redeem himself with women, starting with writing the Violence Against Women Act of 1994, and the "It's On Us" campaign to end college sexual assault. His decision to choose a woman of color as his running mate: a masterstroke.

But once the election revelry fades, we will have two well-meaning Democrats who could face a hostile, obstructionist Republican Senate. We must temper our expectations of what this election actually promises, at least in the short run. I'm confident the Biden-Harris administration will make immediate strides against Covid-19 by following the recommendations of the scientists and medical professionals, and mandating necessary guidelines for all Americans to follow. I trust them to develop incentive and relief packages that will reinvigorate our economy and salvage small businesses. But I'm not sure a Biden-Harris administration can do much to heal the racial divide, which has proven to be not a rift or a schism, but an abyss.

Indeed, with nearly half of voters preferring Trump, the first days after the election were disheartening and nerve-wracking. Who are these people who believe that Trump deserves a second term? Did they really vote for him because they believed in him or because they couldn't bring themselves to vote for a ticket with a Black woman on it—no matter how vile they knew Trump to be?

It's alarming that Trump received 11 million more votes this time than he did in 2016, despite Covid-19, his lies about what he knew about the virus, the tanked economy and increasing racial tensions—fomented by him. Many of us had naively believed we had turned a corner this year—that the videotaped and televised killing of George Floyd had awakened something in our collective soul that decried the historical, ongoing slaughter of unarmed Black citizens at the hands of law enforcement. Many of us believed this election would be a referendum on racism.

We thought that White America had finally experienced an "aha" moment: watching a defenseless George Floyd executed in broad daylight under the knee of a callous and brazen police officer while other officers stood by, daring bystanders to intervene. Finally, white people understood "Black Lives Matter." They reacted: marching, protesting, taking a knee—even some police officers. The Reverend Al Sharpton said it felt different; the late Congressman John Lewis said it felt different. Major cities allowed Black Lives Matter flags to fly in public places; some painted murals on large buildings and major streets. Symbols of racism began to disappear: Confederate statues were voluntarily removed. Universities started renaming buildings that had honored segregationists and slave holders. The NFL changed its position on kneeling during the national anthem, and Quaker Oats decided to retire Aunt Jemima after 130 years because they suddenly realized that the image was based on racial stereotypes.

Across industries and institutions, public pledges to tolerate no act of racism and bigotry were constant and swift. We really thought we had turned the corner; that eradicating racism, bigotry and police killing unarmed black people with impunity was finally Priority One. Some may argue that we're looking at the glass as half empty instead of half full. After all, we did succeed in electing the Biden-Harris ticket, which means a majority of voters did the right thing, and we can reasonably expect a tamp-down of racial acts and insults. There is a lot being said about the difficult conversations that we need to have about race.

But, quite frankly, I'm weary of the conversations about the need for more conversations, and how we need to try to understand each other better. We've been having those conversations for as long as I can remember. For me they go back to growing up in Wilmington, North Carolina, during the late '60s and early '70s when all hell broke out after the assassination of Dr. Martin Luther King Jr. And that same summer when violent protests followed the unceremonious closure of our beloved Black high school to force a one-way integration. We had riots on a pretty much daily basis for a while. Amid the turmoil, I was appointed a youth member of the New Hanover County Human Relations Commission. There was a lot of talk about how things won't change until we take the time to listen to and understand each other. I even got an award from then North Carolina Governor Bob Scott for all my efforts in human relations during a time of turmoil. Well, I've learned that human relations efforts and honest conversations don't carry us far. Racism is an evil monster that never dies, it simply sleeps until it is awakened by friendly forces.

I agree that we need to have conversations about race relations; there is always some benefit to open, honest discussions. It's nice when people are able to walk away feeling heard and understood. But what Black Americans need is protection—from racist and reckless police officers and white vigilantes who feel they can deputize themselves to rid their neighborhoods of "suspicious-looking" people of color. We need laws to protect us from excessive use of force, and people "standing their ground."

Kamala Harris, former San Francisco district attorney, understands this and is uniquely equipped to offer realistic objectives. She does not support outcries to defund the police, but she does say that we need to reimagine policing and take a look at how cities apportion police budgets versus social services, job training and mental health resources. She was one of the four members of Congress, along with Senator Cory Booker, who introduced the Justice in Policing Act of 2020, a bold piece of legislation designed to hold police accountable, change law enforcement culture and build trust between police and the communities they serve.

In her introduction of the bill, Senator Harris stated: "America's sidewalks are stained with Black blood. In the wake of George Floyd and Breonna Taylor's murders, we must ask ourselves: How many more times must our families and our communities be put through the trauma of an unarmed Black man or woman's killing at the hands of the very police who are sworn to protect and serve them? As a career prosecutor and former attorney general of California, I know that real public safety requires community trust and police accountability. I am proud to join my colleagues in introducing this historic legislation that will get our country on a path forward."

Among other things, the bill bans choke holds, carotid holds and no-knock warrants at the federal level, establishes a National Police Misconduct Registry to prevent officers who are fired or placed on leave for misconduct from moving on to another jurisdiction without accountability, and it creates law enforcement development and training programs to establish best practices. The House of Representatives passed a similar bill, dubbed the George Floyd Justice in Policing Act (H.R. 7120), in June; the Senate companion bill (S. 3912) has 36 cosponsors. I fully expect that Vice President Harris, with the full support of President Biden, will get the sponsors needed to enact this crucial legislation.

I dare say this is a priority for most African Americans who have grown fearful of blue lights in their rearview mirror, sending their teenage sons to the grocery store, or even calling police when they are in trouble, afraid the police will shoot first and ask questions later. That doesn't mean we aren't concerned about climate change, education, guns, health care and taxes—we are. Just that we want no more cries of "I can't breathe." And Vice President-elect Kamala Harris has given us a reason to exhale.

NEW YORK, NY

If you don't know who **KEITH OLBERMANN** is by now, this paragraph isn't going to help you: politics, dogs, sports, television. Google it.

DÉJÀ VU ALL OVER AGAIN

BY KEITH OLBERMANN

For five years, nearly every time Donald Trump would appoint somebody to some job, I would repeat the job title and the name aloud to see if it was real. And then I would repeat both again with a combination of disbelief, disdain, and disrespect. Sometimes this catechism wound up with an ironic laugh or a rhetorical question mark or almost any sound in between.

"Campaign manager Kellyanne Conway. Campaign manager Kellyanne Conway?"

"Presidential lawyer Rudy Giuliani. *Presidential lawyer* Rudy Giuliani."

"Secretary of Education Betsy DeVos. Secretary of Education Betsy DeVos!"

I never got the tone exactly right.

It's an ineffable sort of thing. It requires all kinds of qualities I do have, like a sense of the ironic and a sense of the absurd. But it requires something more: A kind of soul-deep optimism that as moronic as it might sound to conjoin an important title with the name of this ill-suited idiot or that Dunning-Kruger Effect Poster Child, that the heelot in question would ultimately be driven from the landscape and all would be well.

On the Tuesday after he clinched Pennsylvania and thus the election, Joe Biden listened as a reporter recounted that day's rantings of Mike

Pompeo, a six-year former congressman who'd accomplished nothing but lunch. Pompeo had been pressed about a smooth presidential transition and had said "there will be a smooth transition to a second Trump administration." The generous interpretation of Mr. Pompeo's statement was that it was the kind of thing that his kind of moron would think was a good joke, without thinking of the effect on the other countries with whom he dealt on behalf of our nation. The slightly less generous interpretation was that it was part of the GOP attempt to delegitimize the Biden administration before it started. The ominous interpretation was that it was another harbinger of a potential coup by count or court or corporals.

"So far," the president-elect said placidly, "there is no evidence of any of the assertions made by the president, or Secretary of State Pompeo." Here, Biden broke into a brief, calm, almost cordial laugh that seemed unconnected to what he had just said—until he did that repeat-the-name-and-title-thing I'd been working on for five years. "*Secretary of State Pompeo.*"

He nailed it.

I was so jealous.

And I loved Joe Biden even more.

Having first met Donald Trump in 1984, and worked in the same television company with him, and owned an apartment in a building with his name on it, I had also spent five years trying to warn people that Trump's brain didn't work right. In February 2016 I wrote a piece for *Vanity Fair* called "Could Donald Trump Pass A Sanity Test?" (they published it in the July issue). In March 2017 I wrote a follow-up video commentary for *GQ* called "Could Trump Pass A Sanity Test?" And in October 2017 I published a book which dropped the premise of the question and cut straight to the chase and was called *Trump Is F*king Crazy.*

None of these were metaphors and none of what's in them was hyperbole. I meant it, and mean it, literally. I didn't predict all of the horrors of the Trump administration, but I got a lot more of them than I thought I would, from the concentration camps along the Mexican border to the certainty even before his election that he would never leave office without at least trying to stay even if he had to burn democracy to the ground. So, I was waiting even a longer time than many others for the formal conclusion that he had no legal basis to stay past January 20, 2021. When that word finally came down I was—naturally—asleep. Once Trump had announced Giuliani's Total Landscaping news conference with the "vote counting fraud" witness who turned out to have gone to jail for flashing little girls, next to the Fantasy Island Sex Shop and across the street from The Crematorium and da uther side of thah spressway from Sweet Lucy's Smoke House, I needed a nap. When I realized what I had awakened to, the 30 minutes or so of snooze suddenly seemed like my best night's sleep since 2015.

That day, in addition to rediscovering the will to actually do things like clean out closets or balance checkbooks or make TikToks, I found myself thinking even more about Giuliani and his resurrection by Trump and a pattern so prevalent in administration personnel that it's actually true of Trump himself. A stunning number of the key people have been like Giuliani. They had not just once been in a spotlight. At least briefly, they had once been the *only* person in a spotlight.

Trump was like that. "The Apprentice" was the seventh-best rated show in television in 2004. It then steadily descended to 67th in Trump's last year. There has been considerable reporting that the presidential run itself was merely a brand-boosting gambit by Trump after the television collapse and other business failures. This isn't exactly how the Roman Empire ended, but it's close enough.

In the days that followed the news from the Pennsylvania count, as I discovered that I *didn't* have asthma and there *was* another fraction of an inch in my lungs that had evidently closed off from stress, I thought a lot about Trump and Giuliani and all the others Trump had dredged from live burial in the mudbanks of well-earned obscurity and put front and center in his gothic horror version of the American political scene. They were all like Bob Shawkey, a popular ex-pitcher who spent one year as manager of the New York Yankees in 1930. He was fired, and in the next 45 years his successors would win 23 league championships. At the age of 85 he was invited back to throw out the ceremonial first pitch at the remodeled Yankee Stadium. Escorted to the mound by team Publicity Director Marty Appel, he coldly surveyed all the success since his ouster and said, "I should still be managing this team."

Giuliani was last viewed having his chimerical presidential

aspirations vaporized by Biden's priceless comment about how the ex-mayor's entire campaign was made of sentences solely consisting of "a noun, a verb, and 9/11." In fact, few had realized that Giuliani's political career had actually ended (certainly this never dawned on Giuliani himself) when weeks after the 2001 attacks on democracy, he suggested throwing out democracy, by delaying his legally mandated departure from New York City Hall for three months because who wanted to sit around acting rationally when the situation called for panic?

Trump had found countless other people who had drifted off into nothingness, and who would thus do anything to get back in the game. Giuliani's deputies included the husband-and-wife team of Joe diGenova and Vicki Toensing, refugees from the Clinton Scandals cable telethon. One of Trump's other attorneys was John Dowd, last seen driving baseball's Pete Rose into the ground in 1989. Still another was Alan Dershowitz, a running joke since the O.J. Simpson trial. At various times, Trump had the staggeringly unsuccessful Ken Starr and Newt Gingrich as informal mouthpieces. Hell, his first henchman was Roger Stone, who acted (and dressed) like a "Batman" TV series villain in a bad episode. Even Trump's television flying monkeys were those who had been serially fired or shunted to the side like Lou Dobbs, Sean Hannity, and Tucker Carlson before signing on board Trump's version of the *Pequod*.

But three names above all others filled these specifications and I knew them all and thought of what happened to the Undead after you killed them again. In a previous century I had once dated Laura Ingraham. She had boasted to me of breaking into her ex's home to put back all the photos of them which he had removed. When she returned to finish the job, she found the locks changed, so she instead grabbed the garden hose, shoved it through the guy's front door mail slot, and ruined $10,000 worth of new hardwood floors. She mocked Hillary Clinton's "Vast Right Wing Conspiracy" by snorting at me and saying "Vast! It's just me and my brother and a few guys and Drudge!" And all this was on the first date. Unsurprisingly, the second "date" was more of a low-key hostage-taking.

Though she'd been in cable news for 20 years, Laura had just never clicked. She'd had her own show on MSNBC and she was Bill O'Reilly's top sub on Fox but only Trump took her from promise to success.

Next thing I knew Laura was stiff-armed saluting Trump at the 2016 Republican Convention. Next thing I knew after that, I was watching a bank of three televisions in a Washington sports studio one day. On the one on the left, up popped a woman with whom I used to live, anchoring on MSNBC. In the middle, suddenly there was another woman with whom I used to live, punditing on CNN. On the right, Fox News was in a commercial, but I was certain that if they returned to the studio and Laura was on it, casino lights and bells would go off and gold coins would come spewing out of the monitor.

When we, in the Bill Clinton days or the Iraq War days, couldn't get Ingraham or Ann Coulter or the late Barbara Olson to be that night's management-designated conservative blonde, we would turn to Kellyanne Fitzpatrick, now Conway. She wasn't just literally fourth-string; she seemed to philosophically define the concept. When it's down to maybe cancelling the segment, the show, or maybe the network, you call Kellyanne. And now *she* was the first defending anything Trump did, at any time, on any network. And *she* was the one who was the off-the-record source for every reporter at every news outlet this side of *The Daily Racing Form*. Because only when you've been fourth-string will you agree to say anything, no matter how heinous or immoral, just so long as the boss guarantees you're *first*-string.

Lastly among this group—The Walking Political Dead—was William Barr. He had been the boy wonder attorney general of the first Bush presidency. He was just 41 when he ascended to the pinnacle of active lawyering, and then Poppy managed to not get re-elected and suddenly Billy was working for the phone company. If you're Barr and you're a theocrat-on-the-rise cut down in the morning of your ascendance and suddenly your 69th birthday looms, it's not hard to begin publicly bleating that the Mueller Investigation was unconstitutional and Trump was a victim, and just wait for him to notice and call you in and give you *your rightful job back, the one those bastard Democrats stole from you a quarter of a century ago.*

I have never met Barr and hope not to. But I knew of him, in another one of these all-too-close-for-comfort personal connections. My last scoop as editor of my high school newspaper had been the revelation of the man who had been chosen to succeed the headmaster who would retire the very day I graduated. I dug up the story with the help of a really sharp underclassman reporter of mine named Bill Bunch, who is now *Will* Bunch of *The Philadelphia Inquirer.* The new headmaster was named Donald Barr, and our reporting was really good except we didn't know what everybody else didn't know: that Barr had been ousted in a virtual coup from his previous job running The Dalton School for being a martinet, a bully, a financial disaster, and a religious nut. Lost in the haze of forgotten cause-and-effect, just as Barr left Dalton an inexperienced kid with no degree was hired as a teacher and let loose among the teenaged girls. His name was Jeffrey Epstein. At my alma mater, Hackley School, Barr The Elder would be ousted in a virtual coup for being a martinet, a bully, a financial disaster, and a religious nut.

Back in this timeline, Barr The Younger issued his infamous memo breaking DOJ precedent and encouraging his prosecutors to pursue voter fraud allegations, while Trump continued to roll out more obvious farces. After the Giuliani Press Conference (Trump started with "American Carnage" but ended with "American Pornage") came the ludicrous swamping of the "Voter Fraud Hotline" by hundreds of callers who simply insulted Trump, then hung up. There was the Trump Recount Legal Defense Fund, in which the fine print at the bottom indicated that the donations could actually be split 60-40 between the campaign's general fund and the Republican National Committee with no guarantee that a dollar of it would actually be spent on recounts. There were the hapless appearances of Lindsey Graham, Marco Rubio, Ron Johnson, and the aforementioned Pompeo, all insisting Trump had won or at least might still win, and all acting either like kidnap or blackmail victims.

So, as soothing as the Pennsylvania triumph might have been, it still felt like the days after a concussion. You knew you weren't dead and you knew you weren't brain-damaged, but you would be damned if you felt like anything was really right. And for me, mixing in the personal connections to Trump and Giuliani and Ingraham and Conway and Barr and all the rest, it still felt like I was hitting my head on an hourly basis.

And then a photograph reminded me of the details of another personal connection: Joe Biden once took me to lunch, to ask for advice.

The further in time I get from it, the less I believe it really happened.

It was early in 2007 and he started talking about commentaries I had begun to do the previous summer on MSNBC. "Those special comments!" he said, with first a smile, then a whistle. There was then, and there remains now, almost no space between the public Joe Biden of the campaign or the president-elect speech, and the guy who talks informally to some knucklehead off the streets—which in this story would be me.

"I watch the commentaries you do. And people send me the videos. And my staffers tell me about them. And every time, I think the same thing: You express anger, but as close as it comes to the line, you never cross the line. I say to my staff, 'Folks, is he too angry for you?' and they all say 'No, just right.'

"So here's my question. And then we can enjoy this great lunch. When I am passionate about something, and I speak, on the Senate floor or anywhere else, I get told by my friends and my enemies: 'You're too angry!' And when I really *am* angry they all say 'You're *really* too angry!'"

And here Biden laughed.

"Now you, you go on TV, far larger audience, far longer speeches, and people say, 'That Olbermann, he's righteously indignant!'" With a mixture of laughter, astonishment, and curiosity, he then said: "Me? *I'm* angry. You? You're righteously indignant! How do you do it? How do you do it, man? Can you tell me?"

Without thinking, I replied. "You have been in the Senate for how long now, Senator? Thirty-four years?" He nodded. "And you're only just asking this question *now*?"

The words were barely out of my mouth when I froze. Politicians are seldom known for their senses of humor about themselves. In the brief pause that followed I actually thought Joe Biden might get up and leave. But then the corners of his mouth turned up and, to my great relief, he burst into laughter. He rocked back into his chair. He slapped the table with a palm. "My God that's funny." More laughter. "And, my God, that's true." Louder laughter.

I didn't really have advice for him. I had never analyzed my process. But he kept asking for details, and soon I realized that I *had* a process, and it did filter down anger (it is basically the simplest of laws: *write* the anger tonight; *say* the anger tomorrow night)—but that I never would have understood myself without Biden's kindly cross-examination.

Those who know him far better than I do keep saying the same thing: His laughter at himself and those probing questions that educate both people "are so *him*."

There are two photos of Joe Biden and me. They're at a Democratic debate I moderated in Chicago in August 2007. We're both beaming. I looked at them the day after he became president-elect and suddenly remembered what we were smiling at. He has just asked me if I've noticed that he's been doing his best to turn his anger into righteous indignation. And he's also asked me if I think he's succeeded.

"Secretary of State Pompeo." Laugh. "*Secretary of State Pompeo.*"

I think he has.

Washington, DC

JACOB HEILBRUNN is editor of *The National Interest*, a contributing writer for Spectator USA, and a senior writer for the Absolute Sound. He has written for *The New York Times*, *The New York Review of Books*, *Washington Post* and a variety of other publications, and was a senior editor at *The New Republic* and a member of the *Los Angeles Times* editorial board. He is vice-chairman of the Arthur F. Burns Fellowship and has published in *Die Zeit*, *Der Tagesspiegel* and *Süddeutsche Zeitung*.

COOLING OFF THE
MORONIC INFERNO

BY JACOB HEILBRUNN

"If I am out of my mind," Saul Bellow's protagonist Moses Herzog muses, "it's all right with me." It's a sentiment that more than a few Americans may have felt tempted to express during the past four years of Donald Trump's presidency. Trump, as the astute critic David Bromwich observed in *Harper's*, possessed the "remarkable ability to render large numbers of people as crazy as himself. ... The furor has also infected the media, the Democratic Party, and the activists in the streets."

Not me. Ever since he descended down the golden escalators with Melania in tow, I've oscillated between cool detachment and disdain for Trump's serial shenanigans. His presidency, a prolonged exercise in nostalgia for a mythical past, has represented an attempt to rebrand America in his own image—grasping, petty, vainglorious. His restless impulses bring to mind the 17th-century poet Andrew Marvell's description of Cromwell as a revolutionary who sought "To ruine the great Work of Time/And cast the Kingdome old/Into another mold."

What surprised me wasn't Trump's behavior but that of the Republican establishment in kowtowing to him almost immediately. It was hard not to feel a kind of morbid fascination about Trump's camarilla. While I don't mean to suggest that the Trump regime was tantamount to a new Third Reich, there were some evocative parallels, most conspicuously in the rush to curry favor that took place then and today with the high and mighty. In his memoir *Defying Hitler*, the great German journalist and historian Sebastian Haffner emphasized just how quickly the country preemptively capitulated to the Nazis. The universities, the legal and medical professions, and the government bureaucracy—all made their accommodations. The issue, in other words, wasn't resistance but how speedily Haffner's brethren tried to assimilate to the Third Reich. Haffner recounted that he himself had not been exempt from cowering before the new regime in 1933: As he worked in the library of Prussia's top court, brownshirts showed up, yelling "Out with the Jews!" One SA poltroon inspected Haffner's nose and demanded to know if he was an Aryan.

He blurted out, "Yes."

"What a disgrace to buy, with a reply, the right to stay with my documents in peace!" Haffner wrote. "I had been caught unawares, even now. I had failed my very first test. I could have slapped myself."

America's elites failed their Trump test long before he even contemplated becoming president. In a brilliant essay in *New York Magazine*, Frank Rich showed that Trump has been able to rely on the benevolence of a variety of establishment enablers, liberal and conservative, from the outset of his career. "Trump practiced bigotry on a grand scale," Rich wrote, "was a world-class liar, and ripped off customers, investors, and the city itself. Yet for many among New York's upper register, there was no horror he could commit that would merit his excommunication." Small wonder Trump believed, or appeared to believe, that he could act with sovereign impunity as president. His January 2017 conversation with FBI Director James Comey asking him "to let this go" on behalf of his former National Security Advisor Michael Flynn was emblematic of Trump's approach. Comey resisted. He was fired. So was Attorney General Jeff Sessions, the most fervent and valuable lackey that Trump had early on in his campaign. His service bought him nothing but Trump's scorn after he failed to resist the appointment of special counsel Robert Mueller. Soon enough, a steady stream of *Mitläufer*, or fellow travelers, appeared on the scene, from the eminently forgettable Matthew Whitaker to the oleaginous William P. Barr.

The capitulation to Trump was not confined to government. Quite the contrary. For me, one of the more telling moments in the 2020 campaign arrived when the paper I'd grown up reading, *The Pittsburgh Post-Gazette*, endorsed Trump for president in an editorial portentously titled "The Man and the Record." The *Post-Gazette* had for decades been a complacently liberal newspaper. No longer. The endorsement itself offered the usual conservative folderol about Trump not always employing the most delicate language but having the right instincts and aspirations. He is, we were told, the kind of guy who delivers the goods: "Donald Trump is not Churchill, to be sure, but he gets things done." Joe Biden and Kamala Harris, by contrast, represent a lot of "Cuckoo California dreams" about the environment and job growth. Harrumph!

The editorial stipulated that the newspaper had not endorsed a Republican since 1972, but its troglodytic owner, John Robinson Block, seized upon Trump's presidency to transform the once-proud liberal stalwart to mirror his own hardline views. A few years ago, he installed a conservative named Keith C. Burris as editor. Burris created a stir by publishing an editorial on Martin Luther King Jr. Day in 2018 that was titled "Reason as Racism." Its pearls of wisdom included defending Trump's allusion to "shithole countries" in Africa and arguing that racism is the new McCarthyism. Next, Block and Burris fired the paper's cartoonist, Rob Rogers, for lampooning Trump, which they deemed an unpardonable offense. Eventually, the newspaper guild responded with an official statement, "Keith Burris, John Robinson Block and his twin brother Allan, BCI chairman, have declared an unprecedented scorched-earth war on their employees and the culture of the PG newsroom."

The conversion of the newspaper into a pro-Trump organ came as a jolt to me. It had been a staple of my childhood. For over a decade, I was a paperboy, reading the *Post-Gazette* between lobbing it onto the front porch of subscribers. Its pro-Trump stance constituted a form of apostasy. Put otherwise, I couldn't escape the sense that I was being gaslighted by my old hometown newspaper. Trump's vaulting ambition meant that everything that I thought I knew about America was upended almost overnight.

My own family background served as a kind of distant early warning system about the rapidity with which historical tremors can manifest themselves. The Steel City has a large Jewish community and a number of refugees from Germany, my father among them. 2020 is the 80th anniversary of my father's emigration as a six-year-old from his birthplace of Kassel, Germany, to the United States.

"*Den Jungen werden wir nicht wieder sehen*," his grandfather lamented on the morning of his departure. ("We will not see the boy again.") He sailed by himself from Genoa in May 1940 and turned seven somewhere over the Atlantic on an Italian ocean liner bound for New York. His parents, unable to obtain a visa to enter America, were murdered in the Nazi concentration camps. His middle name, Israel, bestowed upon German Jews by the Nazis as a verbal badge along with a yellow star, was not expunged until he became a U.S. citizen in 1954 upon his 21st birthday.

The reverberations of those events were inescapable. For one thing, I grew up with an intense interest in how the past related to the present. Punitively restrictive immigration policies had combined to make it impossible for Jews in Europe such as my grandparents, who had even made a last-ditch attempt to settle in Alaska, to escape the Third Reich. These weren't distant events for me. They were pregnant with contemporary significance, not just because of their implications for my family but also because I was fascinated by another modern totalitarian regime and its similarities to the Nazi dictatorship.

This fascination is not very hard to explain. As a classics professor, my father sometimes liked to pretend that he was aloof from quotidian politics, but liberal anti-communist magazines like *The New Republic*, *The New Leader*, *Encounter*, and, perhaps most fatefully, *Commentary*, were strewn around the house. I devoured them. It was heady stuff. If you wanted someone to condemn the Soviet Union or Arab hostility to Israel, I was your man, or, to put it more precisely, kid. In sixth grade I read Alexander Dolgun's memoir of living in Stalin's Soviet Union. Dolgun, an American who worked as a file clerk for the U.S. embassy in Moscow, was arrested by the Soviet secret police in 1948 and vividly describes his torture and imprisonment for eight years in Stalin's archipelago of slave labor camps. Early on I was inoculated against any illusions about the totalitarian nature of the USSR. In high school I received a booster shot after purchasing a battered copy of the essay collection *The God That Failed*. For me the belief in a socialist paradise could never fail because I never believed in it in the first place.

After I graduated from Oberlin College, where I regularly jousted with students and faculty about the true nature of the Soviet Union, I wanted to join the anti-communist cause. In 1989 I became an assistant editor at *The National Interest*, which was edited by Owen Harries, a former Australian diplomat and professor, and Irving Kristol, the godfather of neoconservatism and a former Trotskyist. No sooner did I arrive than the Berlin Wall fell. Communism was on the way out. Capitalism was in. One of the first essays I helped edit was Francis Fukuyama's "The End of History?" Fukuyama went big, prognosticating the inexorable rise of liberal democracy. His remarkable sally foreshadowed the rise of a second generation of neoconservatives, led by Paul Wolfowitz, William Kristol and Robert Kagan, who championed American hegemony. In retrospect, their crusade to export democracy to every nook and cranny around the globe ended up poisoning it at home. That very danger was something that Fukuyama was quick to recognize as he publicly broke with his old comrades, shrewdly anatomizing their failures in his book *America at the Crossroads*. How, he asked, could disciples of the political philosopher Leo Strauss, who had inveighed against the dangers of social engineering and radical change, champion it in the Middle East?

Someone who recognized this danger at the time was Harries, a shrewd analyst of international affairs. Harries was a Burkean conservative, not a radical. All along he regarded the neocons and their dreams of reordering the globe with the utmost apprehension. After 9/11, he predicted America might well lurch into a nationalistic fervor that would rebound upon itself. He cited a famous maxim of Burke's to warn Americans not to overreact: "Among precautions against ambition, it may not be amiss to take one against our own. I must fairly say I dread our own power and our own ambition. I dread our being too much dreaded. ... Sooner or later, this state of things must produce a combination against us which may end in our ruin." Harries's adjuration was to no avail. The George W. Bush administration, spellbound by neocon fantasies of democratizing the globe, plunged into Afghanistan, then Iraq. America has never extricated itself from either country. The stage was inadvertently set for Trump. During his 2016 campaign, Trump was able to posture as a fresh breath of air in the GOP by branding the war a "big fat mistake" and attacking the Republican poohbahs who oversaw it.

The Republican establishment initially viewed the rumbustious Trump with horror. At a 40th gala dinner at the St. Regis Hotel held by the Ethics and Public Policy Center, where William Kristol was emcee, I recall him joking that Trump had called him "dopey" and concluding, "This should be a Trump-free evening, so that's enough." It wasn't. Later that evening, a shudder went through the crowd as Trump's triumph in the New York primary was announced. The barbarian was at the gate. But as Trump ascended, more than a few conservatives made peace with him. No longer did they espouse capitalism and liberty and democracy. Rather, they threw in the towel. Illiberalism, in one form or another, became the new mantra.

None other than Irving Kristol, who never thought much of Fukuyama's original essay, had set out the lineaments of a more authoritarian credo in an essay in *The National Interest* in 1993. For Kristol, anti-communism appeared to have been no more than a pitstop. Now that the Soviet Union had vanished, it was time to march against the true enemy: liberalism. In "My Cold War," Kristol wrote, "so far from having ended, my cold war has increased in intensity, as sector after sector of American life has been ruthlessly corrupted by the liberal ethos. It is an ethos that aims simultaneously at political and social collectivism on the one hand, and moral anarchy on the other. It cannot win, but it can make us all losers. We have, I do believe, reached a critical turning point in the history of the American democracy. Now that the other 'Cold War' is over, the real cold war has begun." He couldn't have been more wrong. It is revanchist conservatism, to borrow a term from Sam Tanenhaus, that poses the greatest internal threat to American democracy.

As the historian Christopher Browning observed in the *The New York Review of Books* in October 2018, there are some unsettling parallels between the decay of democracy in Weimar Germany and America: "No matter how and when the Trump presidency ends, the specter of illiberalism will continue to haunt American politics." Browning predicted a politicized judiciary would remain with hotly contested future judicial appointments, racial division, cultural conflict, and political polarization inflamed by Trump. Gerrymandering, voter suppression, and uncontrolled campaign spending would continue to hollow out our democratic legitimacy. What Biden will be able to accomplish domestically if Republicans continue to control the Senate is an open question. To shift course from Trump domestically, he can issue a variety of executive orders on immigration and the environment. In foreign policy he seems likely to enjoy a lot more maneuvering room. Trump's defeat represents a significant setback for the nationalist and populist forces that have sought to pose as the avatars of a new political age. Under Biden, America will not leave NATO. It will strengthen it. What's more, Biden will rejoin the Paris climate accords as well as the Iran nuclear deal. Autocracies will be on notice. America is back.

Or is it? Max Boot, a chastened neocon, noted in *The Washington Post* after the election that the fact that Trump did as well as he did in the election is astounding. He attracted more voters than in 2016. He continues a magnetic attraction for his base. A substantial conservative media apparatus continues to depict Biden as a dangerous radical and corrupt leader who stole the election from the valorous Trump. A Republican Senate might well launch investigations of Hunter Biden's putative dealings in Ukraine and China, not to mention the 2020 election. For Trump's pursuivants, defeat is victory. "For them history has stopped," as Orwell put it in *1984*. "Nothing exists except an endless present in which the Party is always right." According to Boot, "the election reveals that nearly half of the nation inhabits an alternative reality ... where Trump is a successful president and Biden a socialist."

But there is room for hope. More often than not, Trump's America resembled what Saul Bellow called a moronic inferno, but Joe Biden's decisive victory suggests that a cooling-off period could loom. Biden has been badly underestimated ever since he started running for the presidency. Firm leadership and competent government officials can go a long way after the incessant tumult of the past four years. As Tocqueville put it, "The great privilege of the Americans is to be able to have repairable mistakes." It's time to start repairing them.

NEW YORK, NY

JOAN WALSH is *The Nation*'s national affairs correspondent and a CNN political contributor. She is a producer of the award-winning 2020 documentary *The Sit In: Harry Belafonte Hosts The Tonight Show,* about the legendary week in 1968 when the activist-entertainer took the helm from Johnny Carson, and the author of *What's the Matter With White People? Finding Our Way in the Next America,* which the *Philadelphia Daily News* called "one of the best books of 2012—and even more relevant now." *Salon*'s very first news editor, Walsh served as editor in chief for six years. She's written for publications ranging from *Vogue* to *The Nation,* and for newspapers including *The New York Times, Washington Post, Los Angeles Times,* and the *San Francisco Chronicle.* Walsh lives in New York with her dog, Sadie.

GROUNDHOG DAY

BY JOAN WALSH

Have you ever thought about what an influential film *Groundhog Day* was? The actual Groundhog Day has always been a silly holiday, mostly observed by children plus the fine folks of Punxsutawney PA, where we are every year supposed to believe a groundhog seeing its shadow could predict six more weeks of winter—or not. But Bill Murray's 1993 film implanted that strange civic tradition in our psyches, as a metaphor for vexing situations that would never end, be they crises or opportunities or ludicrous life conditions.

Most of the first week of November felt to me like Groundhog Day. I woke up with the sun, every morning, assuming the presidential race would be called for Joe Biden. I'd jump up and turn on the TV and grab my laptop. And it simply wouldn't, didn't happen. I'd stay on the couch most of the day and wait. For four days CNN tortured me by saying the decisive votes from Pennsylvania were about to come in. In a few hours ... and they never did.

Overall, the days developed a mostly dreary sameness. A few highlights: I walked my dog. I called my daughter, who ran Katie Porter's victorious Orange County House campaign. I texted my friends who own the restaurant downstairs. After their Tuesday night "election party," every day they insisted they were leaving early; but then they stayed late, waiting, like me, for the call, the call, the final call. So I'd run down, grabbing my Biden-Harris mask and my laptop. I'd down a glass of wine (or two or three), then we'd feel pranked, and we'd go home.

We were not being pranked. I still do not entirely know why the networks took so long to call the race for Joe Biden and Kamala Harris. I repeatedly watched CNN's David Chalian, who I admire, explain how many ballots were still out there in Pennsylvania. Yet Chalian always told us that all the votes they knew about were going 70 to 80 percent plus for Biden. It felt so callable. But as someone who urged networks to count first, make calls later, I guess I was reminded of my life motto: "Be careful what you wish for." We asked them to wait. They waited. You're welcome. I fell asleep at about 2 a.m. Friday night.

So would Saturday be different?

I woke up around 6 a.m., Groundhog Day again, and ran to the TV. The numbers were similar—with CNN again saying the decisive votes from Pennsylvania would, again, be coming "soon." I fell back asleep at 8. And then, at about 11:30, I was awakened by screaming, honking and clapping. Outside, Harlem was crazy with joy. I instantly knew what it was about. I dragged myself out—without coffee, but with my dog, Sadie—and joined the insanely joyous crowd outside.

I've always had a secret wish to dance to "Ain't No Stoppin' Us Now" in the streets. I got to do that, and more. There was music and dancing everywhere. I danced down to Frederick Douglass Plaza, a much neglected, glorious New York landmark, and watched people dance around the huge bronze statue of Douglass, while he kept his stoic gaze north, still looking for the North Star. My friends opened their restaurant downstairs early. We drank Champagne. After a few hours, being a journalist, I had to go back to work. A tiny bit tipsy, if you must know. But I felt loose-limbed and liberated. It wasn't the alcohol.

The next morning, I told a friend: It's as though my joints, my muscles, ligaments, fascia—all were mysteriously released. This is the part where I guess I should say: It seems like the Democrats did not win back the Senate. There is trouble ahead. But my body didn't register that. Being freed from the pussy-grabber in chief was what viscerally mattered. When Kamala Harris spoke that night, in her suffragette-white suit (thank you, Hillary Clinton) and her sly pussy-bow blouse, I also knew that electing our first female vice president, also a woman of color, was the perfect rejoinder to Trump. Joe Biden was not my first choice, though I ultimately voted for him proudly. Watching him talk to Harris's nieces on stage that night didn't quite equal seeing Sasha and Malia Obama come out with their parents in 2008, but it was something close. Their blended extended families—Black, white, Catholic, Jewish—this is who we are.

Trump continued to blather on about nonexistent voter fraud. I continue to be proud. We vanquished that miserable loser with a ticket led by only our second Catholic president, and our first woman vice president, the daughter of Jamaican and Indian immigrants. *This is who we are.* If it continues to feel like Groundhog Day, I can live with it.

SACRAMENTO, CA

MARCOS BRETÓN is a *Sacramento Bee*
columnist. The son of Mexican immigrants, Bretón
has been a working journalist in California for 30
years. A graduate of the San Jose State University
School of Journalism, he is a past Alicia Patterson
Foundation fellow and the author of books on baseball.
He was featured in the 2010 PBS documentary "The
Tenth Inning," co-directed by Ken Burns. He lives in
Sacramento with his wife, Jeannie Wong, and their
twin daughters.

'DADDY, YOU SAID HE COULDN'T WIN'

BY MARCOS BRETÓN

I had just gotten dressed that Saturday morning when my phone buzzed with the news: Joe Biden had been elected as the 46th president of the United States. I ran to tell my twin daughters, who were 12 years old four years earlier when Donald Trump beat the candidate they found inspirational: Hillary Rodham Clinton.

Leading up to the November 2016 presidential election, my girls had asked me for weeks before if a vile man like Trump really had a chance to be President. Four years ago, they understood Trump in a way I didn't. They had been subjected to bullying in their sixth-grade class.

My girls were shocked when other children they considered friends were silent as boys and girls at school acted like bullies. Some of their friends even seemed drawn to the bullies. The friends became friends with the bullies. They sought their approval and laughed at their taunts. My daughters had felt let down by teachers who excused the behavior of bullies because, on some level, the teachers liked the bullies and chose to tolerate intolerable behavior in the bullies because the bad kids had engaging personalities.

Candidate Trump reminded them of sixth-grade bullies. Clearly he was not as qualified as Clinton. His behavior as a candidate was boorish. He didn't follow the rules in debates. He engaged in name-calling, labeling Clinton—a woman they admired—by the childish nickname of "Crooked Hillary." And, like the bullies in her class, he got away with it again and again.

When they asked me if Trump would win, I said, "No way." I've encountered people since then who swore up and down they knew Trump would win, but I didn't. So when he did, when I had to break the news to my daughters the morning after Trump's unbelievable Electoral College win, I faced the hardest moment I had ever encountered as a father.

"Daddy, you said he wouldn't win," they said.

"Well, clearly Daddy was wrong," I replied.

"Daddy, you always told us that bullies don't win," one daughter said.

"Trump is a bully," the other said. "He won. He is the president of the United States."

All I could think to say was, "It's terrible," as I read their faces and understood the emotions of betrayal they were feeling.

I'd always known a day would come when my girls would realize their dad was not infallible, but I never imagined it would happen like this. Donald Trump had demonstrated to my daughters that I could be wrong about really important things and powerless to do anything about the biggest bully of all.

Then one of my daughters said something that I will take to my grave.

"I hope I live long enough to see a woman president of the United States," she said.

The words hit me with the force of a blow to my abdomen. They were sadly profound coming from a 12-year-old girl who, in that moment, considered her own mortality as she realized something dark about her country.

She was angry at her country and for the next four years she only got angrier. Her sister hated Trump as well, but she internalized it. But with my daughter who worried she wouldn't live to see a woman in the Oval Office? For her, Donald Trump became a living manifestation of how unfair, unequal, unkind and unrepentant America could be. With every lie, every insult, every taunt, every betrayal of norms and rules we adults once believed to be quintessentially American, my daughter grew more angry.

She would rail about Trump every week for four years, sometimes every day. The beginning of her teenage years coincided with the time of Trump: a time of trolling and character assassination carried out from the highest office in the land. My daughters remembered the presidency of Barack Obama, who I consider to be the finest president of my lifetime and a deeply inspirational man despite his limitations and failings as a politician.

But my twin girls were only four when Obama was elected and only 12 when he termed out. Their transition out of childhood and into the academic realm of studying American history coincided with a man who could go down as the worst president in American history.

My kids didn't get an inspirational president to meet their innocent ideals and open hearts. They got a con man, a racist, a buffoon, an incompetent, venal, simpering pile of cruelty and corruption. They got a liar, a bully, a cheat, a misogynist, a homophobe. His cynicism colored their optimism. The specter of his corruption invaded our happy home.

My teenage years growing up in San Jose, California, coincided with the election of Jimmy Carter, a man of peace and hope. I was 13 in 1976, the Bicentennial of America, when an explosion of reclaimed patriotism put some distance between us and a Vietnam era that I had been too young to understand. When I came of age, I did so with a good feeling about my president and my country.

My hero, Muhammad Ali, had won his battle with our government—a fight I was too young to remember. All I saw when I came of age was Ali the Greatest.

I was 17 when the U.S. Olympic hockey team won its gold medal at the 1980 Winter Olympics. That sound of Al Michaels screaming "Do you believe in miracles?" rang in my ears and made me weep for decades whenever I recalled the moment our ragtag college kids beat the mighty Soviets at their own game.

I would learn the hard truths about my country, but later, when I was older. My beautiful memories of the "Miracle on Ice" team would later be soiled when a majority of that squad donned red MAGA hats and proclaimed allegiance to Trump. They were dead to me when that happened, their memory no longer cherished, but I was a graying grown man by then.

For my kids, and for their generation, hard truths about the darkness of the American soul came very early. As a parent in the time of Trump, I've tried to balance the disappointment my children felt for their country with my urge to correct them and remind them of all the wonderful things America has achieved and stood for.

But I had to tread lightly on correcting them because their guileless and apolitical assessment of Trump was spot on. They believed the biggest jerk in the world was the president of the United States, and they were right. How could I try to tell them differently when I would mute the TV whenever the president spoke for the last four years?

I'm an opinion journalist. It's my job to be informed. But I can't stand the sound of Trump's voice and every time I did listen, I would catch him in multiple lies and distortions mere minutes into his diatribe of the day.

Since I was 13 or 14, I had never missed a State of the Union address. Though I didn't vote for Ronald Reagan, the man could speak beautifully and always told inspirational stories about our country. The first George Bush seemed like a kind and decent man, so I always watched. George W. Bush was a baseball guy like me and, unlike his Republican Party, he did not care to demonize people from Mexico—my ancestral homeland. I never missed a State of the Union until Trump. I haven't watched one since Obama's last nearly five years ago.

I accepted Trump's election out of respect for our electoral process and even tried to give him the benefit of the doubt until he debased his office day after day with no end in sight until the 2020 election. There was no bottom, no end to how low he would go, requiring me to try to explain to my children once again that they were living through a trying time in our nation's history.

Because of Trump's incompetent handling of the coronavirus pandemic, my girls were yanked out of high school near the end of their sophomore year—just when they felt they had mastered the tricky social piece of the high school experience. There would be no end-of-school-year dance, no summer trip to Disneyland, no college visits. The summer before their junior year, which they had hoped to spend in Chicago with relatives, was instead spent at home. Their junior year of high school—the most pivotal year in their academic careers—has been spent learning remotely, an education via Zoom.

They've had to grow up faster than I would have liked. We hope at least part of their senior year can be salvaged in 2021. They know they are blessed by having two parents who have remained healthy and employed. They know kids in their own community who have it much harder than they do. But their formative years have been darkened by Trump. Their world is more dangerous because of him. They never got to live through a time of naive patriotism like I experienced when I was their age.

I've tried to lift their spirits while trying to lift my own. I've seen firsthand how the pandemic has exacerbated inequality in my own country. I've seen how Mexican workers deemed essential have been ravaged by the pandemic and how these vulnerable people have been vilified by politicians like Trump.

Monkey see, monkey do: My voicemail filled up with taunts and racist catcalls of Trump supporters every time I wrote about the undocumented whose work is valued and exploited in California even as the workers themselves are blamed for the ills of our nation.

I can remember writing about farm workers in the early 1990s and feeling heartened by generous outpourings of concern from readers of my newspaper. I heard from some bigots too, but they were in the minority. Far more people wanted to help and did. But that was then. Today it's almost exclusively bigots I hear from when I write about the plight of Mexicans in California.

Pledges to support needy people have been replaced by the same Trumpist script: "What about 'illegal' don't you understand?" It's a script of intolerance that Trump has magnified with the full weight of the Oval Office.

I get called an "enemy of the people" in my own community because Trump used those words against journalists and his worst followers were only too happy to repeat them on my voicemail. What happened to my country? Or was my country always like this and Trump has simply been the manifestation of our racist past?

The patriotism of my youth faded a long time ago and has been replaced by an understanding that I was too naive about American history that I was never fully taught in high school in the first place. What we are living through now is a time of reckoning in America. And so I've continued to tread lightly when speaking with my children because I know now that I've been wrong about more than Trump's election prospects. I've been wrong—or rather, I've been uninformed—about a fuller picture of America that was less glorious than I understood. So by the time the 2020 election approached, I was having fuller, more honest discussions with my kids.

That's really OK. In fact, it's been a good thing and I have learned as much from my now young ladies of 16 as they have learned from me. The only frightening question was: *Do you think there is any way we get four more years of Trump?*

It unnerved me to think that my kids could be 12 when Trump was elected and 20 by the time he left office. Their entire high school years with Trump? And the beginning of college? The years when they learned to drive? Began to date? Dared to dream?

We talked about it the day before the election.

"Are you scared," they asked me.

"Yes," I said. "But I'm hopeful."

"So am I," each told me.

I had stayed up until 4:30 a.m. on the Friday after the election, but no announcement. I worked all day Friday. Still no announcement. Then my phone buzzed on Saturday. I ran and found my children to tell them Joe Biden would be the next president.

"I feel good about my country for the first time in a long time," one daughter told me.

So do I. We can build on that. God bless America.

DETROIT, MI

STEPHEN MACK JONES is a published poet,
award-winning playwright and winner of the Kresge
Arts in Detroit Literary Fellowship. Born and raised in
Lansing, Michigan, he moved to Detroit upon graduation
from Michigan State University and has remained
in the metro Detroit area. He worked in advertising and
marketing communications before turning to fiction.
In 2018, the International Association of Crime Writers
presented Stephen with the prestigious Hammett Prize for
literary excellence in the field of crime writing. Stephen's
first adult fiction book, *August Snow*, was named a 2018
Michigan Notable Book by the Library of Michigan. The
Nero Wolfe Society awarded August Snow the 2018 Nero
Award. His second book in the *August Snow* series, *Lives
Laid Away*, was shortlisted for the U.K. Crime Writers
Association's 2019 Ian Fleming "Steel Dagger" award.

SCHLEPPING TOWARD TOMORROW

BY STEPHEN MACK JONES

A toasted Everything bagel, buttered with a shmear of cream cheese. Half of a banana, tolerated only for its potassium. Coffee, black. And it begins.

Another day slouching half-awake toward one more season in pandemic/political hell. A day like so many others spent in a stupefying fog of amorphous dread, murky bemusement, unfocused anger, reductive embarrassment and shame.

Couldn't watch any presidential vote returns on TV.

Couldn't do it.

Won't.

The convoluted Technicolor maps. Multidimensional green-screen graphics. Wide-eyed, breathless pundits exuding excitement and urgency where there's only speculation, stagnation and deeply imbedded rot. The continuing deluge of candidate attack ads/tweets/ Facebook posts, rivaled only by the drowning flood of pharmaceutical commercials touting drugs people didn't know they needed. I am pining for the long-ago days of the Barack Obama presidency. I need "Beer Summits" and hard-ass stares at that murdering thug Vladimir Putin. I want someone who will say "*We* are One," not "*I* am the One."

And I need more "Rockford Files."

I creak and crouch my way, coffee, bagel and banana in hand, to my family room chair—a big, overstuffed, leather affair complete with complicated hydraulics and USB port to charge a mobile phone I barely use save for the occasional curbside pickup order of Chinese, Greek or Mexican food. My wife thinks my chair is some sort of a Jabba the Hutt abomination. My third *August Snow* book came out of sitting in that chair. So darlin', I may love ya—but piss off. I debate for a moment whether or not I should turn on the TV. At least make a wan effort to see where the American Ship of State is sailing in hopes it has finally—*finally!*—steered clear of rocky shoals and every rumored Kraken, Orc, Devil Whale and Charybdis.

Five minutes into election coverage on CBSN, it becomes depressingly apparent the good ship USS *DEMOCRACY* is still rudderless, the crew clueless. It's still battered by relentless headwinds of its own bloviated making. I turn the news off, left to feel helpless, hopeless and, strangely enough, soiled.

I eat my modest breakfast in silence, staring at a black 50-inch rectangular screen. Time was, I would read two, three newspapers (a strangely antiquated word) at least four times a week. I once listened intently to NPR's "Morning Edition," drank coffee and argued with MSNBC's Don "Nappy-headed hoes" Imus. Upon Imus's justified demise, I argued with the bobblehead political dilettantes of "Morning Joe," pausing only to listen—really *listen*—to Mike Barnicle. He seemed the only one of the crew who wasn't an Upper East Side Manhattan "Limousine Liberal." I took pride in being informed. Knowing which way the political winds blew.

These days?

Not so much.

For my sanity's sake I have retreated from the tempest of news media. More correctly, I have recently joyfully regressed; MSNBC's Joe Scarborough has been replaced by *SpongeBob SquarePants*. Newspapers and the multitude of online news sources have been replaced with crime fiction, comic books and graphic novels. I long-before-her-passing kissed the Grand Dame of "PBS NewsHour," Gwen Ifill, farewell and stared in wide-eyed wonder at reruns of "Stargate-SG1." My blood pressure came down. My blood sugar came close to unmedicated normalcy. I, not unlike a majority of Trump supporters, embraced willful ignorance. Deliberate stupidity became my friend. And the occasional Xanax turned those dark roiling fascist clouds that had settled over America's purple mountain's majesties into sugary pink cotton candy and unicorns.

And why *not* make the conscious choice to embrace ignorance, idiocy and two-dimensional cartoon lunacy?

I had certainly earned this right!

After all, I was matriculated from a highly respected university. I'd worked suit-and-tie in advertising/marketing communications for over 30 years and had acquired various company shares and a 401(k). I could well afford to join the ranks of middle-class automatons performing garage maintenance on John Deere riding mowers and Husqvarna snow blowers. Or squirting pungent lighter fluid on expensive beef briskets lying helplessly on the rack of an outrageously priced designer propane grill. (My MAGA neighbor to the east of me does this at least twice a week during the summer and fall months, gifting the subdivision with the flesh-melting scent of a long-ago napalmed Vietnamese village.)

Unfortunately, my experiment with willful ignorance didn't last very long.

It never does for a Black person in an American society determined to remind you on a daily basis that you are tied to the socioeconomic whipping post. A stinging lash from a white boss-man bullshitting you about why you lost a promotion to a lesser qualified white candidate. A bloody lash from a white Human Resources boss-lady who, with a Hollywood-white perfect grin, gleefully admits to having created fictitious middle-management Black people for Chrysler and who has now been tasked to explore "diversity" programs for a software company. The freckle-faced 18-year-old white department-store sales associate who dutifully skulks eight feet behind you, scrutinizing everything your eyes settle on, refolding that Pierre Cardin sweater you gently ran your fingertips over. Your Black-hand touch must have somehow soiled the garment.

Willful ignorance is a quick death sentence for a Black human target.

"Read books, boy," my dearly departed father reminded my brother and me. "Get yourself an education. That's the only way you're ever gonna see inside the mind of America. You'll see how it sees *you*."

He would issue a bitter laugh, take a pull from his bottle of Carling Black Label beer and, with his eyes flooding, say, "Go to church on Sunday with your mother. But when Monday comes 'round, watch your ass, boys. Watch your ass."

Helluva way to grow up: Knowing your skin, your nose and lips and hair were tantamount to a bull's eye.

From deafening factory floors to 20th-floor conference rooms, constantly searching for the assassin's perch. Feeling the red targeting laser dot on your temple. Your forehead. Your chest or back.

I can feel myself holding my breath.

All of me for nearly four years, holding my breath.

Hearing the echoes of my father's prescient warnings shiver across my skin, raising the hair on my forearms.

Votes are still being counted. Maps are still being plotted out in the binary anachronism of Red States/Blue States. All I've ever seen on the Technicolor, 3D, 4K maps are states that may bite their civilized tongues for a tenth-of-a-second when it comes to uttering the word "nigger" and states where the word "nigger" rains down like hydrochloric acid from torrid skies, burning and killing those who dare brave the storm. I will not be going to Indiana anytime soon. Or Tennessee. Or Wyoming. Or Louisiana. Same with Idaho, though they do produce delicious spuds.

For that matter, you won't see me in *any* MAGA shithole.

Then again ...

... in the fall of 1968, George Wallace, the notorious snarling bigot and governor of the snarling bigoted state of Alabama, ran for the office of president of the United States. On a Michigan campaign stop was a blue-collar rally at the Lansing GM Oldsmobile factory. Wallace had whipped his blue-collar crowd into a fiery frenzy, ending with a call to come up and get and proudly wear one of his "Wallace for President" campaign buttons. My Black father had shouldered his way to the middle of the crowd and hollered, "I'll take a couple of those buttons!"

He managed to get to the head of the line—perhaps within eight feet of the diminutive Wallace—and walk away with a couple of "Wallace for President" campaign buttons, leaving in his wake some very confused, gobsmacked white UAW brothers.

Later in his 10-hour midnight shift, my father's first-generation Czech friend—inexplicably nicknamed "Dutch"—said to my father, "Jim!

Why you *do* this? George Wallace, he is *not* a friend of the colored man!"

"Oh, I know, Dutch," my father told his friend. "But *some*body's got to show these backwoods pecker motherfuckers they don't put the fear of God in *every* colored man. Got to leave 'em guessing *which* colored man'll go toe-to-toe with 'em."

So, on second thought, Indiana, Ohio, Tennessee, Oklahoma, Wyoming, Louisiana and Idaho, maybe I *will* visit y'all for a spell.

Leave yo lil chilluns copies of Alex Haley's *The Autobiography of Malcom X*, James Baldwin's *The Devil Finds Work* or Attica Locke's *Bluebird, Bluebird*. Maybe I'll continually lobby your public school boards to permanently put Howard Zinn's *A People's History of the United States* on middle and high school history curriculum reading lists. Maybe I'll GoFundMe "Black Lives Matter" billboards in your states and laugh every time you burn one down knowing you got a hundred corn, wheat, cattle and alfalfa miles to go before you get to the next one ... and the next one ... .

Oh, hell—maybe I'll just sit in my overstuffed leather chair that resembles Jabba the Hutt and conjure up stories that let you, let the world know I've seen the wizard behind the curtain—and he ain't that big and he for damn sure ain't that scary.

No, I refuse to be a victim of fear.

I will stand in light.

Take your shot.

If you haven't already noticed, Black folk have been around for over 400 years. We've been surviving, prevailing, creating, procreating, fighting and dying and rising up like Lazarus for over 400-goddamn-English-colony-and-American-years. You put a bullet in Martin and Medgar, and we still show up. You busted John's skull at the Edmund Pettus Bridge, and *he* still showed up. And—big mistake—you came for one of three of my *true* heroes: my father. For nearly 40-GM-Oldsmobile-UAW-years, you came after him. Told him he couldn't, so he did. Said he shouldn't, oh, but he would. Threatened him with a screwdriver gut-stabbing and he told you to make the first thrust count because if you didn't, you'd be the one bleeding and hurt just seconds before you were all the goddamn way dead. He took your jabs and punches because he knew he could take the punishment. And when the punishment became too much—when it threatened the love of his life, my heroic mother, or what he hoped were incarnations of his better self, my brother and me, he came out swinging. Thunder in one fist. Lightning in the other. And a mind that danced with the muses through the corridors of Alexandria.

I am many things.

But I am no one's victim.

I, like my father before me, am God's healing hand and the devil's punishing fist. I am Jesus in worn sandals on the dry and dusty road to Galilee and Robert Johnson standing at the crossroads. I am John the Revelator reaching for the Seventh Seal and Bass Reeves unleashing thunderous justice from twin Colt single action .45s. I am Harriet Tubman, spy for the Union Army and—realizing it was *all* bullshit— ferrying beaten and bloodied slaves through dead of night to Northern hopes. I am my miracle of a mother producing everyday hope and inspiration while laying healing angel's hands on her weary husband's battered and bruised body and soul. A body and soul always tested in the pursuit of a United Auto Worker's hard blue-collar labor wage. And I stand on my heroic older brother's shoulders as he has always wanted me to see many sunlit roads ahead.

I am all these.

I live in this stolen land of America navigating through an ongoing experiment called "democracy." An experiment who's guiding Constitutional principles never went beyond referring to me as property. But then, isn't that always the problem with the syphilitic disease of colonialism? It's either fecklessly incapable or lazily unwilling to imagine a future where the human property becomes—by parts warm kiss and spilt blood, rape and holy matrimony—kith and kin. The horns of differing beasts locked in constant battle over the Gordian Knot of Democracy.

9:05 A.M.

My bagel is gone. The mushy fruit of the banana has been incorporated. Coffee's lukewarm. The vote count drags insufferably on. A mentally feeble old white man versus a decrepit old white man. Militias are loading AR-15 semiautomatic rifles. Proud Boys are letting their MAGA freak-flag fly in the streets. Boogaloo Bois are scratching their Cro-Magnon nuts and just getting fatter and hairier. Kanye West has delivered his concession speech to Zardoz. Neighbors have moved their "Trump 2020" signs closer to their houses, as if retreating once again from reality. And my elderly Syrian neighbor has packed away his "Vote for Jesus" sign until the next election cycle. (NBC's Chuck Todd has no idea what numbers Jesus pulled in Maine, Massachusetts, South Carolina, Montana or Iowa.) The elementary school sandbox squabbling between Regular Middle-of-the-Road Democrats and Progressive Hair-on-Fire Democrats has bubbled over into public domain. And jittery, pearl-clutching Republicans are arguing over which one of them gets the dubious honor of taking dementia-addled Uncle Donald home to live with the family (until, that is, his cell at Rikers Island is painted gold.) My bet—$5 cash money!—is Dumpy Don goes home with either Senator Mitt Romney, Senator Ted Cruz or Little Marco Rubio. Whichever one, I want Hollywood producer/master sitcom creator Chuck Lorre to acquire the reality-TV rights.

In a country that has sent men to the moon, invented Post-it Notes and spanked France with canned *spray*-cheese, we seem to have made a helluva archaic mess of electing effective, responsible, strong leadership. Like the song says, "Money for nothin' ... ."

I glance at my watch again. Way too early for my go-to presidential election drink, an "Ulcerated Cowboy" (equal parts bourbon and Pepto-Bismol), so maybe a long walk at the local park will help relax me.

Yeah.

A walk will do me good.

And should a president actually be announced/anointed/coronated/confirmed while I'm communing with nature?

Remember: 1600 Pennsylvania Avenue is *my* house. My ancestors built it at a cost of blood, soul and labor. I pay my taxes every year to feed you, clothe you and your family and staff and fly you around the country and the world in *my* tricked-out private jet. If you violate any aspect of your four-year lease—*any* aspect—Lord Jesus so help me, I will do everything in my power to kick yo narrow ass to the curb.

Amen, I say amen.

New York, NY

BRONWEN HRUSKA runs Soho Press, an
independent book publisher in New York City, and
was named 2020 Publisher of the Year by the Strand
Critics. She is the author of the novel *Accelerated* and
has worked as a screenwriter and journalist.

MORE COWBELL

BY BRONWEN HRUSKA

This morning, just before 11:30, the first whoops and cheers erupted outside my window. Heart pounding, breath held, and as close to praying as I get, I stepped onto the balcony to investigate. Across 110th Street, I watched my neighbors in their windows, clapping and dancing, drumming and screaming—with pent-up nerves or boundless joy? Probably a bit of both. One middle-aged woman on the seventh floor with crazy hair unfurled an American flag and with some effort, began to wave it and wave it. Below, horns honked with euphoric abandon, rounding out a symphony of percussive excitement as bodies in windows banged on pots, pans, yes, even a cowbell.

I ran inside and refreshed CNN to confirm it. They'd called the election for Biden and Harris. I stared at the screen, stunned, relieved, paralyzed. A smile broke slowly across my face, feeling foreign there after so many days of dread. Then I climbed back onto the balcony, where I stood in glorious 70-degree November weather and breathed a huge sigh of relief with my fellow New Yorkers. It wasn't a decision but pure reflex when I started clapping and howling right along with them. I raised my hands over my head and pumped my fists, yelled at the top of my lungs. I didn't realize I was crying until my cheeks were wet. I couldn't—didn't want to—stop.

Pennsylvania, of all places, had done the trick, and I was reminded of an old boyfriend who lived in Lycoming County, one of the small rural rectangles on the Electoral College map I'd come to know so well. I knew without a doubt that he'd voted smarmily for the wrong candidate.

During the beginning of the pandemic, when Manhattan was a hot zone and Covid-19 rates were through the roof, there was citywide celebration from windows and fire escapes at 7 p.m. every night to thank essential workers for putting themselves in harm's way to care for the sick. The celebration this Saturday morning—from our apartments, balconies, the safety of our socially distanced spaces—reverberated with the same sense of sweet community. But today I didn't want to be inside, sealed off from the rest of the world.

I grabbed my mask, jogged down five flights and ran outside, following the commotion. I found myself on 111th and Broadway in front of Famiglia Pizza, in the middle of a spontaneous street party. Like me, these 200 masked Upper West Siders needed to share the moment. Not only was Trump out, we had our first woman in the White House. A woman of color. The moment was far too long in coming, but I pushed that thought aside for now—this was a moment to savor.

The residents of my neighborhood cheered and hollered and erupted in standing ovations as cars drove by honking in solidarity. Parents, kids, Columbia students, grandparents, this was a happy blend of humanity. I recorded the spectacle on my phone. For posterity? For proof? I wasn't sure, but I needed to soak it in every way I could. People danced, hopped, clapped, shouted. "Celebration" blared from someone's speakers. One guy held a professionally manufactured sign with white campaign lettering on that familiar Biden blue that read simply, "Bye Don."

A voice called "Congratulations!" from behind me. I turned to see a frail white-haired lady I didn't know. Her eyes above her batik face mask were crinkled in a smile. I looked around to make sure. Yep, she was talking to me. What was the right response? Thank you didn't feel quite right, so I raised my fists in the air. "Woohoo!" I responded and crinkled my eyes back at her.

I thought of Haley, my son's girlfriend and one of my favorite people, in graduate school at South Dakota State University. She'd quietly watched the election Tuesday night with the one other Biden supporter she knew at school. What could it possibly feel like to be one of only two blue dots in a red Trump swamp, with no random people congratulating her in the street? Were her classmates spewing conspiracies of voter fraud and a stolen election? Could she enjoy the moment at all? "It's hard, but it's better than Trump winning," she texted pragmatically that night as she cooked herself a victory steak dinner for one.

I am trying to empathize with the more than 70 million Americans who cast their ballots for Trump. I imagine they are as devastated and forlorn as my Upper West Side neighbors and I are relieved and happy and hopeful. And while the toddler in me (egged on by four years of this particular president) is telling me to gloat and taunt, I stop. Okay, Melania, this is not what you meant by "Be Best" (or gosh, if it was maybe I love you), but I'm going to try it. I'm going to give that toddler in me a time out. Yeah, I'm going to rise above the level of the man we just voted out of office. I'm going to realize that each of those grieving Trump supporters in every state in the country is hurting and worried. My hope for them is that they open themselves to the possibility that things can be better, calmer, more sane with Biden and Harris running things. We've all been held hostage by a spiteful megalomaniac who was as bad a winner as he is a loser. I want to say to the Trump people: You don't have to live that way anymore. You'll see—having compassionate adults in the White House will be *good*. You might even like it.

Think about it, the first lady knows of what she speaks. Maybe she was onto something, grammatically challenged as she was, after living with Trump for years. God willing, Biden and Harris will find a new working slogan, but I like to think there was a coded, transgressive message coming to us from inside the White House this whole time. America, it said, we can be better than my husband's tantrum politics. We can move past the terrible twos behavior that got us into this mess. No bite. No scratch. No hit. Let's use our words. Let's not only be good, FLOTUS was trying to tell us with her misleadingly simplistic two-word manifesto, let's be better than that—let's get rid of this joker once and for all.

Tartu, Estonia

WILL RAYMAN is a professional basketball player living and working in Göttingen, Germany. During the elections, he was playing in Estonia for Tartu Ülikool Maks & Moorits. He was named the 2020 Patriot League Defensive Player of the Year while at Colgate University.

FIRST PRESIDENTIAL VOTE, FROM ESTONIA

BY WILL RAYMAN

I didn't vote in 2016. I don't know why exactly. I guess I didn't know how bad it could really get. I was 19, had just gotten to college as a first-year student at a small liberal arts school in upstate New York called Colgate University. You probably know it as "the toothpaste school." Anyway, I was just starting college—I'd gotten a D1 basketball scholarship, and I was trying to be the best college player I could be. So I was distracted, for one thing. But truthfully, I didn't think my vote mattered that much. I wasn't fully aware of how having one president over another could impact me personally. Not only that, but going to a liberal arts school like Colgate, all you heard every day was F*** Trump. So I thought that my vote didn't matter. He wasn't going to get elected anyway. I thought Hillary was going to win, regardless, because who would want a joker like Trump in the office? Obviously, I was completely wrong. Even though I would be a New York voter and the state would be blue regardless, I now realize that I could have used my platform as a ball player to influence my classmates and peers who live in swing states to vote as well.

Anyway, we know the rest of the story. Trump won and over the past four years he's brought out the very worst in our country, the exact opposite of his fake promises to make the country great. Not only has he encouraged racism and sexism among Americans, but he has also shown an egregious lack of care for the many thousands of Americans who've died from Covid-19. If nothing else, these past four years have been a harsh life lesson. I will never take my vote for granted again. I have a voice, influence, a platform, and I'm going to use them to convince other people to use theirs, too. This election has felt personal. It's made me more interested in politics than I have ever been in my life (much more so than in any history class I've taken). Even though I don't know how Biden and Harris will do in office, I'm comforted by the fact that it won't be Trump.

I'm currently living and working in Europe, playing basketball in Estonia. Leading up to the results, everyone on my team kept asking me who I thought would win. I always said Biden, even though secretly I was worried—for most of the week the news made it look like Trump was ahead. I think I was trying to speak a Biden win into existence. About halfway through the week, a Lithuanian teammate was taunting me, saying Trump's percentages were up and he was sure to win. When I found out my teammate had bet money on Trump, that just set me off. I'm a pretty calm and measured person for the most part, but not this time. I exploded.

"It's not your country!" I shouted at the poor guy, who was clearly uncomfortable and maybe a little scared of me then. "You have no right to bet on something like that. And to put money on Trump, of all people? On that despicable human!?"

It wasn't until I blew up—I actually feel terrible about it now— that I realized just how personally I was invested in this election. The Lithuanian didn't understand what it was like for me to have my country represented by a president who's made our country into a joke all over the world, something I might not have seen clearly if I'd stayed in the U.S.

When I learned that Biden had won, or at least that Trump had lost, I was just so happy. But it was a lonely feeling, too. My family and friends (and from what I saw on Instagram all of New York City) were celebrating. My girlfriend, Haley, was multiple time zones away in South Dakota. The only other person around me who could understand just how big this was to me was the one other American on my team. He's from Nevada, a swing state, and was extra excited that his vote might have helped change that state to blue. The non-Americans on my team asked if we were happy, but that was about it. They couldn't understand the overwhelming sense of relief. For me and my American teammate, this victory felt like we'd won a championship game against our fiercest rival. And while it was sweet, I also felt very far away as I texted my family and friends back home. From the videos and pictures that I saw, there was music, dancing, singing, just an overall sense of happiness and joy.

But it would be too easy to say everything is fixed now. More than 72 million people still voted for Trump, almost half the country. The Biden-Harris victory is a step in the right direction, but in no way is it the end-all-be-all. Now we need to put out that fire that Trump started and continue the conversations about equality that he was so keen on neglecting. Biden and Harris just need to tell the truth and listen to the struggles of the American people. It's going to take all of us, but I think if we work together—and keep voting—we can create real change.

Afton, VA

DENVER RIGGLEMAN III was born in Virginia and grew up in Manassas, graduating in 1988 from Stonewall Jackson High, where he played football. In 1989, he married his wife, Christine, who also grew up in Manassas. Denver earned an A.A. from Burlington County College in 1996, an A.A.S. degree in Avionics Systems from the Community College of the Air Force in 1996, and a B.A. (with Distinction) in foreign affairs from the University of Virginia in 1998. Between 1992 and 1996, Denver served in the Air Force as a C-141 Starlifter enlisted avionics technician at McGuire AFB, New Jersey. After graduation he served as a commissioned officer with the 366th Fighter Wing and 34th Bomb Squadron at Mountain Home AFB, Idaho, and in the National Security Agency at Fort Meade, Maryland. Denver was first elected to Congress in 2018. He and Christine live in Nelson County and have three children, Lauren, Abigail, and Lillian.

WHAT HAS HAPPENED TO THE REPUBLICAN PARTY?

BY REP. DENVER RIGGLEMAN III

The morning after President-elect Biden's victory, an adult film star, a mortuary worker and landscaper walk into a bar. They order a whiskey laced with adrenochrome and pull out their mail-in ballots and lay them on the bar. The hidden watermark on the ballots not only gives them a discount on their drinks, but allows them entry into a private basement where they can interact with members of the Democratic, "Satan-worshipping cabal of pedophiles." They march single file down a dimly lit stairwell into a room covered in WWG1WGA wallpaper. A Comet Pizza box container has been framed and hung above a roaring fireplace. Donuts made into the shape of a "Q" are aligned neatly on tidy rows on top of a large roughhewn oak table in the center of the room, inside a newly bought chinoiserie tray. The basement dwellers savor the donuts, symbolic of their hatred for the digital prophet that has dragged them screaming into the public square. Those already milling in the basement giggle about Biden's victory, all of them wearing blood-red high school letter jackets embroidered with a large golden "R," signifying the venerated last name of "Rothschild."

I could go on and on about the insanity I have encountered in my two years as a congressman from Virginia in the 116th Congress. Above is only a snapshot into real conspiracy theories, although the narrative was my own. Since the election has been called for Joe Biden, my social media accounts have been flooded with conspiracy theories from Republicans I hardly know and those who I called friends. The insanity of the belief systems is something I have worried on and warned about for years. Whether QAnon, or the weaponization of beliefs from left to right in the political spectrum, the contagion of conspiracies and falsehoods has gripped this great nation in ways that were unfathomable only a decade ago. The crazy virus is spreading faster than the coronavirus.

The morning after this historic election I tried to convey a sense of normalcy to all those I communicated with, texted or phoned. My underlying message was: "It's all going to be OK." Friday afternoon, I texted someone very close to me, simply expressing my desire to move on and noting that the split in voting between the presidency, the House and the Senate could create a stalemate. I then mentioned tongue-in-cheek that "less government is better government." Earlier that week I had reiterated on a CNN segment that although I was a GOP congressman, as a free-thinker I would consider all options when voting, Republican or Democrat. I also condemned QAnon and conspiracy theories with brutal verbal gusto, utilizing my military jargon to unequivocally express my disdain for all conspiracies in general. The person I texted had watched that CNN interview. The text that came back my way was as brutal as my takedown of QAnon. This individual accused me of the deepest betrayal. Considering a vote for someone other than President Trump was a betrayal to my constituents and the president. I had been played by the liberal media, used as a pawn by the left to destroy the Constitution. QAnon believers had no choice but to react to the Deep State coup, and by the way, many of the QAnon theories were undoubtedly true. When I referred to QAnon grifters and pushers as "mouth-breathers," I personally insulted many of those who supported me in my election. I had now lost their support. In short, if I was a Republican I must support President Trump regardless of his words or deeds. Because, like many Republicans, this person believed that Donald J. Trump had been ordained by God and placed in his position to save the United States of America from the Deep State and those tyrants who would subjugate all under the blue banner of Socialism.

I needed to ask forgiveness. To their horror, that I would not do. Would never do.

After my initial shock of sadness and terror over the loss of critical thinking and common sense, I realized something the morning after. If I were a Republican, I was not a DJT Republican. I was a free-thinking independent Republican, or for 2020, something completely different.

As someone who self-identified as a constitutional republican with a libertarian streak, I found my unique brand of live and let live did not work in today's GOP. Obviously there are many who agree with me, but many who followed (and still follow) President Trump have embraced a peculiar kind of hero worship, as if Xerxes the God-King had been elected president. Anyone that strays from the path of exalting President Trump is automatically labeled an Ephialtes—humpback and all.

Hell, I know that much of this raging sycophancy is political. Attaching oneself like a remora fish to the man or woman in charge is not surprising in politics or business. Especially for those where ladder-climbing is their only option based on career choice (like politics) or an exquisite lack of talent. What frightens me is when those who attach to others with a vice-like sucking maneuver refuse to acknowledge anything outside their self-interest. "Service" becomes an empty word when one can become an elected official over and over as long as they swear fealty. For me, that was never an option. I am new to politics, learned quickly what I had to do to stay in the *inner circle*, but simply refused to conform.

The two-party system is a disaster, exacerbated by the continuing onslaught of social media and misinformation/disinformation. The pronouncement by President Trump that he had won with all the "legal" votes and that only "illegal" votes would beat him didn't exactly surprise me. And, to be fair, elections can be rigged. It's always possible. But intelligence professionals like me know the difference between the possible and the probable. It's possible that every state could coordinate a massive fraud on Election Day, but not entirely probable. And if the Deep State could pull off a presidential theft, why not steal the Senate too and ensure a supermajority in the House of Representatives? And since those on the GOP side have nowhere else to go if they are to stay in power, they must conform to the message from on high. Where else will they go? There are only Democrats left. And, Democrats have their own crazies to deal with. God forbid that someone has an independent thought. Our country is only R and D and everyone has to pick a side! If you have an R behind your name, then there is no choice in your decision-making. Biden stole the vote.

Like the Immortals under Xerxes, those who must obey rush into the breach, armed with an absolute truth that the election was illegal. White vans with no windows invaded election areas and swapped ballots. Biden took drugs to fix his brain—probably adrenochrome. Watermarks prove fraud. The NSA administered secret programs to switch electronic votes to favor Biden. (This is a particular favorite of mine. I worked for NSA. The NSA conspiracy theory is bullshit and perpetuated by the cognitively impaired, the easily led and the type of half-baked grifter who wouldn't know an original insight if it walked up to them at a bar and goosed them.) Trump golfed because we all must "Trust the Plan." Mail-in ballots were burned. Mail-in ballots were forged. Arizona should count all the ballots! Pennsylvania should stop counting! Nevada must COUNT THEM ALL! Georgia must STOP THE STEAL! President Trump must win because President-elect Biden has a secret plot to assassinate the president! Dems stuffing ballots caught on video. Election workers changed ballot names (and why not change ballots for all the Democratic Party candidates? I guess the spelling challenges were too much to overcome). Dead people voting everywhere. There are more votes than registered voters! Sharpies were handed out to Trump supporters to invalidate their vote. (How did poll workers know that certain voters were Trump supporters? A secret handshake? A hip wiggle? Two knocks on the table and a thumbs up?) Sharpie-gate lives.

I have been the subject of conspiracy theories and disinformation from Republicans and Democrats, so I can speak to this in a very honest way. As the first sitting GOP representative to officiate a same-sex wedding, I was accused of leading the charge to re-educate children into the homosexual lifestyle. I was called the "tool of the Antichrist." One intrepid conspiracy theorist called me the "General leading the Sodomitic armies." I was labeled a Soros spy and plant. My wife was called the spawn of Satan. To be fair, if I was indeed a tool of the Antichrist and my wife was the spawn of Satan, we would rate as the world's new *power couple.*

And my Democratic Party opponent accused me of Bigfoot Erotica. Completely made up. I laughed, though. Kinkshamer! I would never alienate those elusive Bigfoot voters.

I was aligned with President Trump on many policies such as trade, deregulation, criminal justice reform, infrastructure, fighting addiction and taxation. But I was not aligned on pandering to anti-Semitic-based conspiracy theories, dehumanizing language, immigration, foreign policy and health care. The morning after can be exhausting. Just hours ago on Facebook Messenger, I received a rambling 1,000-plus-word treatise on the *conspiracy* about what "really happened" during the election. I'm sharing this portion of the screed in all its glory, no changes to syntax or grammar.

"Trump has a plan and watch it play out. He asked for a recount which they will fight. He had the real ballots marked before hand with a secret water mark; the forged ballots do not have this. [From Evelyn – only 12 toss up States got the watermark. Special ink is only observable with UV light or military night vision goggles]. So in the recount they will sort out the real ones from the fake ones. Trump was prepared. He knew Biden was in China's pocket. His NSA told him what was going on at the Houston Chinese Consulate that is why he ordered it closed 6 months ago and there were reports of them burning papers in the yard when he announced the closure. That is here they were storing the forged ballots to turn Texas blue on election day. What better place to store fake ballots then at a foreign consulate where you can not get a warrant to search because of diplomatic immunity. Because of closing this consulate Texas remained Red. So the intelligence agencies have been doing their jobs behind the scenes. So do not worry – we already won; we are watching a movie play out. That is why Trump always says grab the popcorn and enjoy the show. #WATERMARK #TheDemsFellIntoTheTrap."

Evelyn must be connected. Maybe she's Q. Most likely, a cover name. No one would reveal their real name, right? Maybe it's a male named Evelyn? Why would this person writing to me about such dire mischief reveal the source? Now, I can track Evelyn and insert a tracking device under the skin while she or he sleeps. You know what's really weird? James Rothschild's father is named Sir *Evelyn* De Rothschild. A conspiracy, indeed.

Relief. Sadness. Hope. Apprehension. That's how I felt the morning after Joe Biden became president-elect. I am no fan of progressive policies. I am no fan of over-the-top far right policies. I am a fan of the Constitution. I enjoy facts. I despise conspiracy theories and the directed use of disinformation to radicalize people online. I cannot suffer those crazy enough to believe that *Lord of the Rings* was a documentary. Grifters abound in the digital universe and pretend to be prophets of a glorious future. Charlatans and the deranged feed off one another inside an electronic maelstrom of bad ideas and dangerous tropes. As elected public officials we cannot spread disinformation to pander or consolidate support. It's dangerous. The spread of conspiracy-laced falsehoods will rot the very core of a fact-based representative system. Every elected position is bigger than the person occupying it—and that includes the presidency.

On this morning after, my objective is to stop the super-spreaders of radicalization and hate. I hope it's something we can all agree on, left and right.

CHARLOTTESVILLE, VA

SUSAN BRO, a nationally acclaimed speaker and coach, is President and Board Chair of the Heather Heyer Foundation, formed in honor of her daughter, killed in August 2017. You can find her on Twitter @SusanBro7 or at the foundation website www.heatherheyerfoundation.com

REVELATIONS

BY SUSAN BRO

Reality reveals the lie. I say I'm not stressed, the Thursday after the election. I say I'm taking it all in stride and waiting patiently. My husband and I avoid glimpses of election results. There is no point yet. On Election Day, a young grandchild was having surgery, which had me in enough of a tizzy. I woke up on that day with tears on my face from crying in my sleep. The grandchild is fine now. I hope the country will recover as quickly as the child seems to be. But it really can't without intervention.

Reality reveals the lie. Before this election cycle, I would have said my husband was apolitical. He quietly chose a candidate, voted, and did not say much about it. I'm not sure he even voted before we met in 2010. Both sides were equally mocked or tolerated. This year, he's wading into the fray on his social media groups. For safety, he had largely remained anonymous. Now he's calling out BS on those pages, asking for patience, asking for sources, citing sources, and identifying himself as Heather's stepdad. He would tell you that none of it bothers him.

Reality reveals the lie. Both of us are coping with stress-aggravated medical conditions. My sugar is up, and pain stabs without warning. We are both fighting chronic infections, our sleep peppered with much tossing and turning. I'm very involved with writing, talking, posting, managing the post responses, checking on friends. And that means I'm stuck in one spot most of the day, which does not help the sugar issues, does not get dishes done, groceries ordered, or laundry finished. Reality is shaped by the stress.

Reality reveals the lie. We say we care and want to make the world a better place. Earlier today, I shared Stacey Abrams's photo on my FB page to respect and honor her outstanding work in Georgia. This was done at the request of my Black mentor. Then she had second thoughts and suggested that could be a taken as a digital form of blackface. So I promptly took it down, and posted an explanation why. Also today, I reshared a post asking for 20 people to donate at least $5 to help a Black mom who was about to lose her home. Guess which one got the bigger response? The blackface page is up to 75 likes and hearts, and comments are moving into a third page. Helping the mom with an urgent need has engendered two shares, three likes and three responses. We're better at talking about justice and reparations than enacting them.

A fellow activist laughed at me for taking that profile photo down and wanted to defend me from whomever had attacked me. We became annoyed with each other and I basically yelled at him. Later I wondered why in the world I lost it. I rarely lose my temper. I think we patched up, somewhat, although he promptly put Samuel L. Jackson as his profile, in defiance of being told it's not OK with some people. So I'm annoyed again. And this from a fellow activist!

Reality reveals the lie. I tell people I stand for justice and equity. I believe that we can do better. They tell me they stand with me and they want these too. They listen to me talk and say how great it is what I am saying. They send me hugs, thoughts, prayers for my loss.

But how many of them contact their elected officials to let their voices be heard? How many of them are engaged on the local level? Do they know what is happening in their own cities? Do they care that incorrect history lessons are still being taught to their children? Do they take the time to educate themselves? If they cannot do more than offer lip service to a cause that affects the very right to life, freedom, and safety for others, they are not truly engaged. They are spectating. They are dabbling. They are wearing the mask of privilege.

Reality reveals the lie. People fervently avow they are pro-life.

They insist life begins at conception. They celebrate the seating of a conservative Supreme Court justice hoping maybe to overturn Roe v. Wade. I'm not here to debate when life begins. I just want to point out that pro-life is not the same as pro-birth.

Pro-life means cherishing and protecting life until death do us part. Pro-life would also include affordable housing, economic opportunities, quality and affordable health care, access to healthy food, elder care and hospice care. Support of life should include the right to freedom and a desire to offer assistance to those hurting and dying everywhere—especially those coming to us in search of asylum.

Reality reveals the lie. People have said we are in a post-racial society, since Obama was elected. People tell me All Lives Matter as if it is in opposition to Black Lives Matter. People say they do not see color at all and are nonracist. Yet whole communities live knowing from early childhood that they are not safe, even in their own living rooms and bedrooms.

Don't tell me about Black on Black crime here—those are apt to be investigated and prosecuted. I'm talking about excessive policing and brutality. Frankly it took me a few years to believe it when my daughter and a Black friend were trying to convince me. My head was buried so far in the sand, it's a miracle I could breathe. My typical response was generally to say I didn't know the whole story.

Comparing judicial treatment of white people with Black people, you pretty quickly get the picture. The total population in the country is only 13.4 percent Black, but our Black prison population continues to be larger than either our white or Hispanic prison populations. Read Black history. Listen to Black lived experience. When you hear of a white person committing a crime with a slap on the wrist, imagine the scenario with Black face on the perpetrator. Do you see the same outcomes? Do you see the same reporting?

We said we wanted a Blue Wave and were sure we had one. We said we wanted to heal our democracy and to have a united country with representative leadership. And yet the voting is close, so close that we are waiting for results with bated breath while half of the country is in a clamor over a "stolen" election. (If we could steal it, then would we have left it to outcomes this close?)

Did we reach out to have difficult conversations? Did we listen to why people wanted their candidate? Did we choose candidates who were representative of the population? My head and heart feel the truth. We did the very thing I feared. Conversations were held primarily with people of like mind. We spent a lot of time reinforcing our own beliefs online, in panels, in conversations.

Most of us avoid difficult conversations with family and friends, for fear of damaging relationships. I was super dismayed recently when a respected family member informed me we don't take sides. Really? Was that part of my childhood? I struggle to remember if that was true. If so, when did I change?

The closeness of the election is on white people, especially women. For it to be close like this shows that we have not connected. We have not had enough honest discussion of what we need, particularly with marginalized communities. I am deeply grateful to Stacey Abrams and the numerous others like her who have organized Black voters who have hopefully saved the day this election. But even after watching the news tonight all I can say is we have work to do the next years leading up to the 2022 midterm elections. We cannot afford to gloat. We have to reach out and connect with people across the way.

I can keep my convictions while talking to others. My personal goal is to get them to come across to my way of seeing things. But I also acknowledge that I have not been listening to them. I have not been paying attention to what they liked about Trump. I have not been hearing what they fear from Democrats. I have yet to take the time to watch Fox, read conservative newspapers, or have more than a handful of real conversations with conservatives about religion, politics or the economy. So I need to practice what I preach.

I decided to go back to read conservative posts that were skimmed past on my feed. Fears are that gas prices and taxes will soar. There is fear of Kamala Harris taking office, although no one says why they fear her. They are convinced all guns will be banned and confiscated immediately, which has literally caused a shortage of ammo supplies and a run to purchase guns. One cousin stated we should all be experiencing the same feeling as when watching buildings crash and burn on 9/11.

Points of praise for Trump were brokering two Middle East deals. They say he was the first president to not engage us in war since Eisenhower. Per the posts, he brought the greatest jobs and economy and lowered the jobless rate the best of all the presidents. He, according to them, exposed deep and longstanding corruption in the FBI, CIA, NSA, Republican and Democratic parties. To their way of thinking, he turned NATO around and made them pay their dues, neutralized the threat of North Korea, and jolted our relationship with China to bring back business. He revived the economy, lowered taxes, increased our standard deduction, etc. etc. etc.

My word! I could spend weeks trying to validate all these claims. I only listed half of his supposed accomplishments. This is from a lengthy copy-and-paste rant on Facebook, so I'm sure each of you can go find it on your own. While we can shake our heads at this, these beliefs are absolutely true to them. So far, they have been thoroughly convinced that mainstream media is lying to them. Convincing them of the truth, even with facts, is going to be difficult.

Can we please add civics back to school curriculum and tell the truth in history class, going back to 1492 moving forward? At least start at 1619. As a former educator, I can tell you that many believe changes to curriculum take a great deal of time. During the pandemic, the whole country managed to adjust curriculum in three weeks.

Parents have the power of change in their own hands. Most don't realize curriculum decisions are made at the state level. They can contact their state representatives and state board of education to change curriculum. School boards are elected officials that will listen to parents.

Think how differently this election would look if everyone understood authentic history and civics. There would be a better understanding of the needs of marginalized communities. People would be less gullible about vote-counting schemes with prematurely declared victories or discussing stolen elections. Can we do remedial adult classes in both? What perks could we offer upon passing the course—a tax credit, extra points on driver's licenses, a free coffee with a pastry?

I watched the late news as usual and heard Biden was going to speak. I waited, thinking it is still a bit early in the counting process. But no speech showed up on my channel. The headlines popping up on my iPad mentioned the White House chief of staff tested positive for Covid. I posted that the White House will need disinfecting before the end of January. Then I questioned myself if that would be off-putting to people

I want to reach. But I left it.

Now I wonder what Trump will do in parting shots if he loses. What legislation will he have time to push through Congress between now and late January? Will there be enough in Congress to hold any further damage at bay? And that unscalable wall—will that keep him from being removed if necessary?

What will Washington be if we have a new president? Will Congress work with a new administration to push through initiatives we need and not block legislation? Will they be able to move forward in any meaningful way while trying to undo the damage done since 2016? A key feature to positively moving ahead is not only offering clean, affordable energy alternatives, but also economic replacement opportunities for fossil-fuel industry workers. We have to provide a better life for our Indigenous population. We owe reparations to our Black communities. And there must be some very substantial fixes to our health-care system.

So set your sights firmly on the goals. Make sure to listen better. Recruit and train others to join you. Because talking and writing about it will be little more than dabbling and spectating. Reality will tell the lie. It's 3 a.m.—going to bed finally.

SATURDAY

Woke up at 8 and checked my notifications. Nada. Back to sleep. I am resigned to not knowing until next week.

Up at 12:30 p.m. to see my stepdaughter asking if I've seen the TikTok of Biden and others dancing. Searching, searching, scanning all the reports. I so much want to believe, but don't want to get my hopes up. People call and text about it, but I am numb. I post on Facebook a bit and then just sit and read the posts, check Twitter, read the news, read the posts, check email. Somehow I get brunch made and start the laundry. But I just can't feel comfortable about it yet. Anxious thoughts keep playing out in my head. Can the Electoral College yank this away from us? Will there be shenanigans from D.C. to stall, in addition to the court cases filed?

On the days that Ahmaud Arbery, Breonna Taylor and George Floyd were killed, I sat frozen at my computer, shaking in rage, posting and reading reports all day. It feels a little like that today—not rage, but deeply emotional somehow. Running from Twitter to Facebook to emails to Messenger to texts. People let me know they are thinking of Heather today. None of my family asks except my stepdaughters. I did not think the others would reach out. Most of them are Trumpers or say they are nonpolitical. I draw more comfort from strangers sometimes. I'm used to it, mostly, by now. My husband sees the look on my face and asks if I'm OK. I am not there yet.

Biden gives a sane speech calling for us to work together. I see his plans for action on my newsfeed, and I feel a tightness in me relax a bit. I wish Heather were here. I wish I could call her. But I'm pretty sure she knows. As soon as I wrote that, a friend sent me a photo from D.C. where someone made a little sign that says, "Remember Heather." I take it as a sign she knows. And I am good. We will be alright.

Northampton, MA

HOWARD BRYANT is the author of nine books,
Full Dissidence: Notes From an Uneven Playing Field,
*The Heritage: Black Athletes, A Divided America and
the Politics of Patriotism, The Last Hero: A Life of Henry
Aaron, Juicing the Game: Drugs, Power, and the Fight
for the Soul of Major League Baseball, Shut Out: A Story
of Race and Baseball in Boston*, the three-book *Legends*
sports series for middle-grade readers, and *Sisters
and Champions: The True Story of Venus and Serena
Williams*. He is a two-time Casey Award winner (*Shut
Out*, 2003, *The Last Hero*, 2011) for best baseball book
of the year. The Heritage received the 2019 Nonfiction
Award from the American Library Association's Black
Caucus. A two-time finalist for the National Magazine
Award for commentary in 2016 and 2018, he has been
a senior writer for ESPN since 2007, and the sports
correspondent for NPR's *Weekend Edition Saturday*
since 2006.

ONE FOR THE ELDERS

BY HOWARD BRYANT

I was not in Harlem that late Saturday morning, just before noon, when word spread that the election had at last been called, Joe Biden was now president-elect, and more urgently, the one-term, terrible reign of Donald Trump was very soon coming to an end. I was not in Harlem, but as the video texts, of the dancing, the drum-banging, the cowbells, the spontaneous, V-E Day-style outbursts of joy from friends arrived, one in particular was accompanied by a message: "People are acting like a dictator has just been taken down."

Harlem, Los Angeles, Philadelphia, Detroit, San Francisco, Atlanta, jubilation everywhere—but not exactly happiness. Happiness was Grant Park, 2008, when Barack Obama was elected and even the most futuristic, optimistic rarely believed they would see in their lives a Black president. The Obama election was aspirational. A hope. A realization. A marathon finally, exhaustingly completed.

This was a release. A relief. A rescue. In my college town of Northampton, Massachusetts, horns honked into the evening, the way horns honk not when something is won, but when something is defeated. It was a *liberation*. The November morning had become a

November afternoon that was a record, 74 degrees, which felt like some form of divinity; 74 degrees three weeks before Thanksgiving. Heads popped out of sunroofs. People looked one another in the eye, masks on, waving rainbow flags and American flags. They wrapped them around their necks and wore them down the street as capes. They carried signs, profane signs, profanely vindicated, bidding a resounding and unambiguous *adieu* to Donald Trump. People acted like a dictator had just been taken down.

It was too early to reach conclusions. I had only thoughts. As the hours passed, it became clear why this day was producing such a collective exhale for so many people, especially those Americans who hung on so tightly to the myth of its exceptionalism, desperate for some concrete sign that allowed them to believe that Donald Trump did not represent America. For four years, they had been looking for proof of America's *goodness,* waiting for this day to deliver the evidence. For all of Election Night, as the votes were tallied and the races drew closer and it became clear that this day that had been anticipated for so many months, expected to do the job of removing Trump that impeachment did not, that the facts did not, that emoluments violations and sexual assault and tax fraud allegations could not, the evening did not cooperate. The numbers piled up for Trump—topping 73 million votes in all, more than any Republican in the history of the country, 11 million more than in 2016. There would be no cascading rejection of the last four years, which meant there would be no mandate against the Proud Boys, the killer of Heather Heyer, the snarling and defense of whiteness so many of the good white liberals believed was just a fringe, a cult to be mocked by Facebook memes and late-night jokes. It was no fringe. It was you, a majority of that 73 million that wanted for him to win again, and that majority that allowed him to refuse to concede. If the repudiation would never come in the form of a cleansing landslide, and it did not, at least the victory of his defeat would, by one vote or 1 million. Victory was the last chance. Victory allowed them to breathe. And for this, they danced.

I have often said that to be Black is to be a dissident. It is to dissent against the country that had made it at various points on the historical timeline illegal for Black people to read or write, to live here or there, to sit at this lunch counter or drink at that water fountain, for the purpose of fighting to secure the right to be—or, to dissent against the aspirational lean-in, the constant naïve hope, the soaring rhetoric, to believe in the better angels of our nature when for so much of our time here our nature has been an eight-minute, 46-second long knee on the neck of George Floyd. It can be a dissent against a relationship that has become unsatisfyingly toxic: subjugation of the Black grievance in exchange for individual firsts.

I have grown so terribly weary of the firsts while the group falls further behind. This year produced the first Black vice president, who happens to also be the first Black female vice president. The first Black photographer to shoot a *Glamour* cover. A Black person's exceptionalness in a given field, skill or aptitude, to do something no Black person had ever been capable of doing, is certainly worth celebration, but these milestones have virtually nothing to do with the pioneer and everything to do with exposing the totality in which Black people have been excluded from the everyday successes of life. In 2020, firsts are not triumphs. They are indictments.

And yet within that indictment was the incessant demand for Black people to do more. The Black electorate, or at least its lack of enthusiasm, was blamed for Hillary Clinton's defeat, even as the white majority that has been solid Republican in every presidential election since Lyndon Johnson last won it in 1964, was not. In the following days, when the Black people had come through, in Georgia and Pennsylvania, Wisconsin and Michigan, the satisfaction was tempered by the knowledge that their candidates desperately craved their votes without much commitment in return, for this predictably has become commonplace and given rise to the counterinsurgent argument that Black people are better without the Democratic Party. And it must be acknowledged that this reality doesn't make the Republicans more attractive; it simply leaves Black people stuck between two truths: The successful Biden strategy of relying on the math he knew (winning the center moderate whites he knew would head to the polls) over the math he did not (attempting to activate 2016's 90 million nonvoters with a riskier but more progressive agenda) brought victory but is unlikely to bring justice in the form of sweeping progressive positions on policing, reparations or education. Unlike the historical political exchange where delivering a key voting bloc is rewarded in return, the Black electorate is expected to vote, and faithfully, but not to be listened to.

If Baldwin believed that to be Black in America is to be in a constant state of rage, it is also to be in a constant state of conflict, for certainly the defeat of Trump was in and of itself a victory, and it must be said that over the past 12 years we have seen things that many of us did not expect to see, many things some of us desperately wanted to see but did not live long enough ever to, and the benchmarks of a Black president and vice president cannot be dismissed. My mother, for example, never lived to see it.

When the race was called, and the horns honked, I felt like I had been here before. It was 1992, when Bill Clinton had defeated America's last one-term president, George H.W. Bush. I was at Murio's Trophy Room in San Francisco, in the Upper Haight neighborhood. People were hugging and dancing and raucous. They also had been liberated, not simply from Bush, but from 12 of the cruel and emotionally violent Reagan years that serve as today's conservative foundation. It was a first victory, for four years earlier, in my first election of voting age, when the promise of voting mattered in a way it only can for the young, my friends and I sat in a circle in the offices of the Temple student newspaper, underage drinking, deflated by Bush's destruction of Michael Dukakis. Heads bowed, hollowed out, beaten—supposedly on the side of good and beaten by men who would ignore the AIDS crisis, unleash a homelessness epidemic on cities from which most have still not recovered, embedded the false equivalency that affirmative action gave Black people shut out of opportunity a handout. Belief in being right culminated weeks earlier, when a group of us students attended a rally in Washington, D.C., sat with Jesse Jackson, and he looked at us and said, "When young America moves, *all* of America moves."

Two decades later, sitting next to Dukakis at a dinner in San Diego, the former Massachusetts governor had not truly recovered from losing to Bush. "He was an empty suit," he said to me over dessert. "Such ... an empty suit."

People are acting like a dictator has been taken down. I felt like I had been there before, but I hadn't. Throughout the year, from Breonna Taylor to Ahmaud Arbery to George Floyd, the America narrative existed within the twin frameworks of a pandemic and a racial reckoning. When dictators fall, so, too, do their monuments, and in anticipation of this rejection of the last four years, the people tied ropes and chains to the statues and tore them down, into the rivers, onto the concrete. The act of physically toppling symbols of white supremacy was being called a *racial reckoning.* As the dictator grew cornered, Trump resolved to turn the American military against its own citizens, threw protesters into unmarked vehicles, and deputized prison guards to American streets. And, when the day of anticipation finally arrived, 73 million Americans supported what he had been. The 78 million who did not saw, finally, what Black people and their ancestors saw and have seen all their lives— what this country is capable of. They saw the brink, and for surviving it, they cheered.

These final months and days have always been white people talking to other white people, lifted by the soaring oratory of the great Black voices—King, Lewis, Obama. They talked about *saving democracy,* which they never really talked about when Black people were the ones suffering under it. They talked about *the end of the republic,* as if the current republic had ever displayed fairness, especially to Black people. My white friends would despair over the last four years as if they were living an apocalypse. I would not share in this performative show of fear and grieving, telling them the ancestors would be ashamed of me if I couldn't handle this. Who had more hope, I would ask: me in 2020 or a Black person in 1825? Even my closest white friends and colleagues treated democracy as something that was supposed to work for them, that they promised would one day work for Black people, too. What white people saw from 2016 to 2020 was the possibility that it didn't work for them, either.

When the Black voices made it their duty to save a place that had inflicted so many wounds upon them, they were stirring, in the great oratory traditions of the Black church. *The moral arc of the universe bends toward justice.* When John Lewis talked about Black involvement as a "down payment" on justice, people were activated, recognizing they were part of a titanic struggle. They were good words, certainly, but who were the words really for? They were for the whites, to remind them to stay in the fight, to remain in anticipation of that Saturday, four days after the election, when they could honk horns and feel normal again. As the normalcy of the past began to coalesce into a goal, all of this celebrating to go backward, but away from Trump, I felt something else: none of this is ours. With that came a question: How can something be yours if you have to fight like hell just to have the smallest piece of it? For all of the internet memes thanking Black people delivering Wayne, Allegheny and Philadelphia County, calling Black women "auntie" and "queens" for saving democracy, the American Dream for Black people remains, even at this late date, an IOU. The ideals may soar, but the check is still in the mail.

Walking around town, surrounded by euphoria, my emotions during the day were not a revelation but confirmation of a secret fear. After four years, the anticipation and emotion that stirred in me were not rooted in the belief of Joe Biden and Kamala Harris to be transformative. Neither received my vote in the primary, and throughout the campaign I did not acquire the sudden conviction that the Black position in this country will greatly improve under them. Neither ran with the Black grievances that welled during the summer as a priority, but more to restore the feeling of decency and goodness, common sense and leadership America has believed it has always possessed—which if it has, it must be said, has also coexisted with Black suffering. For me, the victory was more micro: it was for Black people, the Black elders of my world, in their 70s, 80s and 90s, the ones who waited in line to vote not just this year but in all the years, took the humiliations, got redlined, wore the uniform, still believed in the promise of the country, and saw fulfillment in a Black president and were told it was the gateway to better. It was devastating enough to think about the Black people I did not know personally who died with Donald Trump as the final president of their lifetimes, a cold repudiation of the Black president they never thought they'd see. For the Black people I did know, the retrograde messaging of Trump being their last image of life in America was a dread I carried deeply and quietly for four years, too heavy to face. I spent the entirety of his presidency prepared to never forgive this country for its historical confirmation of itself in anticipation. But the moment never came. The elders survived, and for my ears, the horns honked for them.

NEW YORK, NY

REVEREND AL SHARPTON is the host of
MSNBC's "Politics Nation," founder and president
of the National Action Network, a leading civil rights
organization. With over 40 years of experience as a
leader, minister and advocate, Reverend Al Sharpton is
one of America's most-renowned civil rights leaders.
Sharpton also hosts the nationally syndicated radio
show, "Keepin' It Real," and recently released his new
book *Rise Up: Confronting a Country at the Crossroads*.

WHAT PAIN TEACHES

BY REVEREND AL SHARPTON

I was just sitting down at my desk to eat that Saturday morning at the House of Justice in Harlem when I noticed I had a call. "House of Justice" is the name my mentor Jesse Jackson gave the National Action Network headquarters at the ribbon-cutting ceremony years ago. I'd led our regular Saturday morning rally to inspire people, with tens of thousands of activists who had worked so hard to elect Biden-Harris watching and listening on radio and television. I was literally getting ready to pick up my fork to eat my kale salad when I saw that Phil Griffith, president of MSNBC, was calling.

"Rev, can you fire up your phone and go live now on FaceTime to react," he said.

"React to what?" I said.

"They just called the election," he told me.

"Really?"

"Yeah, hang up and put on FaceTime."

So within 15 minutes of me finding out they called it, I was on MSNBC live from the House of Justice. Joe Scarborough had been the one to make the call on MSNBC, stopping short before an interview with author Jon Meacham to declare: "OK, we have an announcement to make. Joe Biden is president-elect of the United States." I missed that, but soon I was on with Joe and Mika Brzezinski as the screen showed a picture of Joe Biden with a total of 273 Electoral College votes and a list of the states that helped get him there.

"It is a real moment here at the House of Justice," I told Joe and Mika. "But I feel vindicated because Joe Biden really connected with people and if there's anyone that can heal this country, it is someone that has been through the pain, has had to grow, 'cause we fought over the Crime Bill 30 years ago, and he's grown."

The screen next to me at that point shifted to a large portrait of Biden.

"You have the poetry of him winning in his home state, from Scranton, Pennsylvania, but you also have the poetry of here was a man who was the vice president to the first Black man that was president that is now bringing in the first Black woman to be vice president. He is the bridge to bring this country together. ...

"This is the kind of healing we want. I was in the room, Joe and Mika ... I was there when he met with George Floyd's family, the day before the funeral in Houston, and only Joe Biden could show the empathy and compassion and took George Floyd's young daughter to the side and talked to her one on one like she was a head of state. She said to him, 'You know, my dad's going to change the world.' And he quoted that everywhere. That's the kind of man we need to bring this country together. We're not going to always agree, but we're going to have to trust the one that convenes us and I think he's earned our trust because he understands pain."

Mika had been trying to cut in. She had news, the first statement of our next president. "Well, the president-elect of the United States, Joe Biden, just issued a statement, reading, 'I am honored and humbled by the trust the American people have placed in me and in vice president-elect Harris,'" she read.

"'In the face of unprecedented obstacles, a record number of Americans voted, proving once again that democracy beats deep in the heart of America. With the campaign over, it's time to put the anger and the harsh rhetoric behind us and come together as a nation. It's time for America to unite and to heal.'"

It was a great moment. Obviously I had prepared myself that I thought Biden was going to win, but it wasn't like the impact of what it is to hear it officially. Joe Biden and I worked pretty closely together during the Obama years and I got to like him a lot. He's a decent guy. I like his wife, Jill, a lot. He's going to bring a new direction.

When I finished talking to MSNBC I texted Kamala Harris to congratulate her. I've known her since she was San Francisco District Attorney, running for California Attorney General in 2010. We gave her a National Action Network award in 2011 and brought her to New York for an event at Lincoln Center. In February 2019 when she was running for president, she came to New York and I took her to lunch at Sylvia's Soul Food restaurant in Harlem. I'd sat at the same table with Barack Obama when he was running for president in 2008. There was a lot of press there. She had a similar situation to what Obama did. People said Obama wasn't Black enough and he wasn't taking an aggressive stand. Her thing was, she was Kamala the cop. She was putting people in jail. We'd talked about that and how she could handle that issue.

The day the election was called, I got into the car to drive downtown to appear in studio on MSNBC, and on the way down Kamala called me. She thanked me for always being there for her. We teased about when I brought her to Sylvia's.

"You've come a long way from me having to support you and say you are all right," I told her.

She laughed.

"But what's really striking me today, Madame Vice President-elect, at 18 years old in 1972 I was the youth director for Shirley Chisholm for President in Brooklyn," I said. "I remember the misogynist stuff I would hear as a kid, what Black leaders and Black elected officials would say about Shirley. I lived to see a Black woman as vice president. And Shirley has got to be smiling from where she is in heaven."

I think Kamala got a little choked up, listening to me speak.

"That means a lot to me, Rev, and I know you've been fighting this stuff a long time," she said.

"We've had to deal with sexism and racism, and you've brought us another block or two toward what we've got to do," I told her.

I felt a lot of promise. I feel that the Biden-Harris administration is going to have a lot of challenges. Like Obama, they won't be able to do everything. They will probably disappoint some of the people that voted for them, because government does not work the way that you get everything done.

But here is how I would sum up how I felt that day. When I was working as youth director under Jesse Jackson, years ago, I heard a story about an old man in Mississippi being asked what he thought about the Civil Rights Act of 1964 passing. Did he think it was going to change his life?

"I don't know," he said slowly, thinking it over. "It ain't like it's going to be, and it ain't like it ought to be, but thank God, it ain't like it was."

That's how I feel. Whatever it's going to be, at least it's not Donald Trump. We knew what that was.

MOBILE, AL

CYNTHIA TUCKER is a Pulitzer Prize-winning syndicated columnist whose weekly column appears in newspapers around the country. Tucker has spent most of her career in newspapers, working as a reporter and editor. For 17 years, she served as editorial page editor of *The Atlanta Journal-Constitution*, and was also the paper's Washington-based political columnist. She later spent three years as a visiting professor at the University of Georgia's Grady College of Journalism and Mass Communication, where she was also a Charlayne Hunter-Gault writer-in-residence. She is currently the journalist-in-residence at the University of South Alabama, where she teaches in the English and political science departments. In 2006, she was named Journalist of the Year by the National Association of Black Journalists. In 2011, she was inducted into the NABJ's Hall of Fame. A graduate of Auburn University, Tucker was a Nieman Fellow at Harvard University in the 1988-89 academic year. She's a native of Monroeville, Alabama, and lives in Mobile with her 11-year-old daughter, Carly.

WHITELASH

BY CYNTHIA TUCKER

Dedicated to data, I believed the polls. So on Tuesday evening, November 3, I awaited the Blue Wave, the clear repudiation of Trumpism, the cleansing of a civic fabric sullied by a corrupt and incompetent narcissist. I didn't think there was any such thing as a "shy" Trump voter. There didn't seem to be any such species here in south Alabama, where I live. My neighborhood was dotted with Trump-Pence signs; a few huge Trump flags hung from second-story balconies or front porches. One Black man I talked to—a working-class employee of a defense contractor—said he might support Trump. He had bought into the widespread belief that Republicans are more favorable to military spending. Shy Trump voters? Hardly.

Alas, I was so, so wrong—wrong about the polls, wrong about Trumpism, wrong about my country. I didn't start drinking until Wednesday evening, as Senate races were called for Republican incumbents and the Blue Wave receded to mirage. Trump won GOP strongholds such as Texas easily, with help from Mexican-American voters along the Rio Grande. Florida went red as Cuban-American voters helped to oust a Democratic congresswoman, Donna Shalala, whose Republican opponent, former television journalist Maria Elvira Salazar, had campaigned against "socialism." I poured another glass of wine. The presidential contest was too close to call.

I woke up on Thursday attempting to come to grips with the grim reality that nearly half the country wanted to give President Donald J.

Trump another four years in office. Whatever excuses they may have had in 2016, whatever assumptions they may have made about the sort of leader he would be, they couldn't use that as cover. They knew exactly what sort of leader he would be, and they wanted four more years of just that. Trump received millions more votes in 2020 than in 2016.

So this is where we are: Trump relied not on dog whistles to express his bigotry but a foghorn, campaigning as the heir to George Wallace, yet half the country wanted him back. Trump was defeated, but Trumpism was not. I am stunned. I am dismayed. I am embittered. I am having difficulty trying to muster a kernel of the optimism that animated the late, great John Lewis, whom I covered as a reporter and who represented me in Congress when I lived for several years in Atlanta. He famously endured so much more than I could imagine, starting with his impoverished childhood under the cruel lash of Jim Crow, but he never gave up on America. He believed in the "beloved community." He lived by the quote adapted by the Reverend Dr. Martin Luther King Jr.: "the arc of the moral universe is long, but it bends toward justice."

He and I were both ecstatic when Barack Obama was elected the first Black president of the United States, although neither of us believed it represented a "post-racial" America. I thought Obama's election represented several steps forward on the continuing journey toward a more perfect union, toward a nation that finally lives up to its creed.

A month after that historic election, my adopted newborn came into the world. I was giddy with excitement (and lack of sleep). Keeping a diary during her first months of life, I wrote about watching the inaugural festivities all day on January 20, 2009. She would see a Black president and his lovely family as normalcy. I concluded with these words to my baby girl: "I want nothing but the best for you, and I'm just thrilled that you're going to grow up in a nation that is a much better place for little Black girls than it was just a few short years ago."

Fast forward a little more than a decade, and I've lost that sense of confidence in my country. Other pundits and analysts have pointed repeatedly to former Vice President Joe Biden's victory, which not only saves the nation from a four-year descent into autocracy and kleptocracy but also brings California Senator Kamala Harris into the White House as vice president. She is the nation's first female vice president. She is also a woman of African and South Asian descent. Little girls around the country, especially little girls of color, have already noticed, dressing like Harris in pantsuits and Chuck Taylor sneakers. Yes, her ascent is a very big deal.

But. But. But. As a Black woman raising a Black daughter, I cannot get past a few inconvenient but inescapable facts about my fellow citizens. Approximately 57 percent of white people voted for Trump. So, no matter how much my Trump-loving white neighbors smile and wave, I know they stand against full equality for my child and me. They have applauded a racist, saluted a corrupt autocrat, supported a pathological liar, approved an incompetent, extolled a misogynist.

Nothing that I was taught in high school civics mattered to half the nation—not fealty to the U.S. Constitution, not honesty and transparency in government, not honoring the men and women who gave their lives on the battlefield, not standing up to dictators abroad and domestic terrorists at home. All that mattered was keeping their standard-bearer, their white knight, valiantly fighting the culture wars on their behalf.

Meanwhile, Republican leaders in Congress—men and women who keep repeating their undying fealty to the U.S. Constitution—stood by as the White House and government institutions were taken over by Trumpism, doing whatever it took to remain in power. They said precious little as Trump repeatedly insisted that the election was being stolen from him. Those GOP leaders apparently don't believe anything I learned in high school civics, either.

As happened in 2016, some analysts are still laboring mightily to see economic anxiety as a major reason for Trump's popularity. They labor in vain. Trump's tenure coincided with historic lows in unemployment—3.5 percent in December 2019, before the pandemic—but he inherited good fortune from his predecessor. Obama and his vice president, Biden, fought off the Great Recession, in which unemployment reached highs that hovered around 10 percent, and brought it down to 4.7 percent by December 2016. Meanwhile, Trump's trade wars did as much harm as good to manufacturing jobs, especially in the Rust Belt. Besides, Black voters, whose net worth is far less than white voters, went overwhelmingly for Biden.

Let's be clear-eyed: Racism is the cornerstone of Trumpism, as central to America's civic fabric as it was at the nation's founding. I saw this coming during Obama's tenure, when the Tea Party burst onto the scene claiming a mantra of fiscal conservatism and government restraint. That was never the central concern of its members (who since then have shown no interest in either government or fiscal restraint). Their political banners were steeped in racist imagery, picturing Obama as a witch doctor, among other disparaging symbols.

First Lady Michelle Obama, an accomplished and attractive woman, was subjected to any number of racist memes, some featuring monkeys and baboons. And when the Affordable Care Act passed, Lewis and other Black members of Congress received emails and letters denouncing the ACA in explicitly racist terms.

Political scientists, too, began to see in the backlash to the nation's first Black president—or the "whitelash," as some clever pundits have called it—the racism which fomented it. One group of researchers tested opposition to the ACA to parse racial resentment. When it was described as an idea proposed by former President Bill Clinton, whites in the survey overwhelmingly supported it. When the same proposal was described as Obama's idea, white opposition climbed.

However, racism, while a major factor in Trump's appeal, doesn't explain it entirely. Trumpism is a combustible and dangerous mix of cultural resentments, a rage against modernity. William F. Buckley, founding editor of the *National Review*, once famously declared: "A conservative is someone who stands athwart history, yelling Stop." Trumpism is a movement whose followers are addressing modernity with a primal scream.

Trumpists are unhappy with the 21st century, which has brought not only the first Black president but also the first female vice president, who is, not coincidentally, a woman of color. That has forced them to confront the demographic wave that threatens their cultural hegemony, that will downgrade the significance of whiteness. The 21st century has also brought gay marriage, challenges to police violence and a vocal transgender community demanding equality.

When Trumpists watch television, they see gay couples advertising home insurance, biracial children in cereal commercials and Black couples advertising new cars. In the grocery store, they see magazine covers featuring dark-skinned women such as Viola Davis and Lupita Nyong'o. They see Oprah everywhere.

They claim their political choices are driven largely by a passionate opposition to abortion, but I have my doubts. If they are so devoted to children in the womb, why does that concern for poor Black and brown children stop as soon as they exit the vaginal canal? Their patriarchal, white-nationalist churches preach a theology that opposes allowing women to own their bodies and their choices. Trumpism thrives in those churches.

For all the dangers of the racism and sexism that animate Trumpism, those antediluvian views may not represent the greatest threat to democracy. Living in a bubble of misinformation, lies and unfathomable conspiracy theories, many Trumpists have turned their backs on reason, evidence and facts. No democracy can survive if half its citizens reject the foundations of the Enlightenment, as the Founding Fathers well knew. For all their failings, they believed in reason, in empiricism, in science. Half of this country gave their votes to a man who rejected all those things, repeatedly, publicly, enthusiastically.

In Georgia, Republican voters in a conservative district north of Atlanta just elected to Congress Marjorie Taylor Greene, an ardent promoter of a web of conspiracy theories called QAnon. At the heart of that morass of unfathomable beliefs is the idea that Trump has been secretly doing battle against a worldwide cabal of pedophiles, led by Hollywood elites and Hillary Clinton. (Hillary-hate is a weird beast in its own right.) QAnon has significant support in Trumpist precincts. How can that be?

Even as I think of John Lewis, who gave so much to this nation, I find it difficult to imagine continuing the fight for full equality, for progress, for highly touted American ideals. What to do in the face of this madness? The rise of Donald Trump was not like the rise of Ronald Reagan, whose electoral victories left me depressed, or the rise of George W. Bush, whose disputed 2000 election left me angry. Trumpism is an affront to logic, to facts, to a nation of laws.

How do we move forward together when half of us are ready to follow a man who ignored the deaths of more than 200,000 Americans from Covid-19 and wanted to fire the public health experts who tried to tell him how to curb those deaths? How do we move forward when half the country embraced a man who repeatedly told lies that were easily refuted? How do we move forward together when so many Americans believe in wild conspiracy theories?

Joe Biden and Kamala Harris may have won the election, but the nation has lost something incalculable. Our fragile democracy is battered after this assault on its founding principles—an assault carried out not by one man named Trump but by the millions who supported him.

NANCY E. O'MALLEY is the Alameda County, California, district attorney and is the first woman to serve as Alameda County's district attorney. A national leader known for her innovation and vision, O'Malley has made combating violence against women a high priority throughout her career. She has written more than 40 bills that have become law, and received numerous awards for her leadership, including the ABA Margaret Brent Award, the Lois Haight Award of Excellence and Innovation Award from the United States Congress, and the James Irvine Leadership Award.

KAMALA AS A YOUNG
PROSECUTOR

BY NANCY E. O'MALLEY

On Saturday, November 7, I got an early start, helping a family member move. But I was stopped in my tracks when the news reported that Joe Biden had won Pennsylvania and he was now our president-elect. You see, from the bottom of my heart, I knew that electing Joe Biden and Kamala Harris would be the right outcome for America. We needed to remove the provocateur in the White House—the one who continually exhibited racist and misogynist attitudes, who went rogue from the experts and discounted or disregarded many protocols of the office of the presidency. It had to be "time's-up" for the man who showed utter disregard for those career government employees who were there to serve and protect the interests of the American people. We needed to replace this president who was disrespectful to leaders, in D.C., throughout the states and across the globe. It was time to replace this president who always put himself above country, including pushing his way to the front of the line at the G7 summit in 2017. Time to retire the leader who generally exhibited contempt for everyday Americans, even his own supporters, unless they were kissing his ... ring.

I knew that the combined leadership of Joe Biden and Kamala Harris would heal our country and guide us through our recovery from the economic crisis, the pandemic and the divisiveness that wreaked havoc on America over the last four years. I have long admired Joe Biden. He was the champion in the enactment of the Violence Against Women Act of 1994. That was my first experience of him. More recently, in 2015, I worked with then-Vice President Biden's office to enact the Sexual Assault Kit Initiative. For several years, I had been working in California to rectify one of the great injustices to victim-survivors of sexual assault crimes. Victims would undergo forensic sexual assault exams resulting in the collection of forensic evidence and completion of a sexual assault kit. Those kits could recover vital evidence such as DNA potentially linked to a perpetrator. While there had been federal dollars for crime labs to test the kits, hundreds of thousands of kits remained untested, sitting in police property rooms. As DNA grew in use as a forensic science, hundreds of thousands of kits still languished in police property rooms. Victims, who thought their kits were being tested, were left in the dark.

I brought this issue to Vice President Biden's staff, literally drawing a flow chart to show where the backlogs of untested kits began. Within a few weeks, President Obama and Vice President Biden earmarked $35 million dollars in the federal budget for sexual assault kit testing. We subsequently navigated the initiative through Congress, resulting in an increase in the budget amount. Vice President Biden then created the "SAKI" program that has tested hundreds of thousands of kits across America. Vice President Biden cares for every person and his humanity was in full force addressing this issue. He could see the injustices, as well as the dangers to communities across America by failing to hold sexual offenders accountable. It was a proud moment for me at the press conference with Vice President Biden when he spoke from his heart, using his influence and authority to illuminate and correct injustices impacting mostly, but not only, women.

I was front and center when Kamala Harris announced her bid for the presidency. I met Kamala when she was a student at the University of California's Hastings School of Law. Upon completion of her second year there, Kamala was selected to join the Alameda County District Attorney's law clerk program in my office, one of the first such programs in the country. Law students, under supervision, could try cases, argue motions, work with victims of crime and more. Kamala was one of 12 students selected out of more than 250 who were interviewed. As a deputy district attorney, I had the opportunity to supervise her as she stepped into a courtroom representing "the People of the State of California." There was a true quality about Kamala that made her a top candidate for joining our department as an attorney—a prosecutor. The qualities she exhibited in her early years in my office are the same qualities she has shown America. She is a woman of high intellect. She is perceptive. She has strategic sophistication in assessment, planning and implementing programs to improve and bring about reforms. Kamala has natural charisma. Her heart, like Joe Biden's, is authentic and caring. Her ability to put action to feelings and words has helped her meteoric rise to the top. She was the perfect choice for vice president.

During her time in my office, I made it my mission to recruit Kamala to my team, the sexual assault unit prosecuting crimes against children and adults. I knew her ability to handle cases that were emotionally and factually challenging. With victims, Kamala was gifted at assuaging their fears and anxieties. The touch of her hand, or the kindness on her face, helped victims get through a difficult process. They knew that this confident woman would be the fighter they needed in the courtroom—fighting to ensure justice was achieved. No matter the final verdict, victims knew that Kamala was their "Warrior Woman."

Kamala came into the law with an expansive and progressive view of the criminal justice system. We shared the belief that people were more than just "a defendant" or just "the crime." Her sense of justice was much broader than simply crime and punishment. When Kamala left Alameda County for the San Francisco District Attorney's Office, she made it her mission to reform criminal justice from simply punitive to be fair, equitable and just. As the first woman to serve as San Francisco DA, she broadened the focus, and improved the policies and practices of that office. Her programs produced reductions in recidivism, which was substantial. Kamala's rise continued as California attorney general, and her national presence was enhanced. She earned the respect of her colleagues from across the country. It was Kamala who beat a drum that many followed.

In 2009, I became the first woman district attorney in Alameda County, a position once held by Earl Warren, who eventually became the chief justice of the U.S. Supreme Court. I had always worked with the legislature, having successfully had more than 40 bills signed into law. As DA, I spend considerable time in Washington, D.C., as well. As I thought about the 2020 election, I knew that who sits in the Oval Office and the Eisenhower Executive Office Building would have a dramatic influence on the direction of the country, and the distribution of resources that have become critical to millions of Americans.

As an introspective and strategic thinker, Kamala Harris has learned from her own experiences. She has been a teacher, a model for other leaders but especially for women and even more so for women of color. I have benefitted from watching and learning from her. And while I have been honored to be a partner, a colleague and a worker in Kamala's world, I was also relieved that she would be the vice president of the United States of America, working side by side with President Joe Biden. Why? Because I know the person—I know her character, compassion, drive and integrity. She is a loyal and proud American, but understands the need to work for progress, fairness, justice and equality.

So on Saturday, November 7, 2020, as I was going about my business like millions of Americans, I heard the heartening news that Joe Biden had won in Pennsylvania, giving him more than the requisite 270 Electoral College votes. I was literally stopped in my tracks. I felt great optimism and breathed a great sigh of relief for our America.

As I celebrate the election results, I reflect on my favorite saying: "If you're not at the table, you're on the menu." Joe Biden and Kamala Harris have earned their leadership seats at the Table of America, and it is where they both belong right now, in these times. We need them to lead us back to the proud country we love. As I watched President-elect Biden's speech, hearing him repeat that he will be the president for *all Americans*, I immediately knew that the nightmare of the last four years would soon be over.

I ended November 7 watching "Saturday Night Live." In his profound monologue, comedian Dave Chappelle reminded "everybody who's celebrating today to remember, it's good to be a humble winner. Remember when I was here four years ago, remember how bad that felt? Remember that half the country right now still feels that way." As Joe Biden said, the work will not be easy—we have plenty of issues on our proverbial plate. However, my confidence has been restored. I know that Joe Biden and Kamala Harris will rebuild our stature on the world stage and with our allies, and we will once again reclaim our place as a world leader—led not by someone who puts his own interests first, but by a president and vice president who will show respect, leadership and integrity to the world.

On November 7, 2020, after I had taken several deep breaths and felt joy and thanks, I read a tweet from the mayor of Paris, a city I love. She tweeted, "Welcome back America!"

Très jolie! We can now reclaim the America we deserve, that cares about each other and finds the common ground on which to work. Joe Biden and Kamala Harris cannot do it alone. I will claim my seat at the country's table, as I hope all Americans will. Let's get to work and make it happen.

GENERAL WESLEY CLARK serves as Chairman
and CEO of Wesley K. Clark & Associates, a strategic
consulting firm, and Chairman of Energy Security Partners,
LLC. A best-selling author, General Clark has written four
books and is a frequent guest on TV news programs. He
retired as a four-star general after 38 years in the U.S. Army.
He graduated first in his class at West Point and completed
degrees in Philosophy, Politics and Economics at Oxford
University as a Rhodes scholar. While serving in Vietnam,
he commanded an infantry company in combat, and was
severely wounded and evacuated home on a stretcher.
He worked with Ambassador Richard Holbrooke to
help write and negotiate significant portions of the 1995
Dayton Peace Agreement. In his final assignment as
Supreme Allied Commander Europe he led NATO forces
to victory in Operation Allied Force to stop ethnic cleansing
in Kosovo.

A MAN ON HORSEBACK

BY GENERAL WESLEY CLARK

To borrow a Churchillian phrase, November 3, 2020, could mark the beginning of the end for a terrible four years for our democracy. It has been a period of rank partisanship, selfishness, greed and anger. It has been a period when fewer and fewer Americans believe in their own government, and when our government does less and less to promote the ideals enshrined in our Constitution. More and more abroad questioned the goodness of America and speculated that we were just another declining power. Especially they questioned our president, his bullying, bragging, deceitful character.

But if the election marks the end of the beginning, America will still have a long way to go to restore greater civic harmony, cooperation across partisan lines, and dedication to the public interest, rather than private interests, lobbyists and corporate greed. If Joe Biden becomes president, he will have a hard task before him to restore the decency in public life and at the same time make the material changes in health care, public investments, fiscal policy and the economy that are needed to deal with climate change, China, racism, chronic unemployment, and so many other issues.

To be honest, I have been anxious about the possible outcome for many months. Forget about the polling for a moment; Donald Trump has wide appeal. And to appreciate the threat to democracy, you have to understand the appeal. A majority of Americans are focused mostly on their own issues—jobs, children, marriage and relationships, houses, debt, families. We aren't following the day-in-day-out of politics. So here is Donald Trump: He looks good on the stump, despite his age; he brings celebrity from his TV series, his supposed wealth, and his womanizing; he whips up crowds with a mixture of bravado, scorn and disparagement; he stirs controversies that attract attention—and somehow over 40 percent of the American people stand by his mixture of narcissism, lies and authoritarianism. Meanwhile, lots of businessmen support the Republican push for ever lower taxes (unless Democrats are in power, in which case they then worry about the deficit), even though they might say they disapprove of Trump personally. Never forget that psychological and sociological surveys consistently show that more than a third of Americans actually prefer an authoritarian leader to the checks and balances and the normal back and forth ("bickering," they call it) of everyday politics. And since so many Americans normally don't vote in elections—a 60 percent turnout of eligible voters is considered high—Trump could indeed be re-elected despite his consistently unfavorable polling.

Why is he such a threat to democracy? He has worked hard to "sell" his "achievements"—a tax cut, border/immigration policies, some support for Israel, renegotiation of NAFTA, prison reform, and a few other little things. But he is a threat to democracy because he is all about himself, unbounded by ethics, laws or respect for others. As his niece has said, he will do anything to win. He doesn't play by the rules or live by the law. Indeed, his whole life—4,000 lawsuits—has been one epic journey of gaming the system, seeking ways to bribe, bully, undercut and cheat to get what he has wanted. What he wants is money, power and respect—a government that belongs to him, and his monument on Mount Rushmore.

It is precisely this kind of leader who, in the right circumstances, kills democracy. The Founding Fathers worried about a Julius Caesar, a "man on horseback" who would use the military to seize control. But we have seen in our own times that a Mussolini and a Hitler could appeal to the same blend of authoritarianism, conspiracy theories, celebrity and rhetoric to use democratic means to overturn democracies in Italy and in Germany. Soviet-backed Czech communists did the same in

Czechoslovakia after World War II. Could it happen here?

Today, my family and I are coming face to face with the uncertainty of the outcome. Will it be the beginning of the end of "Trumpism"? Or will it be the end of our democracy, and the start of a new authoritarian government in America?

Tonight, my wife and I watched the early election returns. From 8 until 10 p.m. I had two long session on TV for the Middle East Broadcasting Networks. I tried to explain: This isn't like a football match. The votes are all cast—the excitement and uncertainty is generated by the counting procedures in various states. Isn't it funny how all the networks want to make it like a real-time sporting event?

My son in Los Angeles called and said, "Dad, don't worry, it will be a blowout for Biden."

Friends in Central America and in Europe are asking about the election, "How does it really look?"

We went to sleep, sort of, with the outcome undecided for both the White House and the Senate. We knew a large number of absentee and mail-in ballots remained to be counted. We hoped they were mostly votes for Biden. It was an uneasy night's sleep.

MORNING, NOVEMBER 4

I was awake at 5 a.m. checking the internet for updates. Nothing new, really, other than the president saying the election was over, vote counting should stop, and that he had won. Oh, sure.

A West Point classmate emailed from Europe, concerned, watching on the local news how European statesmen are dodging questions about the American election.

By 8 a.m., I had cleaned up some leaves and begun watering the lawn and the new shrubs in the yard. Gert, my wife, headed out for a walk, and I sat down for breakfast and the morning call with the office.

I was cautiously optimistic. It looked like Wisconsin was going our way, not sure on Michigan. Assuming Biden won Nevada and Arizona, we only needed Michigan, along with Wisconsin, to hit 270. No worries about Pennsylvania, Georgia or North Carolina.

But we are anxiously awaiting the final counts of ballots. It is an unbearably close election. Biden seems to have the clearest path to victory, but it will likely be without overturning a Republican majority in the Senate. Sadly, Steve Bullock in Montana didn't make it into the Senate. Perhaps there will be a runoff election for one or two Senate seats in Georgia.

A little before 8:30, a friend in Washington, closely connected to the Biden campaign, tells me the pollsters really got it wrong. He is quite concerned that Biden may lose. My friend in Connecticut, who knows Trump and has followed him closely, is warning that Trump will fight to the last vote and may well win. My golf buddy texts and asks: Are you following this? What do you think? My office team—three really smart, politically savvy women—are basically holding their breath when we do the morning update call on Zoom at 0830.

I am concerned. Lacking control of the Senate, the president will be crippled in his ability to organize the fundamental reforms of campaign finance and the courts system. He will have difficulty with economic reforms necessary to stimulate growth and job creation. He will lack the votes to deal with climate change. Without control of the Senate, we will see more of the gridlock, partisanship and meanness that have marked the last several years.

It is tempting to begin to analyze what happened but, really, it is too soon. Still, we can't stop. The loss of Democratic votes in South Florida was surprising. What happened? We will know soon. Turnout for Trump in rural areas was probably higher than the pollsters anticipated. Democrats will once again be asking themselves, as they have for the last 20 years, "What's the Matter with Kansas?" to use the title of a popular post-2004 election critique.

When I campaigned for the Democratic nomination for president in Eastern Tennessee in 2004, Congressman Lincoln Davis told me he wasn't going to be "outgunned, out-gayed, or out God-ed" in his own campaign. He had a shotgun rack in his pickup truck when he met me at the airport. At the rally we recited the Pledge of Allegiance, sang the national anthem, and said a prayer, all before we spoke. He knew elections were about culture, not policy details. He lasted in office until the election of 2010, when he was swept away by the Tea Party. When the Democrats lost Lincoln Davis, and the other "Blue Dog Democrats," Democrats lost the ballast in the party that held onto traditional rural voters. We've been struggling to regain that in the face of Fox News, the Tea Party, and other right-wing efforts for the last decade.

At 9:45 a.m. I get an email from the National Security Leaders for Biden team, asking for patience and explaining that the Biden campaign is projecting victory in the election. Michigan is going blue. This does it. Now waiting for official calls. Still do not have the Senate, however.

By noon, the headlines all over show the election tilting toward Biden. My friend from Connecticut warns me that Trump will fight to the bitter end and find a way to get to the Supreme Court. Another friend from Connecticut writes to say: All this has to stop! She is so stressed that she is gorging on gummy bears and nachos, and she suggests: Watch Bill Barr. He will try to avoid Trump's call so he doesn't get further used in pushing litigation to the Supreme Court.

At 1:15 p.m. I am on TV with a famous news anchor from Bosnia. Technically, he is asking about the Dayton Peace Agreement, reminding me that it has been 25 years since that agreement (which I helped negotiate, along with Richard Holbrooke and others) brought peace and an end to the conflict there. But actually, what he really wants to talk about is the American election, and what it may mean for Bosnia and the rest of Europe. He is frankly worried about President Trump, and he fears that if Trump is re-elected he will abandon U.S. interests and commitments in Europe, leaving Bosnia to the Russians, Turks and Chinese. That is the constant theme I have heard from Europeans for three years: unending worry about President Trump; they feel he is abandoning them.

At 2 p.m. I am back on MBN, answering questions for Middle Eastern audiences about the election and what it may mean for American policy. Yes, if President Trump wins, it may mean the end for NATO, but I go no further than I have gone publicly in other articles and statements. I try not to discuss partisan politics with overseas news media.

By 2, Senator Susan Collins is declared the winner in Maine. *How could they?* I think. She has quibbled and squirmed, voting against Trump only when it didn't matter (except for her politics back home). Then a few minutes later a West Point classmate, bitterly opposed to Trump, emails a note saying, *Thank goodness Susan Collins was re-elected.* He is originally from Maine and still follows events there closely. Guess that's how she got re-elected.

I am in and out of various business calls all day, but periodically checking the news feeds and emails. Canadian friends are asking, *Are you safe down there?* I assure them that in Arkansas we have plenty of firearms, not to worry! Actually, Arkansas has been extremely quiet—it is a state totally dominated by Republicans at every level of government. And there are many people with "concealed carry" permits. So, no safety concerns here!

By 3 p.m. Trump is already saying that he will sue to take the Pennsylvania ballots to the Supreme Court. Totally in character.

Wisconsin is finally, officially called for Biden.

EARLY EVENING ON NOVEMBER 4

Slow counting in Arizona, Georgia, Pennsylvania and Nevada has delayed results. Obviously acting on inside or detailed information, the president's lawyer announces lawsuits in Michigan, Georgia and Pennsylvania. Trump says he wants to get the election to the Supreme Court and accuses Democrats of trying to steal the election. Meanwhile, Giuliani says if necessary, he and Trump will sue the whole United States.

After dinner, all I can think about is the coming struggle, litigation, litigation, litigation. And if Trump loses, the lawsuits will continue. Meanwhile, the Democrats will have to struggle through this and aim for a stronger performance in the 2022 elections.

By 8 p.m. it's time to turn away for a few minutes. Have a good series on Netflix and a good book to read, plus time to do my evening chess problems. Silly distraction, I know, but still a distraction. I never had a chance to swim today.

By 11 p.m. it's time for bed. The counting continues, the legal challenges are now in four states, and commentators in the newspapers are recognizing that if Biden wins he faces a nearly impossible task in governing with an obstructionist Senate and a highly conservative Supreme Court. His every initiative will be challenged and thwarted. Meanwhile the increasingly restive Democratic left will only grow more frustrated. All eyes on the 2022 election. Campaigning must never stop. I go to sleep wishing for a better, more hopeful day tomorrow for the country.

A little less stressful today, as the counting continues, and VP Biden steadily cuts into Trump leads in PA and GA and holds on in NV and AZ. It was a busy workday, with conference calls all day. More calls and texts from friends overseas about the election, essentially asking: *What is wrong with the United States?* So painful to see the partisan strife about the election.

Late afternoon, people are asking, *Did I see the President's rant about election cheating? No,* I answer, because: *Why do this to yourself?* You know this is his nature *and* his strategy: discredit the election if he isn't winning, and thereby lay the basis for his retreat and revenge. Poor president, always victimized; people are always against him, he says. Yet something like 70 million people voted for him, for various reasons.

Midnight, no resolution, going to sleep.

FRIDAY, NOVEMBER 6

Awoke this morning to find Biden leading in the Georgia count and, hopefully, two Senate races going to runoff. The local newspaper, which didn't have room for my op-ed two weeks ago but did give four pages to Tucker Carlson conspiracy theories, complains about people on Twitter criticizing "flyover country" folks as "uneducated fools" who voted for Trump. Our local newspaper always feeds a sense of victimization and inferiority among Arkansans. Such nonsense.

Friday was a calm day, for us at least, awaiting results. More calls and texts from overseas asking about the election and hoping that Biden will restore American leadership in the world.

SATURDAY, NOVEMBER 7

Early morning golf, and as I am finishing up, my wife texts me that Biden has been declared the winner. Relief! Well, Trump and I have at least one thing in common—he is also playing golf at this moment. But of course he is refusing to concede, and his minions are answering by discussing cheating and lawsuits. I arrive home to turn on the TV and find spontaneous celebrations for Biden all over the country. Joy, right in front of the White House.

The analysts speculate about what it will be like inside the Republican Party, and how Trump will deal with his loss. In Little Rock, dedicated Trump fans tell the local newspaper and TV that, yes, they believe the election has been stolen by cheating. No one cites any evidence, just their strong convictions. Lou Dobbs on TV interviews supposed experts who cite possible indications of cheating.

Poor President Trump—first he wanted to stop the counting, then he wanted all "legal" votes counted, and now he is all about lawsuits, still claiming he won big.

By 7:30 p.m., VP-elect Harris is on national TV, and she looks ebullient yet controlled, passionate without gloating or anger. She is such a strong symbol, preaching reconciliation, praising her parents, and acknowledging that she may be the first woman to hold the office but she won't be the last. Then President-elect Joe Biden comes on—clear and strong, vowing to work with all Americans, citing this as a time to heal. He says it's not the "example of America's power," but rather the "power of America's example" that makes America the greatest nation in the world. Wonderful speech and celebration. Surely no Republican can suggest that he looks old, or senile, or faltering. No way! It is the fulfillment of his lifelong calling, and he looks fired up and ready to pull the country together and to lead.

I was there in Chicago in 2008 when Barack Obama stepped on stage to claim the presidency—100,000 of us, and what a sense of joy! I wish I could have been there at the "automobile rally" in Wilmington tonight, with that joy. What a relief, what a blessing!

I text my business partner, and ask: Didn't you think it was a great speech, strong and convincing? He says, yes, but now Biden needs to save his energy—he will need it! Yes, but for now at least we can all pause, at least briefly, to enjoy the moment and "smell the roses."

HOUSTON, TX

ADDIE TSAI is a queer, nonbinary writer and artist of color. She received her Master of Fine Arts from Warren Wilson College and her PhD in Dance from Texas Woman's University. The author of the queer Asian young adult novel *Dear Twin*, Addie teaches and lives in Houston, Texas.

DANGER IN
TRUMP-ERA TEXAS

BY ADDIE TSAI

In the context of the Negro problem neither whites nor blacks, for excellent reasons of their own, have the faintest desire to look back; but I think that the past is all that makes the present coherent, and further, that the past will remain horrible for exactly as long as we refuse to assess it honestly.

—JAMES BALDWIN, "Autobiographical Notes"

I had no clear expectation in November 2016 that Donald Trump would be awarded the presidency, nor did I think that Hillary Clinton's win was in the bag. I was newly married, and everything I took for granted about my life before the moment Trump was announced as the winner seems in retrospect shrouded in bubble-gum pink naiveté, but so was my life then.

I had listened for weeks to my ex-father-in-law, who I thought was loving and just and right and definitely not racist, chuckle to himself about how Donald Trump was ripping apart the Republican Party, as he sat in his comfortable suburban two-story house, lawyering from home every morning barefoot in his favorite house shorts. I would listen to my ex-mother-in-law try to convince me that people were inherently good, that no one would really vote Trump in, but if my ex-spouse and I got too heated, she would say, "Enough of that talk. Let's just eat our enchiladas and talk about happy things."

I was watching CNN upstairs in our bedroom while my ex-spouse, who lives with extreme OCD and needed several hours a night to himself to make the thoughts stop spinning, as he put it, watched the same channel on the television downstairs in the living room. Throughout Donald Trump's campaign, he had been insistent that there was no way in hell he would win the nomination. Then when Trump won the nomination, he was convinced, again, that there was no way that Americans would vote for him. I was skeptical and frightened to get too cocky, to assume that Americans weren't gullible enough to fall for someone just because they had seen them on television, or to doubt the white supremacy and racist hatred I knew sat whirring in enough people's hearts. After all, my own white mother had called me Oriental once, when I was a teenager, and rebuffed me when I asked her to call me Asian.

"I had three of them," she said. "I'll call them whatever I want."

Around midnight, as I was falling in and out of fitful sleep, my ex-spouse stomped upstairs to where my head was tossing back and forth on the side of the bed closer to the television, and he said with a kind of theatrical rage: "We're fucked!" I didn't have to look at the television then. All the air slipped out of my body as it shut down, as I dissociated, a trick I had long learned from being the product of an abusive, narcissistic father, and a narcissistic, abandoning mother. I fell asleep.

The next morning, my ex-spouse knew to stay away from me for a while. He knew enough to brace for my rage and devastation at how much my neighbors and fellow countrymen hated me, or at the very least, didn't care about my freedom, peace, or existence. I woke in a daze, but also distraught, and in my car I played Sufjan Stevens, a singer who always gives me comfort, as the tears streamed down my face. As I write this, they stream again, remembering what was to come.

I was on my way to teach in a community college classroom, and as I drove, I wondered how I could comfort my students when I, too, was afraid. Most are Black and POC. It is a rare time that I teach a white student. And I knew, from the conversations I was already moderating in the classroom, that my students were Black Americans,

DACA recipients, queer, children of undocumented immigrants, and immigrants themselves. I knew that they were terrified of this result. Terrified of what Trump would be. Many students asked me, "Where will I live, what will I do, how will I go on?" I had no answers for them. I knew that everything would not be fine. I told them I would always be available to them. I told them their fears and feelings, all of them, were valid. I told them I was sorry. I tried as hard as I could to keep my tears from them. I was not there to be consoled. I was there to provide a space of compassion and understanding.

Over the next four years, teaching in a community college in Texas would become a surreal occupation, one that felt ripe with danger and uncertainty. Over the next four years, Trump's racist rhetoric would become intolerable and open the door for the most hateful sentiments to be thrown around with pride. Hate crimes would flourish. We would be forced to tolerate the unstable and unwieldy words of a sociopathic and narcissistic personality, and for those of us who lived through abuse, every moment of every day would become a trigger. I would be forced to have a student removed from my classroom—on the record, it would be for administrative reasons, off the record, it would be because my daily practice of posting a single quote (sometimes a paragraph) by Black queer writer James Baldwin, which I had been doing every day since Trump was elected, would provoke this self-proclaimed white supremacist student to harass me in electronic messages and attack me for being biracial and queer, among other things. I was told to remind him of the code of conduct. This would happen just weeks after yet another school shooting in Texas. I feared, not at all irrationally, that I could be shot. This scenario would have been unimaginable prior to Trump's election.

During Trump's presidency, I would protest for the first time. I attended the Women's March and I joined a protest at a local international airport where I lived in Houston to contest Executive Order 13769, which prevented the return of refugees and other visitors from seven countries deemed unsafe. I began to use Facebook as a pedagogical tool, consciously aware that my students would not only be made aware of my daily practice of sharing quotes by James Baldwin about white supremacy and racism, and other insights on any given day of Trump's dictatorial presidency, but also that I was queer, nonbinary, and actively pro-Black and anti-racist. I began to affix enamel pins to a jean jacket that I wore daily as a kind of armor against this now harsh, bitter, and terrifying world—pins featuring James Baldwin, Colin Kaepernick, and other Black figures, and Black Lives Matter.

I began to consider more carefully how I curated Facebook, knowing that my students could witness it—and I would post every article I thought would inform them of the kind of country we were living in, and the kind of president that was quickly eradicating the rights of everyone, themselves included. One student, an older, conservative Latina who supported Trump, would never respond to my posts directly, but she would then post on her own wall in obvious reactions to my own, and rated me on Rate My Professor that I was a terrible professor because I "dress like a clown."

By the time of the 2020 election, I had learned just how corrupt the Republican Party's greed for power became, but also how easy it was for liberals to fall into the pattern of mocking Trump: for his hair, for his weight, for the way he walked, for his drug addiction, for his mental acuity, or lack thereof. I learned how easily rights and access could be taken away, how easy it was for the president of the United States to lead a corrupt term and if no one would stop him, then it would just continue, business as usual. Trump's presidency, beyond himself, certainly exposed the holes in our system, a millionfold, but more than that, it exposed how little we could do about it. I had felt helpless every moment of my life up until the time that I was 18 years old, as the daughter of a violent and pathological narcissist as a father. I had worked very hard, and had gone through many, many years of therapy in order to heal from the wounds that were built from that time. But now, it seemed, here I was again, having no control over my life. He was the president. Where could I go? And now that Trump's mismanagement of Covid-19 prevented us from leaving our homes, much less boarding a plane to anywhere safely, even leaving the United States had become virtually impossible, largely due to his inaction. Par for the course, like the one where he golfed the day the election was called for Biden-Harris.

I told my students the Monday before the election to be compassionate with themselves. I extended the due date of a paper I'd assigned. I urged them to reach out if they needed to. On Tuesday, I spent all morning in tears. Tears for the anxiety I felt, tears at the fear that

Trump would be reelected, tears that he would lose, and the country would burn. I lived in Texas, where anything could happen. I braced for race war. I went to my best friend's house just five minutes away from my apartment and made snickerdoodles to while away the time. I refreshed my phone every second as I watched the votes get counted. It was close. It was not a landslide. I finally went to sleep at 4 a.m. with no winner.

On Wednesday, we all shared our stress at how close the race was. I tried to explain to a Black student why people felt that Trump supporters were prejudiced after she said that was an unfair assumption. I tried to explain to her that if a president seeks the erasure of yourself and your community, then it means anyone who supports him either agrees with him, or doesn't care. For me, I said, it is the same either way. Another student, an international student from Nigeria who had been admonishing us for thinking we had it so bad compared to other countries, said that the conversation felt biased to him. I welcomed more discourse from him, more opinions. But I had no understanding of what possible conversation I could have with my students that would not end up sounding one-sided. I wondered if it was possible, in a Trumpian America, to have a conversation that would not include denouncing Trump's hateful rhetoric and policies.

Wednesday evening, I took a dance cardio class on Zoom from my living room. Every time I went to take a sip of water or wipe the sweat from my brow, I checked the results. Still not called.

Thursday, still not called. The entire day passed in a blur, but I remember talking to a friend about her dissertation prospectus and making fried rice for the first time. And refreshing, refreshing, refreshing. Sharing the numbers in Nevada, Georgia, Pennsylvania. Refreshing, refreshing, refreshing.

Friday, November 6, 2020: I wake up to a lead—a LEAD—in Georgia. Because of Stacey Abrams. Because of Black women. I wanted Texas to go blue. It was close for a minute, and the fact that it was close is a comfort. But. GEORGIA!

Just after I share on social media that Joe Biden has a lead in Georgia, I post the following quote from Baldwin: "My vote will probably not get me a job or a home or help me through school or prevent another Vietnam or a third World War, but it may keep me here long enough for me to see, and use, the turning of the tide—for the tide has got to turn." And just after, I reshare a memory Facebook alerts me to, a Baldwin quote, from November 6, 2018: "They were far from the hard apprehension that they simply could not endure being despised, far from the knowledge that almost everybody is, could not conceive that the world, or, at least, the world we know, could be so tremendously populated by people who despise each other because each despises himself. No. They dreamed of safety—I was dreaming, too." This one hits in a different way. Because at that moment, we didn't know how unsafe we would become. Now we were still dreaming that same dream—except this time we knew how dangerous our world had transformed into, but also, what had always been.

Saturday, November 7, 2020: I toss off my new nightguard, which isn't quite properly adjusted, in the middle of the night, and then have a dream that I've ground four of my back teeth so hard that they've fallen off. Then I wake up to some difficult rejections. I feel despondent, so despondent that I'm sure it's the reason for my low blood pressure count—so low that the nurse takes it three times the day before when I go to see my doctor for my first-ever flu shot, my duty towards trying to help mitigate the virus. The race looks clear, but still isn't called, and I know better than to be sure of anything in this climate. It seems all the news networks are now terrified, too, of Trump's refusal to concede the election, of claiming the election is stolen. He really will go down in history as being the only president in American history not to concede an election that he clearly has lost.

I post the following quote on social media: "We must tell the truth till we can no longer bear it." And, not knowing what to do with myself, I stay on social media with my community all day long, obsessing over vote reports, refreshing, refreshing, refreshing. My legs will go numb from crossing them under my desk for so many hours straight. My wrists are tired. My neck hurts. I can't sleep.

I reshare another 2018 memory of a Baldwin quote: "Don't never run from nothing. I swear to you, whatever you run from will come back, one day, armed to the teeth, man, will come back in a shape you don't know how to run from, will come back in a shape you can't deny!" I feel that quote is for all of us. It's for Trump, it's for those who refused to vote because they couldn't reconcile voting for Clinton, it's for those who voted for Trump thinking he wouldn't do anything. But, mostly, I think it's for Trump. Your misdeeds will come back to haunt you. One way, or another.

And then, 10:27 a.m.: The Associated Press finally calls the race when Biden takes the clear lead in Pennsylvania. I put on some coordinated makeup and take a self-portrait with my favorite young adult novel for its title, *We Are Okay*. I text ferociously with friends. I call my best friend and we scream at each other over the phone. I send lots of texts with a string of exclamation points. I can't go out into the world to celebrate, so I take a video of me dancing in my office, the same room where I refreshed, refreshed, refreshed, to "I Wanna Dance with Somebody," and I share it to social media. I send a video message to one of my closest friends in Arizona, a different dance, to a different song, Diana Ross's "I'm Coming Out." I write lots and lots of Twitter and Facebook posts, like this one:

So many things to say about what the last four years have felt like since 2016 was first called. How traumatizing every moment has been as a survivor of a childhood framed by narcissistic abuse, as a person of color, as a queer person, as a professor of students who were both marginalized and threatened by this administration, but also as a professor of students who have harassed me with their racist hateful rhetoric made permissible by this administration. All of these thoughts will collect and form somewhere some day. But, for now, I feel as though the breath inside my body can be let out, and I can finally move again. This is not perfection, but this is a start.

And I exhale like I have never exhaled before. I take a virtual dance class. I edit a dance review for an upcoming publication. But, mostly, I breathe and I cry and I sigh for a new day. Knowing that Joe Biden has clearly won the presidential election is not an excitement. It is a relief. It feels like the day that I left my father's house when I was 18, and my twin and I sat on identical arm chairs on the campus at college, and I looked at her, and I said, "We don't ever have to go back there again." And, at that moment, that was all that I needed in the entire world.

LOS ANGELES, CA

ROSANNA ARQUETTE did an arc of episodes on Ryan Murphy's Netflix series "Ratched" alongside Sarah Paulson. She also played the female lead in the movie *Etruscan Smile*, produced by Academy Award-winner Arthur Cohn, starring alongside Brian Cox. In addition, she played one of the female leads on the Youtube Originals series "Sideswiped" with Carly Craig, which was produced by Jason Sudeikis. Rosanna is one of the stars in the upcoming film *Love Is Love Is Love* alongside Rita Wilson, which was directed by Eleanor Coppola. Rosanna is also one of the stars in the feature film *Holy Lands* with Jonathan Rhys Meyers and James Caan for Studio Canal. She also did an arc of episodes on the critically acclaimed Showtime series "Ray Donovan" and another arc on the HBO Lena Dunham series "Girls." She has starred in such critically acclaimed movies as *Pulp Fiction* and *Desperately Seeking Susan*.

BE LIKE JANE

BY ROSANNA ARQUETTE

FRIDAY MORNING, NOVEMBER 6

Since the election I've gotten up at 3 in the morning every day, and I'm passing out around 8:30 p.m. I wake up again around midnight for about an hour, catch up on everything, and then I go back to sleep. I'm in a weird state of depression and elation, I can't figure it out. My husband was actually really worried about me. The intensity has just been insane, even this morning. I'll take a hot bath a day. I didn't watch anything. It was too crazy-making. I just checked in with people I know who are on the ground and have the good information. I wouldn't watch the polls. I want to know Joe Biden is really the next president of the United States, and then we'll go from there.

I've always been a super positive person, but this last four years has been extremely toxic on so many levels. We're all in a collective state of PTSD. We have to recover from the trauma. Donald Trump is the abuser. If anyone has been in an abusive relationship, this guy is our abuser. It takes a long time to get away from that kind of trauma. We've been collectively abused as a nation and now we have to collectively heal. That's going to take some time. Here we are with a good, hopeful person who can help us heal, and that's Joe Biden, along with Kamala Harris.

Joe Biden wasn't my first pick for president this year. I always thought he was a good man. He just wasn't for me. But as we've gone through this round of him becoming our next president, I have grown to love this man. He's just a very good, honorable man. His message has been wonderful for people. It really is bringing people together. He works for all Americans. He is the kind of center that we need right now, the middle ground. I consider myself a real lefty, but I don't want to hammer home the agenda of that immediately the day he's sworn in. He's got to work with Mitch McConnell. I'm going to let him be president and breathe a little. I want him to be open about fracking, and understand that this is not what we need for the environment, but I think he'll get there, because he's smart enough to listen to scientists. He's becoming more and more open.

One thing we've learned from all of this is how fragile our democracy is. We can never, ever take democracy for granted. We're all so exhausted, but we have a lot of work to do. We can never let this happen again, and it will, unless we are vigilant and on it all the time. I think if everybody does a little something in their own communities, we can have a better country.

I grew up with a mom who was a big part of the Rainbow Coalition in Chicago in the late 1960s: Chairman Fred Hampton, the feeding of the schoolchildren, breakfast and lunch programs they had set up. I grew up with all that. Fred was a good man. He brought people together in Chicago and was one of the top Black Panther Party figures in the country. But the FBI did everything they could to destroy the Black Panther movement, which to me was an incredible movement. They had to galvanize people, to stand up for their rights and justice, and the FBI and Hoover, they just killed it, they did everything they could to destroy these people and make their lives horrible.

It's different now. I think Black Lives Matter is too big to kill. It will never, ever go away. They definitely are trying to do that to the #MeToo movement, we watched that, but this is too big. It's now time for us as human beings to look at systematic racism square in the eye and really do something about it. Unfortunately, to wake everybody up it took watching a Black man be murdered in broad daylight in front of all of us. There were so many murders before George Floyd, but it took that for everybody to say, "Oh my god." This is a daily practice that happens in the lives of all Black Americans. This was the one we saw, that we heard about, that wasn't hidden, that wasn't lied about by the police. We saw in this movement that everybody who is a human being, who believes that all human beings are equal, got up and peacefully protested. It's one of the most incredible movements we've seen in a lot of years.

We have Joe Biden as president of the United States because of Black women, and I will never forget that. I'm always going to honor that. It's time we have a woman president, but especially a Black woman president. It's just time, time for the world to wake up to a Black woman president in the White House. If you really get down to it, Black women have been at the forefront of every social movement there's ever been in this country, the women's movement, the anti-war movement, every movement I've been a part of my whole life.

Young women all over the world are an inspiration these days. Think of Greta Thunberg and the work she's done. She'll turn 18 in January, the month Joe Biden and Kamala Harris are inaugurated, and look at what she's already done. I always try to use my social-media platform to honor important activism, and in February 2020 when Greta was nominated for the Nobel Peace Prize, I tweeted that she had "galvanized a movement around the world to wake people up" that "climate change is real," and added: "Those of us who love our earth love honor this magnificent young woman."

Here in California we live the reality of climate change almost every day, especially during fire season, which seems like it never ends. I live in Southern California, but my favorite place is Northern California. I have a cabin up in Big Sur and it has almost burned down many times. This place is the love of my love, besides my kid and my husband. I'm so lucky it didn't burn down. The fire went right to the fence. It's happened three times, fire goes right to the fence and then doesn't burn.

My Big Sur cabin is a sanctuary for me, I love going there, and in September 2019 I took a road trip from L.A. with a couple friends, and we talked the whole time about climate change and activism. The friends were Jane Fonda and Catherine Keener. They're both great friends and inspirations to me. My mother and I were both grateful to Jane for her activism going way back, and I remember when I finally met Jane in my early 20s, I already felt so connected to her. I was asked to join her on many actions from protecting our water to voter registration to going up to Sacramento with Tom Hayden.

On the drive up from L.A., Catherine and Jane and I were thinking about Greta and her incredible work on the environment. As Jane writes in her new book, *What Can I Do? My Path From Climate Despair to Action*, "Catherine Keener reminded me recently how, on the five-hour drive to Big Sur, she would go on an hourly rant: What can I do? Tell me what to do! Where are the leaders? I need someone to tell me what to do! I felt impotent, angry with myself for my inability to give her the answers she needed because I felt the same way. What can I do?"

The morning we left, Jane had received an advance copy of Naomi Klein's amazing new book, *On Fire: The (Burning) Case for a Green New Deal.* She would read passages aloud to us. "All my life," Jane explains in *What Can I Do?,* "the exact book I needed without even knowing it had come to me at the perfect time and changed my trajectory. Here it was again. I began reading it the next day, and a quarter of the way through I was shaking with intensity."

That's no exaggeration at all. Jane was on fire. I watched her call Annie Leonard at Greenpeace, and watched her call Naomi Klein. I actually filmed her doing this on my phone. That was when she created the idea of Fire Drill Fridays. She decided to move to Washington, D.C., to devote herself full time to climate activism, and jumped right into that work with everything she had. It was incredible and inspiring. Catherine and I vowed to support her in every way we could. Within one month, Jane was living in D.C. and Catherine and I went and were arrested with her twice, in November and December 2019.

Jane has always walked the walk and done it with integrity and grace. She's always done the work to be a great organizer. She has an idea and then implements it and it becomes something everyone can participate in. Fire Drill Fridays created an

Catherine and I getting arrested with Jane in Washington, DC.

incredible awareness around the country. All these young climate-justice activists are part of it. She amplifies the voices of people on her platform, and then we can learn so much from all the people doing such great work.

Catherine and I were there on Saturday, December 21, 2019, Jane's 82nd birthday. The day before, we were all arrested, and the Reverend William J. Barber joined us, and when he started singing "We Shall Overcome," it gave you chills.

Jane turned to us and said: "This is the best birthday I've ever had."

NEW YORK, NY

ANTHONY SCARAMUCCI is the Founder and Co-Managing Partner of SkyBridge Capital. He is the author of four books: *The Little Book of Hedge Funds, Goodbye Gordon Gekko, Hopping Over the Rabbit Hole* (a 2016 *Wall Street Journal* bestseller), and *Trump: The Blue-Collar President.* In 2016, Scaramucci was ranked #85 in *Worth Magazine*'s Power 100: The 100 Most Powerful People in Global Finance. In November 2016, he was named to President-Elect Trump's 16-person Presidential Transition Team Executive Committee, and for a period in July 2017 he served as the White House Communications Director. Scaramucci, a native of Long Island, New York, holds a B.A. degree in Economics from Tufts University and a J.D. from Harvard Law School.

TRUMP IN THE OVAL, LOOKING UP

BY ANTHONY SCARAMUCCI

Thank god Trump lost the election. If he didn't lose, I'm telling you that would have been an unbelievable nightmare. You're one election away from Hungarian-style authoritarianism in the country if we're not careful. Joe Biden repudiated Trump. He got the highest vote count in history. He brought with him a progressive African-American woman to be his vice president, so he made history by crossing the finish line with her. I think he kicked Trump's ass. That's how it looks to me on the Thursday afternoon after Election Day.

I went after Trump at the peak of his popularity when no other Republicans would. When he talked in August 2019 about how members of Congress should "go back" to their countries, I turned on him. I said he's a racist. I said he's an American nativist. People told me I was a kamikaze pilot. They said he was going to win re-election and I was crazy to stand up to him. I said, "I'm not crazy. *He's* crazy. He's not going to win re-election, because he can't handle the presidency." I worked as hard as I could against Trump in the election. I told everyone I could that this is a really weird, unwell guy that was going to hurt a lot of people, just completely unfit and mentally unstable, a danger to the democratic institutions and norms of our society.

I try to learn from my mistakes and working for Trump as White

House communications director for 11 days in July 2017 was one hell of a learning experience. I thought Trump was going to help people like my family and friends on Long Island, working people just trying to make a living, but I misjudged his character. That was an ego flaw of mine. You learn to try to get your ego out of things.

I got my ass shot up after 11 days in the job. I deserved to be fired. Afterward I went through this Shawshank Redemption, I went through this sewer pipe of humiliation, being ripped on late night comedy, having my last name turned into a unit of time. When you have that going on, it's very, very humbling. It makes you perhaps more empathetic, and it probably makes you more aware of other people's issues. I grew up under a lucky star. My parents didn't have any money, but they were good people and they raised my ass right.

Trump never expected to be elected president. The night of the 2016 election, he thought he was going to lose. If we want to revise history, we can do that, but Bannon, Jared and Donald Trump all thought he was going to lose. So did I. I was hosting "Wall Street Week" at the time on Fox Business Network, and I called Trump on Election Night to tell him Fox was going to call the race for Hillary Clinton by 10 p.m.

"No problem," Trump told me on the phone. "I've got the plane fueled. I'm moving the plane from LaGuardia, where I keep it parked, over to Kennedy, and we'll fly out of Kennedy and go to my golf course in Scotland. Let her have her day in the sun. I'm going to get out of the country for a week and then I'll come back and we'll figure out what we're all doing."

Trump was as surprised as anyone when he won. In my mind, even though I'm going after Trump because he's unfit to be president of the United States, I'm not demonizing him and turning him into this two-dimensional figure. So I want to tell a humanizing story.

It was Friday, July 21, 2017, and I'd just been named White House communications director. I was alone with President Trump in the study off of the Oval Office, just the two of us. I had a very good rapport with him. Jared once said to me, "He tells me you're a made guy," meaning self-made. I reminded him of his father's generation, because I grew up with nothing.

"Come on into the Oval Office," the president told me.

It was actually a little smaller than you would think from television.

I'd visited the Oval before, but just briefly. I'd never sat alone with the president, catty-corner across the Resolute Desk. I was looking around, taking it all in, and looked up at the ceiling, where I saw a plaster of Paris seal of the presidency of the United States.

"Mr. President, look at that," I said, leaning over to him. "That's the seal of the presidency. C'mon, my heart's racing a little. You're sitting behind the Resolute Desk, are you unnerved by that?"

"You know, I've got to tell you something," Trump told me. "I was overwhelmed the first day I sat here, and I did look up at the goddamned plaster of Paris seal. But Anthony, let me tell you what happened, I had a state visit. I'm like, 'Jesus Christ, I've got to go get ready. Theresa May is coming to meet me at the North Portico. I'm the goddamned president of the United States.' I've gotta tell you, it was a little surreal."

Then he said, "Let me tell you what's going to happen to you. There's so much goddamned work to do around here, and there's so much action, in about a minute, two minutes, you're going to forget it, and it's going to be just another office with a desk and a phone and you've got to work."

And he was right about that. It was humanizing to him. He is a very flawed human being, and he's malevolent, but if he was not in that position, he would be entertaining, and a raconteur and a good reality television host or a good greeter at Mar-a-Lago, but he's not the right guy to be the president of the United States.

We are living in two countries. There are more than 70 million people who voted for this guy, and that number is just going to go up as they keep counting. This is a culture war for them. White ethnics, remember, see themselves as whiter than Archie Bunker. Many Hispanics also see themselves as whiter than Archie Bunker. They see Trump as the last white man standing between them and a horde of latte-drinking, Hispanic and Black transvestites that are going to come up over the transom and take over their government and their culture.

Trump had a sense for the fact he was going to get his ass kissed and lose. The last week of that campaign was not a campaign, that was a rock-concert farewell tour. Trump was playing his greatest hits, his play list: Hillary Clinton emails, Robert Mueller investigation, I'm a victim, you're a victim. He wasn't talking about what he was going to do for the country or the future.

Now why was he doing that farewell tour? He was doing it because he needs a bargaining chip on the table. He does not want to go to jail. He doesn't want his children to go to jail. He's under investigation, everyone knows that. His move right now is: How am I going to leverage what I've got, this movement of mine, those 70-plus million votes, and the atom-bomb-Molotov-cocktail nature of my personality into a free pass on the Monopoly board, the "Get out of jail free" card? He's not looking for a pardon, just let me be very clear about that, he's looking for a non-prosecutorial agreement, very different from a pardon: Whatever I did, whatever my kids did, nope, you can't prosecute me, I'm going to Mar-a-Lago. That's how I'm seeing it on the Thursday after the election.

These Republicans are a bunch of yahoos. The voting that has just been tallied has sent them a signal, which is: Be Trumpier than Trump. The signal to these jokers and jamokes is that, oh wow, he got 73 million people by acting like an asshole, let me torque up the asshole-ishness. That's not leadership. If you want to be a leader, you've got to be a thermostat, not a thermometer. If John Kennedy was writing a book about these Republicans, it would be *Profiles in Cowardice*. And there are way, way more of them than there are of me.

WASHINGTON, DC

HUSSEIN IBISH is a senior resident scholar at the Arab Gulf States Institute in Washington. He is a weekly columnist for *Bloomberg Opinion* and *The National* daily newspaper in the United Arab Emirates. He wrote the Christopher Hitchens chapter in *One Last Lunch: A Final Meal with Those Who Meant So Much to Us* (Harry N. Abrams, 2020), edited by Erica Heller.

BEIRUT 1975—
WASHINGTON 2020

BY HUSSEIN IBISH

I experienced 2020 somewhat differently from family and friends, because I have childhood experience of what it's like when your country's social and political system suddenly unravels. I was born and mostly grew up in Beirut, Lebanon, and the Civil War years were formative for me. What happened in Lebanon from 1975 to 1990 is not being replayed in the United States by any means. Yet the echoes have often been uncanny and impossible not to hear loud and clear.

The idea that my experiences with Civil War and anarchy in the 1970s would be particularly relevant to the way I process the Trump era emerged immediately after the last election. The day after Trump's unexpected victory over Hillary Clinton in 2016 I wrote a commentary for *Slate* explaining that my experience of social and political disintegration and dysfunctionality in Lebanon in particular and the broader Arab world in general gave me valuable context for absorbing this deeply disturbing development. I wrote that "on election night, the American in me, like so many of my compatriots, wanted to curl into a fetal position and moan. But the Middle Easterner in me shrugged and said, 'Meh, I've seen worse. Much, much, much worse.'" Yet by November 2020 the distance between the two registers seems to have narrowed.

Four years ago, it was readily apparent that a well-situated minority of Americans had elected a peddler of racism, white nationalism, conspiracy theories and autocratic populism. It seemed very likely the American system would probably undergo one of the greatest stress tests in its history. All that certainly unfolded. What wasn't obvious in 2016 is the extent to which most of the presumed guardrails of American democracy—checks, accountability and rule of law—would bend or even crack and fail under the pressure of Trump's brazen disregard for underlying norms and traditions.

The refusal of Trump and his cronies to accept limitations and respect the implicit boundaries of accountable governance vividly illustrated the truism that democracy only functions when everybody fundamentally accepts the underlying logic of shared and distributed power and submits willingly to limits on their own conduct (which is what the founders of the American Republic typically meant by the all-important phrase "self-government"). One after another, supposed guardrails to contain personal and political presidential overreach provided little to no practical restraint. The drift towards autocracy was evident in countless practices ranging from rampant profiteering off of the presidency to the obliteration of any line between official and political activities, to blithely ignoring court orders, and even bypassing the congressional confirmation process for senior administration officials.

The most dramatic failure came at the start of 2020 with the Republican Senate's acquittal of the president at an impeachment "trial" with a verdict that was announced in advance and that allowed no witness testimony whatsoever. Unlike many House Republicans who insisted the president did nothing wrong, many of these Republican senators acknowledged that Trump's effort to blackmail Ukraine into at least pretending to investigate the family of his likely rival, and eventual vanquisher, Joe Biden, by leveraging already congressionally appropriated military aid to that embattled U.S. ally, was inappropriate at best and deeply wrong at worst. This, however, somehow didn't warrant his removal from office, they insisted, even though it was an effort to subvert U.S. foreign policy and deceive the American public in support of his re-election campaign.

So 2020 began with a clear indication that the November presidential elections would be the last remaining guardrail standing in the way of Trump and a wholesale second-term effort to transform U.S. democracy into a personalized autocracy (probably most closely following the model of Turkish President Recep Tayyip Erdoğan and Hungarian Prime Minister Viktor Orbán, strongman leaders who gradually replaced functional national institutions with their own personalized will and cults of personality). The courts and the Congress were clearly not going to stand in his way effectively, particularly if given a second term. Americans, both liberal and conservative, were justifiably petrified, if they cared about democracy and U.S. political traditions, and so was I.

Before the real terror of political disintegration fully sank in, the coronavirus pandemic intervened to provide an earlier uncanny echo from my troubled teenage years. I left Lebanon and permanently relocated to the United States in 1980 when I was 17 and life became utterly impossible in anarchic West Beirut. There was no chance I was going to graduate from high school under those circumstances and it was becoming increasingly dangerous for a young man of my age to walk around streets patrolled by different rival gangs, often teenagers themselves, armed to the teeth and restrained by no authority. I was a dual citizen at birth with a State Department birth certificate of an American born overseas, meaning that although I felt like an immigrant I technically wasn't.

For years in the late 1970s, as a teenager in West Beirut, I didn't go out at night except under rare circumstances and very close to home. So the lockdown that began in March because of the coronavirus pandemic felt oddly familiar. For all the differences, the idea that one was rarely going out and nuclear families sought to stay close together and avoid too much contact with other people while living under a pervasive sense of danger and death was pretty reminiscent of my teenage years. Certainly, for my wife, who grew up in New Jersey, there was no such precedent. But particularly in March, April and May I experienced and frequently remarked on a strong element of déjà vu.

There wasn't much of a parallel between my Lebanese experiences and the racial justice protests that followed the police killing of George Floyd, even though they involved some acts of vandalism and occasional spurts of violence. But to anyone outside of the far-right-wing media ecosystem, it was clear that the overwhelming majority of the protests were peaceful and reflected a broad-based social solidarity that was

extremely reassuring. It appeared, and it still appears, that finally a majority of Americans who identify themselves as white recognized that
"systemic racism," as we now call it, particularly in the form of police
violence against Black people in general and young men in particular,
is pervasive and unacceptable. It was a convulsion, but to me it didn't
feel uncontrolled and didn't feel destructive. To the contrary, it seemed
almost entirely positive, albeit with rare exceptions—often authored
by the authorities or their armed supporters. The most reprehensible
of these was the assault on peaceful protesters outside Lafayette Park
across from the White House engineered by Attorney General William
Barr to make way for Trump to posture grimly in front of a church holding up a Bible and scowling. It was an ample reminder of who and what
posed the real danger to American society.

But what the summer did reveal was the depth of divisions in American society, and particularly the potential for right-wing militia groups,
many of which identify with Trump, to attack and potentially kill their
fellow Americans. The anti-Covid-mitigation-policy agitation, particularly by armed groups in Michigan, which culminated in the thwarted
effort to kidnap and potentially kill Governor Gretchen Whitmer, also
underscored that danger. And in both cases, such groups were both
openly and implicitly encouraged and embraced by Trump in his capac-
ity as president.

The specter of private militia groups and paramilitaries operating at
the behest of the president and his subordinates like Barr was most strik-
ingly revealed by the deployment of a menagerie of various executive
branch security forces, including prison guards, homeland security and
border patrol officers, treasury officials, park police and a range of other
little-known cadres deployed against protesters in city streets across the
country. Frequently not wearing any identifying markings and not responding to questions about who they were, these state security forces
attacked and rounded up protesters with virtually no oversight or accountability. The specter of unaccountable armed men controlling the
streets on which I have to walk was making an unwelcome reappear-
ance in my life.

All these fears built to a crescendo during the campaign season in the
late summer and early fall. Trump made dark hints about potentially insti-
gating violence and intimidation at polling places. He campaigned more

against the election itself and particularly the age-old tradition of postal voting, insisting it was going to be rigged and phony, than against his opponents, although he did call now-Vice President-elect Kamala Harris a "monster" and a "communist." A series of well-informed and very intelligent articles, most notably a lengthy commentary in *The Atlantic* by Barton Gellman, made the vulnerabilities of the American electoral system, particularly in the event of a close result that did not yield a clear, decisive victory in the Electoral College process, terrifyingly evident. And there was every reason to fear the result could, indeed, be close enough in some key states to invite not merely a repetition of the Bush vs. Gore fiasco of 2000 but a series of even more dire constitutional crises.

American society really felt as if it were coming apart at the seams, particularly at the political level driven by ideologies, particularly on the right, driven by fear, suspicion, hatred and rampant conspiracy theories. And, indeed, it may be. The transformation of the Republican Party into a wholly owned subsidiary of the Trump family business was demonstrated by its refusal to adopt a new party platform for this election, simply vowing instead to follow any direction set by the Dear Leader. Worse, the QAnon conspiracy theory was making evident inroads not only among hardcore Republican activists but also among officially endorsed Republican candidates for Congress, two of which ended up getting elected this year. The deranged fantasy holds that the world is ruled by a satanic cabal of Democrats and celebrities who traffic in, molest and eat children, and that Trump is engaged in an elaborate struggle to triumph over this evil. It has endless bizarre subplots, including one about the drug adrenochrome that appears largely cribbed from some of the more absurdist passages of Hunter S. Thompson's classic novel, *Fear and Loathing in Las Vegas.*

This sense of social and political unraveling, underscored by mutual fear and paranoia, wild conspiracy theories about other communities and constituencies, in the presence of large, often unregulated groups of fanatical armed men, was deeply, distressingly familiar. Yet whereas Lebanese society disintegrated in many ways from the bottom up, leaving the shell of a national government to perform, or often pretend to perform, tasks no one else wanted to do while local forces controlled whatever they could on the ground, the U.S body politic appeared to be rotting from the head down.

It's often observed that Trump is a symptom and not the disease. However true that may be in certain ways, the 2020 election as it played out on November 3 served as a striking vindication of the commitment by most Americans to their democratic system. None of the nightmare scenarios played out. Not one, except the refusal of Trump himself and his Republican leadership enablers to recognize the result in the days following (at the time of writing, a tiny handful of prominent Republicans have accepted the outcome). But more Americans voted, although many early or by mail, than in a century. There was no violence, intimidation or disruption at polling places. Throughout the country, local officials, election workers and volunteers cooperated in making the democratic system work without incident or rancor. Indeed, the Secretary of State of Georgia, a loyal Republican, has come under massive attack from both senators, all members of Congress and his own governor, who have demanded that he resign simply because they do not like the outcome of the election he oversaw.

For me what's reassuringly different about how American society seems to be responding to this sociopolitical stress test seems much more significant than what is so clearly reminiscent about the way Lebanese society melted down around me when I was a kid. I don't want to appear too sanguine. As I write, the Republican hierarchy in Washington still declines to acknowledge the evident outcome, the first time in modern American political history that a party is toying with rejecting the democratic process because it has lost. More disturbingly, they have no evidence of improprieties or fraud and are mainly seeking to use technicalities to invalidate massive numbers of lawfully cast votes in order to change the result.

Most likely this is an example of Trump as both disease and symptom. Republican leaders are probably trying to humor him in hopes they can find a way to placate his wrath and that of his supporters, who are also their own constituents, sometime before January 6 when, by law, Congress must hold a joint session to accept the results of the Electoral College vote. This task will fall to Vice President Mike Pence, who has avoided all public appearances in recent days, as it did to Al Gore in 2000 after the Supreme Court handed victory to George W. Bush. But the fact that Republican leaders are willing to "humor" Trump by insisting that he hasn't yet lost and that he may indeed have won, reportedly asking what the harm is when he will eventually give up and go away, reveals their striking lack of attachment to democratic values and processes. If he somehow began to succeed in an effort to overturn the election and stay in power despite the will of the voters and the outcome of the system's regular order, many if not most of them would be delighted and supportive. Otherwise they wouldn't fail to recognize the evident harm in promoting the idea widely at home and abroad that the American election may well have been manipulated, dishonest and fraudulent.

It's fashionable for Americans to fret about the potential for a new Civil War. I'm not about to downplay the danger of right-wing militia groups, who certainly pose the preeminent terrorist threat in the United States under current circumstances (as Trump administration officials and agencies know full well but are sometimes forbidden from admitting because of the president's obvious affection for, and encouragement of, such groups). But those of us who have endured our societies melting down all around us, governance and law and order evaporating, and a terrifying flood of blood and brutality—who know what it means to feel no safety outside, or even often inside, one's own home—can safely say we're nowhere near that, in fact. We're not even close.

These are dark and frightening times, so for me they often invoke earlier dark and frightening times in my life. Yet for all the chaos, disruption, division and strife that could have occurred during or immediately after the recent election, nothing of the kind happened. Instead Americans demonstrated a determination to hold onto their basic mores, norms and values, even at a time of extraordinary political and cultural polarization. The only remaining obstacle is the bewildering and unforgivable refusal of a tiny handful of primarily old men in dark suits in Washington to publicly acknowledge the outcome. When they do, as they eventually must, the 2020 election will be remembered as much for what mercifully didn't happen—any major step towards social disintegration and political violence—as for what, also mercifully, did—the repudiation and ouster of the would-be American autocrat from the White House. I'm not planning to relocate again anytime soon.

ST. PETERSBURG, FL

SANDY ALDERSON has been a baseball
executive for almost 40 years. He is a graduate of
Dartmouth College and Harvard Law School and
served as a Marine in Vietnam.

IN TRUMP'S FLORIDA

BY SANDY ALDERSON

That Saturday began with a Zoom call about New York Mets issues, followed soon after by an hour drive to Sarasota from my home in St. Petersburg, Florida, for an interview with a job candidate. I'd been watching MSNBC since election night (and for many months before that) and had Sirius XM on in the car on the drive, hoping Pennsylvania or Arizona would be called for Biden along the way. No such luck. It wasn't until a break in the interview in the early afternoon that I saw Pennsylvania and Nevada had finally been called.

What followed was not so much a feeling of relief—because vote counts had been trending for Biden since Wednesday—but one of deep satisfaction. Driving through Sarasota after leaving the meeting, I spotted a group of maybe 200 people with signs and noise makers, celebrating the Biden-Harris win. With other motorists, I slowed and honked my agreement. I wore a large grin for the next several blocks and a contented smile for the rest of the trip home.

That's not the way Tuesday started. Polls suggested a "Blue Wave," but that prediction was dispelled early in the evening with Florida going to Trump. Early results from other states were not favorable to Biden either. Mild depression set in. We've lived in Florida for almost two years and can confirm that the state is as odd, unpredictable and schizophrenic as most nonresidents believe. How else does one reconcile a strong majority vote for Trump and, at the same time, approval of a $15 hourly minimum wage? A surprising way to "split a ticket."

This dichotomy is largely explained by the diverse, and divergent, voting blocs in the state. The large white population is a mix of working class, rural and senior voters. That's a reliably conservative bloc in most elections, except when candidates threaten senior entitlements like Social Security, Medicare or maybe Obamacare. The Black vote is consistently more liberal, which leaves the pivotal Latino vote. And the Latino "bloc" is anything but. While much of this vote is predictably supportive of more progressive candidates, the Cuban-American segment of this group is decidedly more conservative. They likely carried Trump to victory in Florida this year.

Cuban Americans as a voting bloc have vexed me for a long time. I was in Cuba many times in 1999, for the baseball game between the Baltimore Orioles and the Cuban national team. It was a controversial event politically, but a fascinating one behind the scenes. Then-President Bill Clinton was in favor, but Secretary of State Madeline Albright was not, and career diplomats on the Cuba desk at the State Department weren't either. Clinton and his strong supporter, Peter Angelos, owner of the Baltimore Orioles, made it happen.

Having seen economic and political conditions in Cuba firsthand at that time, it wasn't hard to understand why many Cuban Americans are so anti-communist and, therefore, more conservative leaning. What's happening in Venezuela today only reinforces these views. I get it. But many Cuban Americans are still preoccupied with the consequences of the Cuban Revolution, when many wealthy Cubans lost vast amounts of their wealth and property. I have no sympathy for them, as they profited from the dictatorial, racist regime of Fulgencio Batista until 1958. What these Cubans lost in the revolution wasn't deserved anyway. But for this and some more legitimate reasons, our relations with Cuba have remained hostile to this day.

Cuban-American voters continue to have an outsized impact on American politics: first, because they are concentrated in Florida, a pivotal battleground state in most presidential elections; and second, because some of the most prolific financial contributors to the Republican Party are Cuban American. Long ago we normalized our diplomatic and commercial relations with Vietnam, a place where I fought 50 years ago as a young Marine officer. Almost 60 years after the Bay of Pigs, however, we are still in an economic conflict with Cuba. Why haven't we tried to address communism in Cuba with something other than an embargo, which has proved ineffective over many decades? I've got a five-word answer for you: Cuban-American voters in Florida.

So Florida as a whole has been a reliably red state in most elections. But there are parts of the state more purple than red or blue. Pinellas County, where St. Petersburg is located, is one of those places. In the weeks before the election, for exercise, I walked five or six miles each day through our neighborhood, which has about 100 houses. Just for fun, I counted lawn signs each day, to track, in an inexact way, the level of Trump or Biden support among my neighbors, most of whom I do not know. By election day, the signs were 14-14, which surprised me given the number of jacked-up trucks in driveways. But this pretty closely reflected the Pinellas vote. Biden won by a percent or so.

By the time I arrived home from Sarasota on Saturday, celebrations of the Biden victory were in full swing in many places across the country. Not so in Florida; what I had seen earlier in Sarasota was the exception. There were some celebrations in Miami, but elsewhere in the state, not much. How ironic that the only large Biden celebrations occurred almost exclusively in Miami-Dade, where a larger than expected number of votes for Trump probably cost Biden the state.

Ultimately, what happened in Florida didn't matter. When Pennsylvania was called for Biden around midday on Saturday, my world view improved substantially. Beginning in January, no more nefarious tweets, no more denials of climate change and no more lies about the extent of coronavirus in this country. But we have 10 weeks or so to get there and I wonder what harm President Trump will inflict in the meantime. Would he try to install another conservative Supreme Court nominee if the opportunity arose? Of course he would, just as he will ram more lower court federal judges into the system between now and then. But better days are ahead. Biden in the White House will reverse many of the policies implemented in the executive branch that have circumvented Congress and have undermined and politicized so many federal agencies, including the State and Justice Departments. Ethical leadership of the United States, I believe, will return.

When I lived in England in the early 1960s, Americans were revered across Europe, especially in Great Britain. The memory of the Allied victory in World War II was still fresh, and America's participation was recognized as pivotal to that victory. Since those days, however, through Vietnam and our involvement in the Middle East, our reputation in the world has diminished. The Biden victory is at least a small step toward restoring our good name in the world.

PIEDMONT, CA

AMANDA RENTERIA is CEO of Code for
America, which partners with federal and state public
servants to create equitable government systems,
and helped launch the civic tech ecosystem 10 years
ago. She has served as the chief of operations at the
California Department of Justice, overseeing 1,000
public servants and an $850 million budget, national
political director for Hillary Clinton's 2016 presidential
campaign, and as a chief of staff in the U.S. Senate.
She was named one of the most influential staffers by
Roll Call and received a number of awards as the first
Latina chief of staff in the history of the U.S. Senate.
She has degrees from Stanford University and Harvard
Business School and serves on several nonprofit boards.

ELEVATION

BY AMANDA RENTERIA

FRIDAY, NOVEMBER 6

I'd been saying for weeks before the election that there was no way we would win Florida. It was not going blue. Not going to happen, not this year. So I called up my mother at the very beginning of the day on Tuesday, before any results were in, and spelled it out.

"Mom, we're not going to win Florida," I told her. "Relax. Breathe. I'm not exactly sure how the rest of the night is going to go, but I'm giving you a heads up that we're not going to win Florida."

I knew how tough Election Day would be for them. They've been reliving their high school days—all this week, and really for the last four years. My parents were farmworkers in their younger years. They spent school breaks and summers in the fields. My father, Trinidad, emigrated from Zacatecas, Mexico, in the 1960s, and my mother, Helen, was born in California to a Mexican-American family. They have always been supportive of me. I moved away from our small town of Woodlake, in Tulare County, to go to Stanford and then went east for grad school. In 2003 when I earned my MBA from Harvard, the Visalia newspaper published a picture of me with my parents, one on each side of me, with the words: "Congratulations Amanda! We're elated with pride!" They were proud of me, and proud of this country—moved by the notion that their daughters, in one generation, could earn master's degrees.

Then, 2016 happened. And the last four years resurfaced all those memories of what it was like for them to grow up in the Central Valley, where Mexican farmworker families were looked down upon. Where my mom's teachers questioned her integrity every time she aced a test. And my dad was pushed aside like all the other Mexican kids from the "camp." For them, the language and style of Trump was all too familiar.

I would tell my mom, "We're going to be OK."

"Oh no, we're not," she would respond. "I experienced this in high school. I know exactly what this is."

I wish I could have changed the channel the day Trump went down the escalator at Trump Tower calling Mexicans rapists and criminals. I was hoping, wishing—more for my parents than myself—that this election would once and for all bury those old high school memories.

But it didn't. It was not a repudiation of a guy who called us "drug dealers, criminals, rapists," who caged kids, who proudly grabbed women, and who made fun of someone with disabilities. For so many of us, women, communities of color, women of color, Latinas and Latinos, it's hard to understand what happened to this country. The one my parents were proud of—that land of opportunity.

As we went into the election day, I did a number of interviews making the point that this was the election cycle where the country would finally get to know Latinos. I reminded viewers that 2020 was the first year Latinos were the largest racial minority group in the country at a rate of a million Latinos turning 18 every year. From the data, we could see the potential early on, especially in battleground states where the margin could be determined by a strong turnout of Latinos. Leading up to this cycle, we had already experienced the power of the Latino vote in states like Colorado and Nevada. As expected, we saw Latino votes turn Arizona blue and boost results in the South and Midwest as well. We are now having conversations about the rich diversity of Latinos/Hispanics. And I'm here for it!

Even the idea that we're talking about Arizona SB 1070 versus economic messaging in Nevada—that's beautiful! It's great that we're expanding the conversation from Cubans in Florida to Puerto Ricans and Venezuelans. It's an indication that we're getting there. People are taking the time to listen and learn about our Latino/Latinx/Hispanic community. Too often, and for way too many years, people have tried to shortcut the listening and engagement tour.

In the political world everything gets reduced to the presidential cycle every four years and the focus turns to a small population of Cubans in Miami. Even in Florida as a whole, the 1.5 million Cuban Americans are only one-quarter of the state's Latino population. Treating that small subset of the population as if they represent all Latinos fails to reflect what we are seeing all around the country. It misses the full picture of who Latinos are and the voting power we possess. That's the conversation that played out on Twitter in the days after the election.

"Wait a second!" people were saying. "Yes, it's great to talk about Florida, but can we talk about Arizona and how Latinos were the tipping point? Can we talk about the hundreds of thousands of Hispanic folks that are in Wisconsin? And the 7 percent of voters in Pennsylvania?"

To go from invisible in past election cycles to a conversation about delivering a win to Trump in Florida is not an acceptable recap of 2020 for Latinos. Instead, it was the largest turnout all across the country because that's where Latinos are—all across America.

As I said to our team at Code for America in the days after the election, "This election gives me hope for our country. People decided to show up."

Despite a pandemic, economic uncertainty, foreign disinformation, aggressive voter suppression efforts at every level of government, and blatant lies, people voted. At a time when surveys showed declining trust in government institutions and four years of disparaging government services, the American people found a way forward, a way to have a voice to decide the direction of the country, *their country*. Groups that campaigns generally ignore were mailing in ballots, standing for hours in line, and doing whatever they could to be seen, all in record numbers: Young voters, indigenous communities, Black, brown, and rural voters decided this was the year to have a say. As a result, the largest number of votes were cast in 2020. And with that we enter a new administration with a mandate to reimagine what this country can be when *everyone* is seen and heard.

Even better, a majority of those voters chose a woman, a Black woman, a Southeast Asian woman, and a daughter of immigrants to be their vice president. Someone who was in the battle from the beginning, unafraid to take on a president who demonized everything she represented.

Joe Biden could have picked a traditional partner. He had a lot of choices. But instead he decided to take on the battle head on —*her* battle, *our* battle—when he chose Kamala Harris. And she was ready, because she didn't wait around to be picked. She elevated herself. She stepped up and stood on that stage long before being chosen. There's so much about that story to me that speaks to the America my parents were proud of— the one where even in the darkest of times, against all odds, we can make progress, we can elevate.

BOSTON, MA

BRUCE ARENA is the author of *What's Wrong With US?: A Coach's Blunt Take on the State of American Soccer After a Lifetime on the Touchline* (Harper, 2018). A 2010 inductee into the National Soccer Hall of Fame, he is in his second season as Sporting Director and Head Coach of the New England Revolution. A three-time MLS coach of the year, Arena has won a record five MLS Cup titles. During his 18-year tenure at the University of Virginia, he led the Cavaliers to five NCAA Division-1 national championships. On the international stage, he coached the U.S. Men's National Team from 1998-2006 and 2016-17, amassing the most wins in the program's history with a record of 81-35-32.

DO WHAT YOU DO, JOE

BY BRUCE ARENA

Probably the greatest honor in my life was coaching the U.S. men's team at the 2002 World Cup. As a nation, we were still feeling the wounds from the September 11 attacks, and when we went to the World Cup, obviously there was a lot of concern about the health and safety of the U.S. team. FIFA countries from around the world bent over backwards to make sure that we felt comfortable and secure in South Korea. I was so proud to be an American. It was wonderful.

Our first game was against Portugal, one of the great soccer countries in the world, and they might have been looking past us. Before the game, I told the team, "When we win today, I'm not going to be surprised." They liked that. "You represent the greatest country in the world," I told the guys. "Have a lot of pride."

We stunned Portugal, 3-2, and made it all the way to the quarterfinals, losing 1-0 to Germany. It was the best World Cup performance in the history of U.S. men's soccer. We were a really patriotic team, so proud of being Americans and having the opportunity to play in front of the world. Today, if there were a World Cup tomorrow, I don't know how the rest of the world would be dealing with the United States. Obviously the last four years, I don't think we've made a lot of friends.

Like everyone I know, I was glued to election results. I saw it as a very important election for our country. We need to change the momentum we've had with this current president, which is not a good momentum.

We need to get back unified as a country, we need to be back in the global community. We've separated ourselves from our allies. I think it's important that we work hard in the future to improve our image abroad. We're supposed to be leaders in the world, and I don't think we are. The part I hate about the current environment we have politically is it's us against them. All the time, it's never "we." We never work for solutions, and that's what our politicians are supposed to be doing.

The job of a leader is to bring all people together. That's what I've always thought as a coach for more than 40 years. You've got to hear both sides. At times you've got to swallow your own ego to make sure you connect people to work together. That's not always easy. Sometimes you're dealing with strong personalities who seem beyond reconciliation. I had that issue coaching David Beckham and Landon Donovan on the L.A. Galaxy starting in 2008. My last run with the U.S. national team, when I came in 2017, that team was a very odd mix. We had to bring both sides together to work together. That's what leadership is, leadership is putting yourself in an uncomfortable place as well, that's part of leadership.

When you coach, there always has to be a compromise. In this current era, a Vince Lombardi my-way-or-the-highway philosophy would never work. It's engrained in every facet of life and business and sports: In this era we have to be changing, whether it's with technology and metrics and analytics or just with people. At the end of the day, it's people who make everything work. You have to find a common ground with the people you're working with.

Donald Trump just didn't have the skills or temperament to be a good president. That's my view. He wasn't qualified to be president, so it was awkward. He's a New York real estate guy, and those are tough characters. You're not real subtle, doing business in real estate in New York. But we elected him. We deserved what we got. It's a democracy and we voted him into office. His inexperience in politics and government was pretty obvious. He's an entertainer. I find him very entertaining. I barely agree with anything he says of any substance. But give him credit, he got elected and he did things that conservatives loved, whether it's judicial appointments to lowering taxes for rich people and multi-billion-dollar corporations. At the end of the day he's probably going to be judged poorly by historians, but he did it his way, that's all I can say.

After these four years of chaos, I think Joe Biden will be a breath of fresh air. He's a people person and he's a great listener. Listening is an incredible skill. Believe me, I've wrestled for years with being a good listener. My wife will tell you to this day, after 44 years of marriage, that I'm probably not a good listener. I'm actually a little bit better than people think. If you don't listen, you're not going to learn.

I'm a big mouth out of New York. At times when I was younger and less experienced, I talked over people's comments. I'm still learning. We learn every day. I'll keep my mouth shut a little bit and listen to what people have to say, then reflect on that a little bit, step back and think about what they've said, and then comment or take action. I think that's critical. Leaders have to be confident enough to listen.

This will be the strength of Joe Biden. He knows how to work with people. He will be able to talk to Republicans and they'll work together professionally. They're going to stand up for what they believe in, but there always needs to be a compromise. If you're the president of the United States, you're working with Republicans and Democrats and many other different kinds of people in the citizenry. That's got to be the charge that the new president and vice president bring to the White House.

I think Biden will do a very good job with McConnell in developing a working relationship and bringing more unity across the aisle. I think that's the recipe for us to move forward. Both parties have to cooperate with each other. They're working for us, the American people, and when there are differences politically, they've got to find a middle ground that works for us. I'm not going to be happy all the time, but it can't be this my-way-or-the-highway philosophy. They've got to work together. There are so many issues that demand urgent progress. First of all, we have to get this pandemic straightened out. From infrastructure to educational issues to the fact that we have millions of people sleeping in the streets in the United States of America, there is so much to be done. We don't mind creating the Space Force, which costs us probably hundreds of billions of dollars, but we accept the fact that we have veterans that are sleeping in the street? Hopefully our leaders in Washington can reach a common ground where we start making progress and taking care of our people and doing it the right way.

Many people talk about what great relationships Biden had with people when he was vice president. Obama, they say, was not the easiest person to work with, nor had the experience. Let's face it, the Affordable Care Act is an unbelievable piece of legislation, to get that through when, obviously, there were Democrats from conservative states who had a hard time voting for it. That will be Biden's strength as a president, the fact he can move legislation forward, I believe, and knows how to talk to people who lead their various parties and run the different efforts on the legislative side.

If I were his coach, sending him into the middle of the action with a little pep talk, I'd keep it simple. I'd tell him, "Joey, the reason you're in the lineup is because we believe in you. Do what you do. You don't need me telling you how to play. You know how to play. That's why you're where you are. Be Joe Biden."

McLean, VA

In 2013, **TERRY MCAULIFFE** was elected the
72nd Governor of the Commonwealth of Virginia.
He restored the voting rights of more than 173,000
Virginians, and served as Chairman of the National
Governors Association. McAuliffe, a lifelong
entrepreneur, is the *New York Times* and *Washington
Post* bestselling author of two books, *What A Party! My
Life among Democrats: Presidents, Candidates, Donors,
Activists, Alligators, and Other Wild Animals* and
*Beyond Charlottesville: Taking A Stand Against White
Nationalism*. McAuliffe was the Democratic National
Committee chairman from 2001-2005. He co-chaired
President Bill Clinton's 1996 re-election campaign
and his 1997 presidential inauguration. He was the
chairman of the 2000 Democratic National Convention
and chairman of Hillary Clinton's 2008 presidential
campaign.

REBUILDING FROM THE WRECKAGE

BY TERRY MCAULIFFE

My feeling in the days after the election was: *I'm ecstatic. We won the presidency.* Some Democrats were wringing their hands. From my perspective, winning the White House and getting rid of Donald Trump, nothing even comes close to that. I love the idea that we won Georgia. Virginia had been the only blue dot in the South. Now you have both Virginia and Georgia as states that are looking bluer and bluer. Here in Virginia, the 2020 election was a blue wave. I'm overjoyed.

Look, I've known Donald Trump for a long time, and know just who he is. He'd been a big Democratic donor going way back. This whole Republican evangelical thing of his was a shtick to win the nomination. He'd have run as a Democrat if he thought he'd had a chance at the nomination. The Republican side looked easier to him. His ego was so large that for many years he talked about running for president and finally did it, never thinking he could win but it would be great for his brand around the globe and he could monetize it.

It wasn't like he made any secret of what he was doing. I was Virginia governor when he was elected and head of the National Governors Association. I sat next to Trump at a White House dinner soon after he'd been inaugurated, and he was kibitzing with me, going on about what the rooms upstairs at the White House were like. I eventually reminded him that I'd seen those rooms a lot more than he had. Right, right, he said. Then he looked over at me and put his hand on mine.

"Terry, can you *believe* I'm here?" he asked me.

"In fairness, sir," I said, "no I can't."

I wrote in my book *Beyond Charlottesvile: Taking a Stand Against White Nationalism* about the phone call I had with Trump on the day of the "Unite the Right" rally in Charlottesville in August 2017. That was a terrible day for America, a day when, as Congressman John Lewis wrote in the foreword to the book, "a thousand white nationalists and Ku Klux Klan followers showed up in broad daylight to preach violence and hate." President Trump called me that day and I gave him the lowdown on the situation on the ground in Charlottesville.

"There was no question in my mind that he was going to do the right thing," as I write in the book. "Foolish me, I was convinced that he was going to clearly condemn the white supremacists and neo-Nazis who had come out of the shadows to march through the streets of Charlottesville, Virginia, in broad daylight, armed and dangerous, screaming some of the most obscene, sickening language I've ever heard in my life."

We all know what happened that day. Trump talked to Steve Bannon or Stephen Miller or some other adviser who reminded him that radical-right hatemongers were Trump's political base. These were his people, which was why David Duke was there that day in Charlottesville, grinning and basically thanking the president of the United States for egging on extreme racists. Trump came out that day as the full-fledged white nationalist we now all know him to be, and it was a national tragedy.

I was working hard on that book when I met Joe Biden for a long meeting in January 2019, and Charlottesville was very much on the mind of the former vice president. Like so many people all over the country, he was horrified by what had happened and how Trump had reacted. Biden asked me a lot of questions about what I'd seen and heard that day, and we went over all of it. He told me that if he did run for president, he'd cite Charlottesville and the need for us to do better as a big part of why he was running. And on the day he announced for president, that was exactly what he did. He also referenced Charlottesville in a major speech on race he delivered in Gettysburg a month before the election that was overlooked by many at the time, but stands out as an important moment.

"I made the decision to run for president after Charlottesville," he said in Gettysburg. "Close your eyes, and remember what you saw. Neo-Nazis, white supremacists, and the KKK coming out of the fields with torches lighted, veins bulging, chanting the same anti-Semitic bile heard across Europe in the '30s. It was hate on the march, in the open, in America. Hate never goes away, it only hides."

Wise words. Now at the time of my lunch with Joe in early 2019, I was very actively considering declaring my own candidacy for president. I've always felt strongly that no job prepares you to be president as well as being governor of a big state. I've been in politics since I worked on Jimmy Carter's reelection campaign in 1980 and I've spent a big chunk of my life thinking about how I could bring the country together as president even as I pushed for bold, progressive change.

Thinking about my chances, I figured I had a tremendous opportunity. I knew I was very popular in the African-American community because of my leadership role as Virginia governor. I restored more felon voting rights than any governor in American history, and got sued by the Republicans. My work on criminal justice reform led other governors to act.

Joe had just gotten a major poll back from his pollster, and we went through almost every page together. It was clear at that point that Joe also had very strong support in the African-American community, with something like a 95 percent approval rating. I thought about it for several months and came to the conclusion that it didn't make sense for both of us to be in the race. I called him in early April and told him I was not going to run and that indeed I would support him. We talked about Beau and his family. Joe Biden is a man of compassion and our country needs that so much now.

I knew Joe's message would break through. As I said for a year on CNN, show me who can build the broadest coalition and that person will be the nominee. I kept hearing about Iowa and New Hampshire. What I said on TV through the process was: *Tell me who is going to win South Carolina.* Iowa and New Hampshire are lovely states, but they're all white. That's not who the Democratic Party is when 95 percent of the Black community votes for us and 70 percent of Hispanics vote for us. You have two states that do not represent either one of those constituencies.

Joe won South Carolina on February 29 and then boy, it was like a match on kerosene. People decided: *We want to coalesce. We need to come together.* Three days later on March 3, we had primaries in 14 Super Tuesday states, and Biden won 10: Alabama, Arkansas, Maine, Massachusetts, Minnesota, North Carolina, Oklahoma, Tennessee, Texas—and Virginia! We had the earliest nominee going back to 2004. And give them credit, Bernie Sanders and Elizabeth Warren and all the other candidates came together and rallied behind Joe Biden and we voted Trump out.

I'm still amazed as I sit here three days after the election: Here you have a president that never once got to 50 percent, a misogynist who made racist comments constantly and screwed up the Covid crisis to the point that millions and millions of people have been infected, and hundreds of thousands died, and he was able to get more than 70 million votes for president. It shocked me.

I do say we as a party have to figure out some things. We didn't do anywhere near as well as we should have in the House, we thought we would win the Senate easily, and the other devastating thing was we lost state legislatures, which will have a big impact on redistricting going forward.

For some reason, many Americans just don't feel that we are talking to them, they didn't see us as the alternative to someone like Trump. We're not talking to people about the things they care about at home every single day. We love these big shiny things. But you know what? They're worried about their kids. Are they going to school? And if they are, are they safe? They're worried about their personal financial situation, health care. That's what we have to continue to talk about.

In December I'm making my official announcement that I'm running again for governor of Virginia. It will be a different kind of race than any I've ever run. Covid has changed everything, including how you run for office, but I'll be talking to people all over the Commonwealth about what state government can do for them and about how the Covid crisis has disrupted their lives. We're all living in a post-Covid economy now. Millions of jobs are lost. Many will never come back. The states that can rebuild their economies will be able to do more for their people. As bad as Covid has been for so many people, the opportunity we now have is to shake up the economy to make it more inclusive. For decades the economy has been stacked against too many people. No longer. It's time to get serious about rethinking education and making sure every child has an opportunity to go into a high-paying job. It's time to work to insure that everyone gets lifted up. It's a big challenge—but I've always loved a big challenge.

INDIANAPOLIS, IN

STEPHANIE SALTER —Born and raised in
Indiana, Stephanie Salter spent 35 years on both coasts,
working for *Sports Illustrated* in New York and as a
reporter and columnist for both the *San Francisco
Examiner* and the *Chronicle*. She returned to her home
state, finished her career at the *Terre Haute Tribune-
Star* and was inducted into the Indiana Journalism Hall
of Fame in 2019.

"HE STOLE EVERYTHING BUT THE SHIT"

BY STEPHANIE SALTER

Back in 1981 when I was making fun of Joe Biden's pathetic new hair plugs, if anyone had told me ...

See, you never know. Even in this country, where knowing is next to Godliness, where you're expected to have the answer, to pigeonhole swiftly, to smugly reduce—to buy the lie that the future is pretty predictable if you're smart—you never really know.

Four decades after I reduced Biden to a visible little plant bed of hair follicles, he became the savior of democracy, the resurrection of reason and decency, the soon-to-be 46th president of the United States. Uncle Joe. The oldest guy ever to win election to the office. The man who saved me and millions from despair or joining a refugee caravan to Canada.

On the sunny morning the numbers made "president-elect" official, I got my first notice from a text that had arrived at 2:25 a.m. from a friend in San Francisco. It began "Hallelujah!" I found my husband, Bill, in the living room, watching CNN. "I guess it's really happened?" I said. He nodded and said, "Pennsylvania. Finally." He was too tired from several nights of fairly bad sleep to jump up and high-five or anything even close to that.

If anyone had told Bill, a staunch Republican until D.J. Trump came along, that in 2020 he would lose sleep worrying over a Democrat NOT winning ... . But Trump was Bill's conversion on the road to Damascus. His disgust for everything Trump outweighed all else. He'd planted our lawn sign for Hillary in 2016 and even gave a post-vote interview to a local TV station, publicly declaring himself an ex-Republican. Biden had been his guy this time around from the beginning, through the primary losses when Uncle Joe seemed to be a sad shadow of yesterday who had no business on a debate stage with all that lefty anger.

It was Bill who kept telling me to have faith that the madness would stop. The retired CEO of a Fortune 500 company, a GE vice president under Jack Welch, a free-market capitalist who worshipped Ronald Reagan, Bill was prepared to vote for Warren or even Bernie if that's what it came to. When James Clyburn and the South Carolina primary reversed the Democrats' engines, no one in America was happier than my husband. He actually sent the Biden campaign *money*.

On the morning "president-elect" became official, friends from Phoenix texted us a Comedy Central sketch we'd never seen. It features an actor-Trump being pulled off a bouncy ball by "Mike Pence" in a roomful of kindergarteners. Trump throws a five-star tantrum, screaming over and over, "I DON'T WANNA GO!" I texted it to dozens of friends and relatives. "You want to watch it again?" I asked Bill later in the day. "Oh, yeah," he said. Our laughter felt like a purge of mercury and lead.

We live in Indianapolis, the state capital of Indiana. Indy is in Marion County, which joined four other Hoosier counties (out of 92) that went for Biden (64 percent to Trump's 35 in Marion). Our house was built in 1939, three years before Uncle Joe was born, and is wedged into a wooded area between two interstate highways. Our mile-long road winds around a small, manmade lake and had only eight presidential yard signs planted this fall. They were all Biden-Harris. We were in a double blue bubble and we knew it.

A pal in Minneapolis was not. Throughout the autumn, she updated her many Facebook friends on her sign wars. Actually, they weren't so much wars as a targeted guerilla action. Someone—who we all referred to as "He"—kept stealing, vandalizing and knocking down her Biden-Harris signs, which were mounted on rebar near a neighborhood trail. The first was stolen. The second, which she covered in Vaseline and glitter, was knocked over and part of the rebar stolen. The third try was that same sign, re-jellied and glittered, affixed to the rebar with wire instead of plastic ties and surrounded by animal shit. "He stole everything but the shit," my friend said.

The fourth effort proved to be the winner. The rebar of a new sign, with more Vaseline, glitter and wire, was sunk into two buckets filled with 100 pounds of quick-drying concrete. It stood through Election Day. My friend had tried to catch the criminal in action with a trail cam, but He stole the camera.

Had I harbored any illusions about our blue Indy bubble, they would have been obliterated two Saturdays before "president-elect" became official. I was driving south on Indiana 39 and saw a line of vehicles with their headlights on, moving north. At first I thought it was a funeral. But it was a Trump Parade: pickups, SUVs, a Hummer (of course), flatbed trucks and regular cars, all festooned with giant U.S. and Trump flags. It crawled toward me for miles. On either side of the two-lane highway, ecstatic Hoosiers were lined up in their own vehicles, lawn chairs and tractors. Men and women, old people and little kids, all screaming, beaming, waving Old Glory and Trump and MAGA banners.

The size of the parade, along with the borderline mania of its participants—every jack one of them as white as the Pillsbury Doughboy—shook me to my marrow. I thought: This is the Ghost of Christmas Future. They hate people like me and they are about to get carte blanche to shut us and our puny, woke, mask-wearing, snowflake, nanny state, "socialist" voices down. And they've got all the guns.

Speaking of socialists, one of my favorite quotes about that came out of the avalanche of Facebook posts and tweets that followed the election. Some guy (I can't find his name now) wrote that he had Cocker Spaniels that were more socialist than Biden. Along with all the self-proclaimed Christians who wouldn't abandon Trump if it meant killing their own children, I remain the most aggravated by the socialism thing. I mean, as if.

Do you know who said this? "All who believed were together and had all things in common; they would sell their property and possessions and divide them among all according to each one's need."

Karl Marx? Try St. Luke. Acts 2:44-45. Of the Bible. You can look it up.

I collected a lot of great quotes over the months leading up to the election. This one was tweeted August 21 by a woman named Eden

Dranger: "At this point, not voting for Biden because he's not your ideal candidate is like finding out Trader Joe's is out of dried mango, so instead you throw yourself into oncoming traffic."

Jesus. What a brilliant simile. I wanted to nail it to the forehead of every whiner who announced they despised Trump but "just can't bring myself" to vote for Biden. Better to sit this one out, they'd say, or write in someone not on the ballot in protest. (My prize for that choice goes to *The Wall Street Journal's* Peggy Noonan, who told her readers she probably would write in "Edmund Burke.")

One other quote I want to show some love for here is about Trump, from an L.A. branding consultant, Anthony Citrano: "It's almost impossible to believe he exists. It's as if we took everything that was bad about America, scraped it up off the floor, wrapped it all up in an old hot dog skin, and then taught it to make noises with its face." If I ever teach creative writing, that one leads the section on imagery.

During the long wait for "president-elect" to become official, I found myself turning away from contemporary thinkers to classic minds. I knew I needed to get out of Now if I was to survive Next, especially if Next was The Ghost of Christmas Future that visited me on Indiana 39. I reacquainted myself with the Buddhist concept of bardo, that very un-fun state between death and the next incarnation. I pulled Thomas Merton's *The Courage for Truth* out of my bookshelves, along with Leo Tolstoy's *A Calendar of Wisdom*, Luigi Barzini's *The Europeans*, and Rainer Maria Rilke's *Letters to a Young Poet*.

"That is at the bottom the only courage that is demanded of us," Rilke wrote to Franz Xaver Kappus in August 1904. "To have courage for the most strange, the most singular and the most inexplicable that we may encounter."

I pulled out Alan W. Watts's 1951 masterpiece, *The Wisdom of Insecurity*. To wit: "A society based on the quest for security is nothing but a breath-retention contest in which everyone is as taut as a drum and as purple as a beet. ... What we have to discover is that there is no safety, that seeking it is painful, and that when we imagine that we have found it, we don't like it."

Such brilliant words. So hard to accept and execute. I had to have some kind of plan for four more years, for all the people I know and don't who deeply believe that every news media figure but Hannity, Carlson,

Pirro and Limbaugh peddle fake news. All the people who believe Donald Trump was chosen by God to stack the Supreme Court and deliver us from Satan's socialism. All the wealthy white bottom-liners who couldn't care less if Trump, unchained, resurrected internment camps and locked millions of blue staters inside, just so long as the stock market soars.

They are all people, humans, citizens, God's children, if you will. Any rude act I commit against them, any epithet I hurl, any denial of their intrinsic worth as brother and sister travelers on this short, bumpy journey is, well, sinful. And it gets us nowhere. Out-hating hate never works for very long. Besides, they have all the guns.

So my only plan was (and is) to remember I'm among tens of millions of people who believe differently, to shrink my world from all I can't control to the tiny circle in which I can help meet the needs of people right in front of me. And to try as hard as I can to be kind. Or at least not mean.

But as I was preparing for the absolute worst, it came: the feeling I heard about from friends and relatives all over the place, from Paris, France, to Poipu Beach, Kauai. From scores of them, the operative word on the day "president-elect" became official was RELIEF. "Like a giant tumor has been removed." "Like a four-year migraine has stopped." "Like I can breathe again." "2008 was an effervescent surprise. This is a release from an underground prison."

An old college pal in D.C. had walked to the spontaneous celebration near the White House, where amiable cops kept expanding the no-traffic zone as the crowd kept growing. "It was an amazing two-square-mile party zone," he said by cellphone. "People dancing, drinking Champagne, playing percussion instruments—99 percent of them wearing masks. This weight was just lifted off all of us because before, it was like, no matter how bad it was, you knew it was going to be worse next week."

No one I heard from thought that what's ahead will be nice. We're still a nation in the throes of a cultural civil war. We really, really disgust one another. Covid-19 is killing and debilitating record numbers of Americans whether they believe it's genuine or a diabolical plot by Anthony Fauci. Black lives still matter, but the sorry truth of systemic racism is the collective sin most of the nation refuses to own. The economy is flying, but on one engine with a damaged wing and fuel running low.

Scariest of all—still—a crazy man who seems incapable of accepting reality has access to the nuclear codes until January 20. We could all go up in an atomic fit of his and Kim Jong-un's pique. And the army of Trump's political enablers would say nothing beyond, "I haven't read the tweet."

I can easily imagine the horrors that could occur. But that's about all I've been doing since 2015. Do I need to be putting my energy and attention into that pursuit right now? Fact: I have no idea if there will be blood in the streets, a Supreme Court debacle or the Trump clan pulling the mother of all Irish Exits and simply disappearing on a wide-body to Dubai. As holy people and sages have been telling us for millennia, the future does not exist.

Do I have hope, be it the audacious kind, the thing with feathers or the one that dies last? I can't say. It's too soon to make that call. What I do know is, Joe Biden, the sublime Kamala Harris and more than 75 million U.S. voters have delivered relief. Uncle Joe, with his veneers, his current hair enhancements, his half-century in politics and his antique but fully functional moral compass, has altered my heart and head. I've gone from "We are totally fucked" to "Maybe we aren't."

Los Angeles, CA

Born and raised in El Salvador, **MARCELO** later moved to the United States to study illustration, and now works making art and children's books.

MI PADRE

BY MARCELO

When Joe Biden won, I didn't hear from my father for about a week. This was out of character for him. Normally we talk almost daily. It was strange, as strange as Trump's post-election silence—unnatural, or perhaps too natural, like wild cats getting quiet when they're about to pounce. Perhaps this is why I prefer to hear these men making noise.

I broke the silence first and called him. He was on his way to the firing range. I was willing to not bring up politics ever again with him, but he had to stir right into it as if our conversation was all one big game of bumper cars. As my father went off on Biden having dementia and his ties with the *comunistas* (no specific country or leader, *all* of the communists), I was watching muted videos of Biden supporters celebrating on the streets, as if viewing this while hearing him vent maintained in me some sort of equilibrium. When he was through, I spoke up (quite foolishly really, because he was just about to run out of fuel)—

"Well, maybe it was the VP that did it for people," I said.

"The Jamaican!"

In the background, I could hear my mother saying, with heartfelt *dolor*, "Holy Lord, Holy Lord." My dad then said we shouldn't talk about this anymore because it depresses my mother.

"Why?"

"Because of the babies."

"Which babies?"

"The aborted babies! She promotes it, that woman! Unbelievable, these gringos are usually so impeccable—she can't love the country, no, not when she's half Jamaican and half who-knows-what-else. Look at our president here in El Salvador, his blood, his roots are Palestinian, and now look where he's leading us to."

I assumed he meant hell, but I didn't ask. We are not even Americans, my family. I moved to Los Angeles 15 years ago while my parents remain in El Salvador, but we, like the rest of the world, cared about this election—I, because of a pending asylum case and my wish to see the country rejoin the Paris Agreement, and my parents, because when a Democrat wins, according to Dad, the whole of Latin America does go to hell—dictators sprout up everywhere, *everywhere*! He made it sound as if Trump had been an eagle all those communist meerkats had been hiding away from and now they would run amok.

I think my father sees a lot of himself in Trump—they're both larger than life, coarse, racists, Twitter freaks, religious when it is financially convenient, and there is in them a streak of fascist kitsch. Masculine, with a Liberace twist—when he is in town, we get pedicures and go to surplus stores to buy Brussels sprouts (his name for ammunition—don't ask). He loves Madonna, perhaps less because of the music than because she is so American. His favorite song is "La Isla Bonita" (the live version from the Sticky and Sweet Tour), and sometimes, when we are by ourselves in elevators, he'll randomly break out into a dance that looks identical to Trump dancing to YMCA, a move that seems to me like a fusion between stabbing and milking a cow.

But what a relief it is.

This victory.

How much so? Well, one of the many reasons I left my country is because I grew up and lived for 20 years in a household that in hindsight I have identified as having been run à la Trump. But I'm glad my father is who he is. He doesn't let me forget the value of exchanging myself with "others"—that if I'm standing on a mountain and I label another mountain as "other," I could easily hike to that other point and look back at where I was just standing, which has now become my new other. My father doesn't let me forget I am my other's other, and that we can still manage to get along. Obviously not having to make decisions that will decide the fate of a nation makes it easier for us, although Ruth Bader Ginsburg and Antonin Scalia, despite their differences, were "supreme friends," Michelle Obama and George Bush share candies at funerals, and Joe Biden comforting Meghan McCain over her father's cancer on "The View" was heart-wrenching. Because of technology, we might be on the cusp of not having to share the same reality ever again, but will we fight and find the worth of holding on to the same values?

So now what?

I'm not sure, but I think it starts with trying to keep in mind that there's an America that will not be dancing anytime soon. With being less hateful, even when there's plenty to hate—Trump's mishandling of the coronavirus and police brutality has led to real deaths, it's infuriating, but houses divided against themselves do collapse, over anyone and everyone in them.

The night of the election I was running errands in Thousand Oaks, a very red city, and before I knew it, somehow, I suddenly found myself driving among a MAGA truck parade. It was one of the scariest moments of my life, but I thought of how, if he'd have had the chance, my dad would have been part of that crowd, with his Brussels sprouts and "La Isla Bonita," and for the first time in years, I felt myself not resisting that which I completely disagree with, and in its place, out of this willingness to listen, there was something I dared to name: hope. And I called my dad, and we talked.

OAKLAND, CA

DOUG SOVERN is Political Reporter at KCBS Radio in San Francisco. The winner of more than 250 journalism awards, he has covered every U.S. presidential election since 1988 and has reported from every continent except Antarctica. He wrote the first-of-its-kind Twitter novel "TweetHeart" and his award-winning short fiction has appeared in *Narrative, Catamaran, The Madison Review* and other literary magazines. He is also a professional bassist and songwriter. He was born in New York City, is a graduate of Brown University, and lives in Oakland, CA with his wife and two children. His Twitter handle is @SovernNation

THE KIDS ARE ALRIGHT

BY DOUG SOVERN

My six-year-old daughter Maya wakes me at 6:47 the morning after Election Day by tapping on my eye mask. This is not unusual. But she is more insistent than normal.

"Daddy!" she says. "*Nobody* won the election!"

I know this already. I worked 14 hours straight reporting the Election Night results on KCBS Radio in San Francisco and tweeting the latest returns like a ballot-powered Gatling gun. I finally went to bed at 4 in the morning, with Joe Biden well ahead in both the popular and electoral vote, but still short of the 270 needed to clinch the presidency. The kids—Maya and her twin brother, Jacob—were fascinated by the whole process, sneaking into my home studio and squatting beneath my desk to watch the televised returns. I gave them a crash course in the Electoral College. Jacob became fixated on the "score" on the TV, the big screen split among four different news channels. Why was it 230-214 on one but only 219-213 on another? When would Biden get more "points"? They would drift in and out over the coming days to check the scoreboard and wait for Biden to score a few more touchdowns to get over the top.

By 8 a.m. I am back at work and on the radio again after less than three hours' sleep. When my kids begin their morning Zoom class, I hear Jacob excitedly bringing the other first-graders up to date on the election, giving them the score and explaining that Biden can't win until he gets at least 40 more "electrical" votes.

In the afternoon, after more virtual school and lunch and some outdoor time, Jacob comes back in. It's been clear to me since the night before that Biden will win. It's only a matter of time, of counting all those votes, of watching a few more grayed-out states on the electoral map roll blue. Jacob wants to know why this is taking so long. He is not alone. I've been fielding frantic, panicked texts and emails from Democrats all over the country since the night before. Relax, I tell them. It's over. Biden won.

By the end of the day, Biden has taken Wisconsin and Michigan. Jacob notes the revised score: 264-214. He rushes out of the room to report the news to Maya.

THURSDAY, NOV. 5

What the hell is going on in Pennsylvania? How long can it take? Trump is slowly erasing Biden's lead in Arizona. Nevada is clearly Biden's, but no one will call it. Finally, Biden overtakes the president in Georgia. In the wee hours, he finally does the same in Pennsylvania. Surely, this thing will be over any hour now. But no.

FRIDAY, NOV. 6

Nope.

SATURDAY, NOV. 7

I'm exhausted after working four consecutive 14-hour days. It's as if we had Election Night four nights in a row. The nation is frazzled. I'm bombarded by Republican conspiracy theorists on Twitter: The Democrats are methodically stealing the election. It's taking this long because they have to forge more ballots and their printer broke. Dead people voted in Michigan. Turnout topped 200 percent in some Wisconsin precincts. Arizona Republicans had their ballots tossed out because they filled them out with Sharpies (each of these claims is easily, and quickly, swatted down with a perfunctory Google search or a simple phone call or email to an election official in the corresponding state). The dead Michiganders are all alive and well. A Sharpie is as legal as any other dark pen in the Grand Canyon State. The only Wisconsin ward where turnout exceeded 90 percent consisted of five votes when only four people were registered, and Trump won it, 3-2.

When I step out in the early morning air to walk our yellow lab puppy, it is bracing. A cold front has blown in overnight. There's a change coming. We've had weeks and weeks of dry, hot days, punctuated by wildfires and power shutoffs, the air often too thick with bitter smoke to breathe comfortably, even with the Covid mask on. Now it's cool and fresh, chilly enough to have to put on a coat. I exhale to see if I can see my breath. Not yet. But I can breathe. The air is different, and so is the light.

I come back inside and check the vote count from Pennsylvania. It's all about Pennsylvania now. The next batch of ballots from Philly and Pittsburgh, from Bucks County and Allentown, should do the trick. If not, then the batch after that. Before Saturday cartoons, Jacob and Maya come in to check the score. Still 264-214. They are frustrated by this, and more than a little confused. They have plenty of company, coast to coast.

At 8:23 a.m. Pacific time, Pennsylvania posts new numbers: Biden's lead has jumped to 31,000 votes, cracking the 30K mark for the first time. I am about to email New York to see if this might trigger a projection when, at 8:25, CNN calls the race: Biden wins Pennsylvania, and with it, the presidency. Thirty seconds later, NBC and MSNBC do the same. Within another minute, CBS and ABC follow suit. It takes the AP nine minutes more. Fox News brings up the rear, six minutes after that.

I run upstairs to tell the kids. They pause Pokemon and check the election channel: 284-214! Jacob is elated that Biden has finally scored enough points.

I hear honking down the hill. Somebody outside whoops. Then someone else. It's finally over.

My dad, Michael Sovern, died on January 20 of this year. He was 88 years old. He'd been deeply involved in the civic life of New York City, and in the Civil Rights Movement. When he was dean of Columbia Law School, he hired Ruth Bader Ginsburg as its first female law professor and Kellis Parker as its first Black law professor. Later, as president of Columbia, he opened Columbia College to women, and divested the university from companies doing business in South Africa. When the apartheid government wouldn't let Bishop Desmond Tutu come to Columbia to receive an honorary degree, my father made the dangerous trek to Johannesburg to give it to him. They became friends for life, and my dad loved to invoke his irrepressible wisdom. "My humanity is bound up in yours," dad told me more than once, quoting Tutu, "for we can only be human together."

As a kid, I got to meet people like Ginsburg and Thurgood Marshall, Fred Korematsu and Ralph Bunche, Indira Gandhi and Jimmy Carter. I first volunteered on a political campaign when I was 11. I started predicting the results of presidential elections in 1972.

I was 18 and a sophomore at Brown University when my dad was named president of Columbia in January 1980. His appointment was front-page news in *The New York Times*, with a "Man in the News" sidebar inside. "Regarded as an incisive thinker, Mr. Sovern, who is 48 years old, has repeatedly shown an ability to elicit opposing views and then achieve a workable consensus," the *Times* wrote. "It is something he is able to do with good cheer, seldom surrendering his sense of humor."

In his inaugural speech, my dad quoted C.P. Snow's observation that "the humanist who cannot describe the Second Law of Thermodynamics is as illiterate as the scientist who has not read Shakespeare." I suspect our outgoing president can do neither.

As an adult, I spoke with my father every Saturday morning, and often those conversations focused on politics. He knew the players, and he knew the plays. As he grew older and his connections began to fall away, the dynamic shifted. Now I was the one with the inside scoop, sharing what I'd learned from interviewing a senator or covering a campaign. My contemporaries, not his, were running the country. He was as keen to hear my thoughts and insights as I'd always been to hear his. We cherished those conversations. More than once, he told me how much he enjoyed them, and how it gave him more pride than I could know to learn from me as I had learned from him.

He has visited me in my dreams since he died. Once, in a waking moment, his spirit came in the form of a golden eagle while I was biking in the woods of the East Bay hills. Two days before this election, he came again, this time while I was asleep. In this dream, I told him how much I missed being able to talk about the election with him, how much there was to share, how I craved his expertise and wisdom.

"Son of mine," he said in the dream, as he often did in life. "No matter what happens, you'll be OK. Don't worry. It'll all be all right." I thanked him and said I hoped he was right, but it wasn't me I was worried about. It's the rest of the country, I said, and the world in which my children will live.

On the first anniversary of my father's death, Joe Biden will be sworn in as the 46th president of the United States. For the rest of my days, I will associate Inauguration Day with my dad's last breaths. I wish he had lived to see this moment, though I'm grateful he was spared witnessing the ravages of Covid-19. It has taken the lives of some of his best friends, and it might well have claimed his, had his heart not given out just as the pandemic was beginning in America. But that heart would have been lifted by the defeat of Donald Trump, a man whose tired act he had seen up close for decades in New York City.

"He's not a serious man," my dad had told me when Trump announced his candidacy. "He's a carnival barker, a con man."

My dad, a respected leader in New York's corporate, cultural and philanthropic circles, said The Donald was never a factor in any of them. Trump's "foundation" was regarded as a self-serving joke by legitimate philanthropists. He wasn't on any significant boards or engaged in civic initiatives. My father, who led the rewrite of the New York City charter and chaired a special joint city and state Government Ethics Commission, who helped found both the Mexican-American and Puerto Rican Legal Defense and Education Funds, and Helsinki Watch, and AMFAR, told me "When people are looking for leadership or engagement on anything involving the public good, no one even thinks of Trump. His name doesn't even come up." In one of our conversations about Trump, we coined a new nickname for him: "the anti-mensch."

My father was appalled by Trump's election in 2016, but, ever the optimist, told me on *that* morning after, four years ago, "Well, maybe he won't be that bad. He's a terrible businessman, but maybe he'll hire some good people. Let's hope for the best." It didn't take long for him to learn those hopes would never be realized.

On this morning after, my kids are not thinking about their late grandfather. They've returned to cartoons. Every half hour or so, in between live shots on the radio, I poke my head in and shout, "Biden won!"

"Daddy! You're so annoying!" they shout back, as any child should. "We know that already! Stop saying that!" At one point, Jacob does check in and notes that Biden's score has crept up to 290, lifted by six by the AP calling Nevada. "He could still get more than 300, Daddy, if he wins one more state," he says. I smile, counting this as a not small victory.

I first met Joe Biden in 1979, when I was a freshman at Brown. He came to my school to deliver a guest lecture on foreign policy. He was 36 and just starting his second term in the U.S. Senate. I was studying American history and political science, and my security policy professor thought I'd be interested in meeting Biden. It was a terrific lecture, focusing on the international issues of the day: Iran, South Africa, the Soviet threat, Nuclear disarmament talks. Biden had taken Amtrak up from Wilmington to Providence.

When the hourlong talk was over, I and several other students went up to Biden to ask him more questions. He looked at his watch and said something along the lines of, "What the hell. There's always another train. What do you kids want to talk about?" He rolled up his sleeves, leaned against a desk and answered every question we had, staying long past dark, talking with us for a couple of hours. All I could think was, what in the world is this young senator from Delaware doing in Rhode Island, wasting his time talking to college students? This guy wants to be president someday. He is playing a very, very long game. I had no idea how long.

He did run for president, eight years later—his campaign collapsing in 1987 after just a few months when he was caught plagiarizing a campaign speech from British politician Neil Kinnock. When he ran again in 2008, I interviewed him, as I did all the other contenders. Before we began, I reminded him we had met some 30 years before.

"We did? Where?" he asked.

I told him about the college lecture.

Biden stunned me by not only remembering the event, but naming the professor and the hall in which he gave the lecture. He recalled the anti-apartheid protest that took place on the lawn outside, and went into detail about the topics we discussed that night. He didn't remember me, but I had much longer hair then—I had *hair*—but he summoned details long since lost to me. I guess that's part of what makes someone an effective politician, and why I could never be one. The interview wasn't great—he had a bit of a cold, his campaign was flailing, he fell back on fairly rote answers—and I thought: *All those years working toward this moment, and he's never going to get there.*

And now, through so many twists of fate and fortune, a dozen years later, he finally has. It's hard to imagine the sense of accomplishment that must bring a person. And the burden of responsibility: Now the work must begin. It is one thing to win an election; it is quite another to govern. Better people than Joe Biden have failed to grasp the difference.

In the minutes and hours following his victory, in my neighborhood, there is a sense of a great weight being lifted off the world. As I walk the dog (again), the Peter Tosh song "Downpressor Man" comes into my head. *Downpressor man, where you gonna run to?* Donald Trump's run is over. The pressure is easing, on our shoulders and on our souls. Everything feels a little lighter. There is reason to hope again, to think my kids might grow up in a more civil and just society, one that turns from darkness and toward love, one that opens its hearts instead of hardening them. But meanwhile, there are still bills to pay and dogs to walk, Zoom classes to proctor and messes to mop up. This day feels like a liberation, but even after a war comes to an end, we still have to put food on the table and make sure the kids get dressed.

Maya and Jacob don't remember it, but when they were two and still in a double stroller, they met Kamala Harris. She was born two miles south of the neighborhood where we live, and grew up in a house five miles in the other direction. I've known her for close to 20 years, since she was working in the city attorney's office in San Francisco and contemplating a run for district attorney. She is the first person from the Bay Area to be elected to national office. The first woman, of course, and the first Black or South Asian person to be vice president. She kicks open a door that has been slammed shut on so many for so long. She may well be the 47th president. The impact of her election feels almost as seismic as Barack Obama's was. It says to so many—young girls in particular—that yes, they have a place in the upper ranks of our society, that they can dream as big as anyone else and those dreams can indeed turn real.

Shortly after 5 p.m. in Oakland, my wife and I gather the kids in front of the television to watch Joe Biden and Kamala Harris give their victory speeches. Harris strides onto the stage, dressed in bright white from head to toe, the symbolic color of the suffragette movement. Maya asks me why. I explain to her, quickly, that when women were fighting for the right to vote, they wore white.

"What?" she exclaims. "Girls and women couldn't vote?!"

No, they couldn't, I say.

"Even if they were 18?"

"Actually, back then, you had to be 21. But only men were allowed to vote. And in the olden days, only men who owned land could vote. And only white men."

"That's crazy," she and Jacob say in disbelieving unison.

"Yes, it was," I say. "Luckily, times change." Nodding at Kamala on the screen, I tell them: "And now they're changing again."

"I'm glad I live now," Maya whispers.

When Harris says, "Because every little girl watching tonight sees that this is a country of possibilities," Maya looks at me and asks, "Daddy? I could be president someday?"

"Yes," I say. "Yes, you can. But you'll have to wait 29 years, because you have to be 35."

"Twenty-nine years!" she says. "How many years did Biden wait?"

"So many," I answer. "He's 77."

"Seventy-seven! And everybody voted for him?"

"Not everybody," I laugh. "Just enough."

Joe Biden has waited decades. The rest of us have waited four long years, and the longest year of our lives ends with just enough votes, just enough hope, just enough light, a change in the weather, the joyful squeals of my children as the speeches end and Maya and Jacob run off to play, and a sense that we are, at long last, closing one of our darkest chapters and moving on to write a better story for our nation, and the world. I sense my father's knowing smile and I hear his voice, quoting his old friend Tutu. We can only be human together.

HENDERSON, NV

KEN KORACH is the radio voice of the Oakland A's, and the author of *Holy Toledo: Lessons From Bill King, Renaissance Man of the Mic* (Wellstone Books, 2013), widely credited with helping earn Baseball Hall of Fame recognition for Bill King, and the co-author, with Susan Slusser, of *If These Walls Could Talk: Stories From the Oakland A's Dugout, Locker Room, and Press Box* (Triumph, 2019). The 2021 baseball season will be Ken's 26th with the A's and 30th in Major League Baseball. He has been inducted into the Bay Area Radio Hall of Fame, the Nevada Broadcasters Hall of Fame and Jewish Sports Hall of Fame of Northern California.

MY DAD (AND FDR) ON
A WAY FORWARD

BY KEN KORACH

My first call the Thursday morning after Election Day was to my dad. It was 8:30 a.m., but I had been awake since 5. The adrenaline of elections is something that's been with me since I first watched Walter Cronkite on CBS in the 1960s. I had a firsthand taste of it in 1982 when I was working for a small radio station north of San Francisco in Petaluma, KTOB Radio, "Top of the Bay." I've broadcast a ton of big games, but nothing has been more thrilling than being on the air that night, tracking races like Barbara Boxer winning California's Sixth Congressional District. It didn't matter that the station cut power to 250 watts after dark and the signal faded to static about five minutes out of town. It was Election Night and it was the same buzz I felt watching TV this morning.

I've always looked to my dad for inspiration and I've been lucky that I've been able to tap into his wisdom for the last 68 years. In the aftermath of the most divisive election season of our lifetimes, my dad's life can help serve as a template for how we might recover and move forward. For example, this is his second pandemic. He was born on Feb. 16, 1919, but all of his official documents say he was born on Feb. 17. That's because of the Spanish Flu. The hospital in Akron, Ohio, was so overrun that there was no time to record his birth on the 16th.

The family eventually settled in Los Angeles. His parents weren't highly educated—they had come from Eastern Europe and the efforts to get settled were a greater priority—but my dad remembers how the discussion of current affairs was a nightly ritual at the dinner table. "My dad only had a slight bit of education at the higher levels," my dad remembered. "But I recall when I was nine the big subject at dinner was the '28 election. Herbert Hoover against Al Smith."

Indelible for my dad was the looming Depression and how Hoover, after winning the election, talked about prosperity being "just around the corner." Sound familiar? We're turning the corner on the current pandemic as daily case counts surge past 120,000, as I write these words.

I was on my way to the golf course once I hung up with my dad. Golf's been my salvation during the last few months. We had 60 games in 66 days during the baseball season and the intensity of it was unrelenting, all of it being played against the backdrop of the virus and the protests that followed the killing of George Floyd. So I pounded golf balls at the driving range. My goal was to keep hitting until my mind turned off.

I met a couple friends and sped around the course in three and a half hours. Our group included the former A's player Mack "Shooty" Babitt, now a professional scout for the team. It was a tough summer for scouts around baseball but thankfully Shooty is back to work. He's a product of the ballfields of Oakland, especially Bushrod Park, where he hung out with Rickey Henderson when they were kids, a park that is a short drive from the childhood home of Kamala Harris.

I talked with Shooty about this book, and the question of "Now What?" He emphasized treating each other the way we'd want to be treated ourselves. It's a simple thing, right? Been said a trillion times, but it rings so true today.

Can Joe Biden's decency rise above the acrimony and the politics of division? I mean, civility and graciousness shouldn't be so hard to find. Can Biden establish enough trust to blunt so much distrust? Is it Pollyannaish to think that we may have more in common than we imagine we do? It seems impossible now, but will his old relationships in the Senate bear fruit when it comes to legislation?

More profoundly, beyond Washington: Can we listen to each other?

Tony Kemp, the A's infielder who was the team's nominee for the Roberto Clemente Award for character and community involvement, initiated the +1 Effect. The goal: Let's have a real conversation about race.

So many of my friends have lost their jobs, including several who worked for the A's as the team reorganized after a truncated season without fans in the stands. This isn't the best time to be looking for a job. It would be great to be able to jump right back into the workforce, but as Dr. Fauci has said, "The virus sets the timeline." Patience is a lot to ask of people who have families and bills to pay, but no work. It may be more than a year before businesses get back to hiring on a broad scale.

I turned on the TV when I got back home around 2:30. John Fetterman, the lieutenant governor of Pennsylvania, was on talking about the virus and how it's turned Americans against each other, bitter arguments developing over things like masks, as if the virus cares whether your side is blue or red. (How f-ing hard is it to wear a mask?) Fetterman talked about how we have to make the virus our enemy and not each other and that a united, concerted effort will be needed to defeat it. It's not going to happen overnight, but when normalcy returns and we can all go back to work and our daily routines, it will be good for the collective psyche. I have this recurring dream focused on the joy we will feel when we can again savor the things we used to take for granted, like hugging our children and going out to dinner.

One of the saddest effects of the last four years has been the erosion of trust in our institutions, including federal agencies. Are they all perfect? Of course not, especially now, because as Michael Lewis explained in *The Fifth Risk,* countless federal agencies have been hallowed out in the Trump years for the sake of shunning expertise. It's a slap in the face to so many people in both parties who have dedicated their lives to trying to make our lives better. I'm also thinking now of the incredible dedication and patriotism of election workers, counting votes around the clock in a pandemic, with the simple but profound goal of facilitating democracy. We're going to need people like them, plus a restoration of the belief that government can do good things, if we are going to defeat the virus and move forward.

Anybody who lived through the Depression was scarred by it and in the case of my dad it framed much of how he's viewed issues like health care. His late sister Margaret got very sick while the country was in the throes of the Depression. The family had no health insurance and almost no money, so my dad was left at home by himself while his parents took Margaret from one doctor to another just seeking someone who would see her. The day seemed to last several days for my dad as he waited alone, scared. How many doctors just flat refused to see her? He doesn't remember, except that it was quite a few. She finally got examined and recovered, but the memories of that night never left my dad. Nor has his belief that everyone should have access to affordable health care. The pandemic has only buttressed his empathy for anyone suffering for lack of health care.

My dad first voted in a presidential election in 1940, exactly 80 years ago today, the year FDR ran for his third term. By 1944 he was stationed with the legendary 8th Air Force outside of London. It look two long weeks for him to cross the Atlantic to get there, and the troops on the ship faced the grim reality that all of them likely wouldn't make it back, but they never wavered in their courage or questioned the rectitude of their mission.

I thought about this later in the evening as I watched Donald Trump attack the validity of this year's election from the White House briefing room. On Saturday, when Joe Biden addressed the nation for the first time as president-elect, he talked about "a time to heal in America." And, "I pledge to be a president who seeks not to divide but unify." The contrast couldn't have been more stark.

Dad was a big fan of FDR. In fact, when he returned from the war and began a career teaching and coaching in high school and junior college, the first school where he coached, Verdugo Hills High, was built by the WPA. From the school's website: "By 1939, there were 78 WPA workers building things on campus." It may not be totally analogous to today, but it is an example of literally rebuilding the country in tough times and also putting people to work.

My dad's 101 now. He's lived through two pandemics, the Depression, a world war, Vietnam, 9/11, his wife (my mom) committing suicide, and yet he's still upbeat. Maybe that's the old coach in him, believing that if you work hard enough an eight-run inning could be just around the corner. He had a great and fulfilling career, a second marriage and a retirement spent continuing to learn and travel. He's never stopped being engaged in his life.

During the hiatus while baseball wasn't played and my wife Denise and I were sheltering like everybody else, my dad usually ended our conversations with this coda: "Keep your chin up." It's that spirit that defined so many of his generation. We should remember how it feels right now.

PITTSBURGH, PA

STEWART O'NAN is the author of seventeen novels, including *Last Night at the Lobster* and *Emily, Alone*. He was born and raised and lives in Pittsburgh.

YOGI AT THE WALL

BY STEWART O'NAN

"It gets late early out there," Yogi Berra said. Most casual fans know Yogi as a catcher, but at the end of his career, when his knees were shot, the Yankees still needed his bat in the lineup, so they stuck him out in left field. Every Pittsburgher knows this, because he's the guy wearing the number 8 helplessly watching Mazeroski's 1960 World Series-winning homer clear the left field wall in Forbes Field. But Yogi was talking about old Yankee Stadium, and specifically left field in Yankee Stadium in October, back when the Yankees were in the Series every year. The first World Series night game wasn't until 1971—in Pittsburgh. Back in the '50s, the games were all afternoon games, and with the sun setting earlier and the orientation of Yankee Stadium's three-tiered grandstand, by the late innings the shadows could be tricky, especially for an aging, bandy-legged catcher-turned-outfielder. When you can't pick up the ball early, it's impossible to know whether to come in or fade back. You can freeze, trying to read the unreadable, and when you don't run well, even the slightest hesitation dooms you.

Joe Biden could have snatched an early victory by taking Texas, Florida, Georgia or North Carolina. In past elections, a Democrat would have had little chance in any of these except Florida, so just that fact that he might steal one was seen as a great opportunity and a sign that slowly but surely the demographics in those states are changing for the better. Progress, the party flacks said. Instead, Texas and Florida were quickly called for Trump. The morning after, Trump is leading in Georgia and North Carolina, and two of the three crucial Senate races in those states are leaning Republican, a bad sign. If those results were to hold, Biden would appear to have just one chance to salvage the race—my state, Pennsylvania. If he loses Pennsylvania, it's over. So yeah, it's frickin late.

On Election Night, trying not to watch the early returns rolling in, I was Zooming with an old friend who now lives in Chile. He was telling me about how the country has decided to write a new constitution. The old one isn't that old—a military constitution instituted by Augusto Pinochet in the 1970s. It sounded intriguing to me, the possibility of a new start, a chance to correct some bedrock mistakes. No. The fear, my friend said, is that the new constitution will be socialist, like Castro's shift in Cuba, abolishing private property, ruining the economy, which he said is doing well. It's a great place to start a business. Besides the riots.

"How's the income gap there?" I asked.

"That's the problem," he said.

Though the news told us all along to be patient and wait for all the ballots to be counted, it feels on the morning after like we've been cheated, conned into believing the country is better than it is. I want to blame the pollsters for raising our hopes again, and Trump voters for being simple and selfish and racist, and any Democratic demographic that didn't get out and vote in big numbers, and the Democrats for not running a better candidate (though who would that be?). I know throwing around blame before the last votes have been counted isn't productive, but it feels like a necessary first step to accept the loss. Gotta put that anger somewhere.

We were so hopeful, so committed. Everything seemed possible, though after 2016, we guarded our hearts, never letting ourselves get too confident, even when the numbers looked promising, especially the massive turnout of early voters. Those long lines seemed evidence of a groundswell, a real hunger for change. Where did all those votes go? Were they all in states Biden was going to win anyway? And if he loses, how do those new voters feel? Will they be back in 2022? 2024?

In fifth grade, we had a mock presidential election. This was in 1972, and I voted for McGovern. The class overwhelmingly voted for Nixon, who my parents also voted for. Why did I choose McGovern? I can't recall, but I remember being surprised by the landslide for Nixon, and feeling bad that I was on the losing side. That Nixon eventually resigned in disgrace still doesn't erase that feeling. Can people not tell the difference between a good person and a bad person? Or are the ends so important that they justify any means? Is that simply realpolitik? Nixon, like Dick Cheney, was a Yankee fan.

Growing up in an Italian-American neighborhood in St. Louis, Yogi was part of a family that voted straight Democratic and worshipped FDR. The ward bosses oiled the city machine in exchange for civil service jobs. Later, as a high-paid athlete, celebrity and entrepreneur (he owned a good chunk of that horrible chocolate drink Yoo Hoo), he tended to vote Republican. As Yogi's son Dale explained in his book *My Dad, Yogi*, "Mom ... was a rock-ribbed Republican. ... And she admired William F. Buckley for his erudite manner. ... he voted for Republicans because Mom said so. No kitchen-table debates were necessary."

During his career, Yogi was a champion of African-American players finally joining the major leagues and late in life supported an organization called Athlete Ally, dedicated to ending homophobia and transphobia in sports.

"Respect others—that's what I learned in sports," Yogi said. "Whatever background, whatever you are, it doesn't matter. Treat everybody the same, that's how it should be."

Now, almost 11 o'clock the night after the election, Biden has taken a narrow lead in Wisconsin and Michigan, which he needs, with North Carolina and Georgia still leaning toward Trump. As most news organizations predicted, it looks like it will come down to Pennsylvania. I take this personally. Will my mail-in ballot swing the election? Or will Trump take me to the Supreme Court and have it nullified?

Joe Biden is from Scranton, but Trump is too, via "The Office." To me, he combines the obliviousness of Michael Scott and the loopy boorishness of Dwight Schrute—neither of whom is ever truly called to account for his actions. Has that lack of self-awareness served Trump well? What about the country? Does it matter to his supporters what kind of job he's done?

My parents voted for Nixon three times, in 1960, 1968 and 1972. They were moderate Republicans, as their parents were. After Watergate, they remained faithful to the GOP, proof that party affiliation means more than the candidate or job performance. At least it did for my mother until George W. Bush took office. My mother thought the war in Iraq was a bald lie and a huge mistake, and in 2004 jumped party lines and voted for John Kerry. After the election, she changed her registration and died a Democrat.

My father is still a Republican but thinks Trump is awful. He didn't vote for Trump, but I guarantee he voted dead red on the down-ballot races without hesitation. It's hard to leave the tribe.

In the past I've explained the political split in the U.S. in very simple terms. In 2000, 48 percent of voters voted for George W. Bush to be our president. In 2008, 46 percent voted for Sarah Palin to be our vice president. In 2016, 46 percent voted for Donald Trump to be our president. This time, when all the ballots are counted, I'll be surprised if Trump gets more than 48 percent, or less than 46. We're just that stable (Thanks, Fox News!). With their built-in Electoral College advantage of white, rural states being weighted more heavily, the Republicans can afford to run weak candidates and let the system reward them, while the Democrats have to overperform just to stay even.

Before 1964, this wasn't a problem. Every four years the Dixiecrats delivered the South for the Democratic candidate (who was pointedly not from the South). It was a pact with the devil, and when JFK broke it by supporting integration, and LBJ signed the Civil Rights Act, the Deep South and its 50-plus electoral votes no longer belonged to the Democrats. Since then, of all the Democratic presidential candidates, only Jimmy Carter and Bill Clinton—sons of the Deep South—had won a Deep South state. George W. Bush, John McCain, Mitt Romney and Donald Trump all carried the region whole, with George W., that fake folksy Texan from effete Connecticut royalty, doing it twice.

I have to tell myself not to give up too soon—just what the news has been advising all along—but the whole process is demoralizing. I don't want to think less of my country and my fellow citizens, and I don't want another four years of Trump and Mitch McConnell (and now the 6-3 Supreme Court) dragging the country back to 1950. I thought Trump would stop at 1980, but McConnell & the Court are definitely down for 1950. A second Trump administration would be a runaway truck, no brakes.

Maybe an even greater fear is if this drags on and PA becomes like Florida in 2000, Cheney's Khaki Revolution blocking the hallways at the state house, trying to shut down the recount, or just the count. I can see the lawyers and lobbyists descending on Harrisburg the way they did Tallahassee. And thanks to McConnell and the Senate obstructing Obama's appointees for judgeships, they have the courts in place to back up their claims. Machiavelli (and Cheney, and James Baker) would be proud. That their ruthlessness will end up costing those who have the least is just the frosting on top.

I've voted for more losers than winners in my life, and win or lose, the job is the same. As Michael Cunningham says, the goal is "to not do anything that makes us smaller," and that takes faith, and hope. We keep fighting, keep running, keep voting. Every setback is temporary. As Yogi says: It ain't over till it's over.

Finally that Saturday morning, after 29,000 mail-in ballots from Allegheny County, where I live, were counted, the news channels called the election for Joe Biden and Kamala Harris. Was my vote the one that put them over the top? It was one of them, and now I'm proud of my neighbors, and proud of my city and my state, and proud of the country again for voting out Trump. The Senate is still in doubt, with two run-offs in Georgia slated for January 5, so there's still a slight chance the Democrats can flip it, but even if they can't, getting rid of Trump is a victory worth celebrating.

That night in Squirrel Hill, where last year the neighborhood held a candlelight vigil after the Tree of Life synagogue shooting, Biden-Harris supporters were dancing in the streets. Crawling past in my car, I joined the party, honking my horn and waving V for victory to the crowd. It's been a long four years. It's a relief to finally have the end in sight.

BLOOMFIELD, NJ

J-L CAUVIN is a standup comedian from New York City, currently living in New Jersey.

SURGERY WAS A SUCCESS—NOW FOR THE CHEMO

BY J-L CAUVIN

I was almost euphoric in the days after the election, but it was a weird kind of euphoric. It was depressing that so many people voted for Trump and that the Republicans actually gained seats in the House and probably held on to the Senate, but the fact is: Trump is going to be out of power. I feel like you get a diagnosis from the doctor, it could have been fatal, but it turns out at least it's treatable. The surgery was a success. The orange tumor has been removed from the system. You're not out of the woods yet. You've got to go to political chemo now, because there are a lot of issues at play. Trump remains a uniquely powerful and malignant force in American history.

I sort of dabbled in a Trump impression as early as 2014. It started with a video impression I did for "The Adam Carolla Show." I don't sit down and practice per se. Trump was just everywhere from 2015 on. It was practically like having a roommate, you know, "I'm picking up on all his tics, because I hear him speaking for six hours per day, five days a week." In 2018 I started doing a podcast as Trump, a weekly, 45-minute ad-libbed show reviewing pop culture and news of the week. That was when my Trump impression got good, but I was doing it for an audience of maybe 500 per week.

Then Covid hit. I was a standup comedian with nowhere to perform, so I had nothing else to do. I was just doing videos in my apartment. A Trump video I did on March 24, 2020, caught on like nothing I'd ever done before. Around 3 million views over the next two days. As NJ Advance Media wrote two days later, "A New Jersey comedian's dead-on impersonation of President Donald Trump vowing to move past the coronavirus crisis by Easter is going viral." They quoted me: "It's crazy. Sixteen years as a standup, and all it took was a global pandemic for me to finally break through." That video totally changed everything for me. Last I checked, it was up to around 7 million views. During the election, I was doing about three Trump videos a day, almost like a comedy wire service.

Being a comedian, as weird as it is, I think helps you understand politics. You get to know what turns people off and what makes them laugh. If the Democrats had held seats in the House and won the Senate, and you had a unified Democratic Party government, Trump would have been out there using his platform to pour lighter fluid on the anti-government energy and you'd have short-term chaos. If Joe Biden passed a $2 trillion climate plan, I'd applaud it, and then whichever Koch brother is still alive would form some sort of unholy alliance with Trump and his followers and that would lead to violence and shutting things down. I think we may be better off short term, in terms of healing conflict, but we are not better off long term. We need real leadership on climate change, and we're not going to get it: We're going to get executive orders and incremental action, like under Obama. We've set ourselves up for longer-term pain with this election by having more gridlocked government. Everybody can melt back into their apathy of cynically or lazily saying, "Nothing ever gets done." There won't be as many riots because we'll just continue down this slow path to Armageddon.

If anyone wonders if I'll miss doing my Trump videos, I'm very happy to see him go. My plan for the Trump podcast is to turn him into the world's worst, insecure political pundit, which is probably what he's going to turn into. If Trump had never been elected, and I'd never had my videos take off, believe me I'd be very happy. If you could put Hillary Clinton in office, I would have traded all of this in a second.

I was very disappointed when she lost in 2016. I was definitely a very strong Hillary supporter, but I think it meant even more to my mom, a woman in her 70s, who found it even more insulting. She's had the life experience of working very hard and going through life feeling at times unappreciated, which I think is common for women of that generation.

You look at Joe Biden. I like Joe Biden, I gave him money, I voted for him. Not to insult the man, but Joe Biden in almost every way is a kind of a lesser version of Hillary, except on the so-called likability front. I don't at all buy into the notion that Hillary is not "likable." But if you accept facts, more people say they like Joe Biden, and more people say they dislike Hillary. Not me. I remain a Hillary fan.

Hillary Clinton, whether you like her or not, would have been a great president—if they let her. She's a brilliant, accomplished, experienced woman who called Trump out. Go back and look at the debates and other clips from the campaign. She was about 25-for-25 on predictions about how awful Trump would be and in the ways he'd be awful.

We unleashed Trump on the world four years ago. I feel like people are so ready to move on from that and take no responsibility. But to have voted for Trump, or stayed home because they're "both bad," that's democratic malpractice. It's weird not to say, "Man, I messed up." It's weird not to have that mea culpa, as a country, and man to man, and woman to woman. I saw a lot of Republicans doing videos during the campaign, saying, "I was a Republican, but I see Trump as bad and I'm voting for Biden." The people I really respect are the ones who can say, "I didn't like Hillary, but I made a major mistake not voting for her." There weren't many of those.

The fact is, we have hundreds of thousands of dead people, we have kids in cages, we have an economy now in shambles, though it's picking back up, and lower standing in the world. We're an international embarrassment. Those are all things that would have been made exponentially better by a Hillary Clinton presidency. Not perfect, but better. It's great if you can love your president, or think your president is awesome, but I want someone who can do the job. Trump is both incompetent and cruel and uncaring. You can't get worse than that.

I always respected Hillary. She had to take all the beatings for being the woman the GOP was focused on. They knew this was a talented, strong woman with higher ambition. She had to take every first hit from a GOP that plans ahead like China to the 10th power. China lays out a five-year plan. The Koch brothers were always like: Hopefully my grandkids will be able to see a destroyed America with libertarianism. These guys go on 40-year plans to change the world. Democrats seem to go on tweet-by-tweet plans. Hillary Clinton was measured tweet by tweet from the left, ignoring the decades-long destruction that the GOP had cruelly, insanely but shrewdly levied at her.

I hope history is kind to Hillary Clinton. I was thinking that maybe I'd get famous enough, doing my Trump videos, that I'd have a chance to meet Hillary. I'd have one favor to ask: *Can we Skype with my mom? So she can say hello?* It would mean a lot to her. Maybe there's still a chance.

PHOTO BY BRAD MANGIN

GRANITE BAY, CA

DUSTY BAKER is the only manager in Major League Baseball history to lead five different teams to the playoffs, most recently the Houston Astros. Baker is the author of *Kiss the Sky: My Weekend in Monterey for the Greatest Rock Concert Ever* (Wellstone Books, 2015), and an entrepreneur whose businesses include Baker Energy Team ("Rethink the way you use energy"), which focuses on solar and other sustainable energy alternatives, and Baker Family Wines. Baker spent 19 years in the big leagues, won a World Series ring with the Dodgers in 1981 and was MVP of the 1977 National League Championship Series. Going into the 2021 season, back with the Astros, he ranks 15th all time among baseball managers with 1,892 wins.

DARREN'S GENERATION

BY DUSTY BAKER

By the time they finally called it for Joe Biden that Saturday I was working outside in the garden. My wife had been watching CNN religiously all week. I was watching, too, but I'd get tired of it. I went to bed a couple times and woke up the next day and it seemed like the vote-counting was in exactly the same spot it was the night before. Everybody was on pins and needles. I was really kind of wishing that they'd make a final decision.

I'm glad the way it worked out. I know there are a lot of happy people on one hand and a lot of disgruntled, frustrated people on the other hand. It's always like that, but it was even more this election. It just seems like the last four years were so full of turmoil, so full of fighting, so full of qualified people getting fired, it brought out the worst in a lot of people, and I mean all the way around. That was what it felt like to me.

You saw sides of people you hadn't seen before. You found yourself looking at people and trying not to judge them on their political beliefs. Everybody can have their own beliefs.

It's just sort of remarkable, sort of bewildering, looking at the vote totals. How can the president have such a following? It appears that the American way is about money, more than anything. Even if you're dissatisfied with someone, if you decide you think they can help you make money, then you can accept anything that they do.

I don't know how we move forward after an election like this. I don't know how we get people talking to each other. We'll see what happens, but there's so much opposition, I honestly don't know if it's possible to step back from the brink. This has all been building for so long. You knew it was there because there were so many people that were totally disgruntled by the job that President Obama did.

I've always felt that there's a racial, economic and intellectual time bomb that we're sitting on. If I'm asked, I'll talk about it. In August 2020, when Jacob Blake was shot seven times in the back in Kenosha, Wisconsin, my son, Darren, showed me a video. I spoke out then and talked about the "racial time bomb" I worry about, especially for Darren and his generation. He turned 21 in February.

"I was just appalled," I told the *Houston Chronicle*. "Boy, it's getting worse and worse in the country. Something has to be done, and something has to stop. It's senseless shootings, senseless killings. Kids are going to have nightmares. You're supposed to feel safe in this country. You're not supposed to feel threatened or afraid. This is nothing new for me, especially a child of the '60s. I'm more afraid for my children and my grandchildren than I am for me right now. They see you as some old man that's harmless versus a young man that's dangerous. That's not the situation of how people should feel."

I grew up in California, first Riverside in Southern Cal, then near Sacramento for high school when my dad took a job there and moved the family. My dad was in the Navy and he believed in nonviolence, but he also believed in protecting your own. I had a tough choice to make in the summer of 1967, my last year of high school. I was offered scholarships to play football or basketball and could have gone to San Jose State or Santa Clara University. I was really looking forward to being a big man on campus. Just before the Major League Baseball draft in June '67, I prayed: "Please, let it be anyone but the Atlanta Braves that drafts me."

As I wrote in my book *Kiss the Sky* (Wellstone Books, 2015), "I did not want to live in the South. I'd been dealing with enough racism in Northern California and I was sure Georgia would be much worse."

The Braves picked me and I was in for an education. My eyes were opened. But you know what? That ended up being one of the best things that ever happened to me. Hank Aaron promised my mother he would look after me, and he did. I was with him constantly. Through him I met so many Civil Rights leaders: Al Sharpton, Maynard Jackson, Jesse Jackson,

Ted Abernathy, Andrew Young and so many others. Hank introduced me to the governor of Georgia, a former peanut farmer named Jimmy Carter, and sometimes before games Ralph Garr and I would drop by the governor's office at the State Capitol down the street from the ballpark. It was two blocks from the stadium. If the governor was tied up, sometimes I'd talk to his mother, Miss Lillian.

Years later when I signed my first big contract, a multiyear deal with the Dodgers, my dad got a call from someone saying they were in the Ku Klux Klan and planned to burn a cross on my dad's lawn. So my dad stayed up for two weeks straight, sleeping in a chair with his shotgun.

"Why didn't you call the police?" I asked my dad.

"You don't know," he told me, "the police could be with them."

That was more than 40 years ago. A lot has changed since then. A lot hasn't changed. Police violence against Black people was in the news all this year, it seemed like. I was in Oakland as manager of the Houston Astros on August 28 this year when we made a group decision not to play that day, and laid a "Black Lives" T-shirt over home plate. It was Jackie Robinson Day and, like everyone, I was wearing #42 that night.

"I'm proud of this generation because in the '60s, it was mostly African Americans and a few white Americans that stood up, but in this day and age, I'm seeing young people of all nationalities and all religions that are standing up together," I told reporters that day. "The young people are a voice to be heard in the country, and I'm very, very proud of the young people in this country."

We all know there are going to be more headlines about gun violence. How many times have you seen people on both sides just openly carrying automatic weapons? It's only going to take one person to do something. If you've got the weapons, sooner or later somebody is going to use them, and then, boy, you've got a race war. And race war is similar to a religious war. Then if somebody kills somebody on this side, well you're not going to rest until you have some vengeance on the other side. It will never end, as long as we're on the verge of violence. You look at survival gear, sales are at an all-time high.

This has been going on for a long time. It just came to the forefront now. It only comes to the forefront when you run out of something. So long as you have it to sell, and people are buying it, a whole lot of people are naïve and don't know what's out there. The populated areas feel one way and the rural areas feel another way. Even in some families, you have people who can't agree on much. I have a close friend who has three sons: One voted for Trump, one voted for Biden, and one voted Libertarian. What do you think their conversation around the dinner table is like?

We all know change has to come. Maybe I'm not politically astute, but I don't understand: Why do we have the popular vote, when it's decided by the delegates? There has to be a way to fix the Electoral College system. But you know what? I don't think my generation is going to solve any of these problems. And I don't think the next generation will get very far either. I'm looking to the young kids my son's age, the ones in their 20s now. They have a lot in common with the 1960s generation, except they're probably a lot smarter than we were.

My son Darren, he's a pretty smart kid with his own mind, and he's not naïve about things. Like a lot of his age group, he knows what's going on. I would suggest that we listen to these youngsters, because this is their world and they know that their world is coming.

San Francisco, CA

KUJI CHAHAL is as an adviser for Plexo Capital, a 100 percent minority-owned emerging venture capital institutional investment firm. Previously he spent 13 years with Fisher Investments, spearheading the firm's institutional capital-raising efforts in the Western United States. Prior to his finance career, Chahal worked in the entertainment industry, where he managed and advised hip-hop and R&B recording artists. Since 2005, Chahal has been active in the philanthropic and political fundraising arenas, raising and donating more than $7.5 million. He was a founding member and served on the advisory board of the Leadership Council, Millennium Network for the Clinton Foundation (2007-2014), and serves as an advisory board member of the i.am.angel Foundation.

THE KAMALA I KNEW

BY KUJI CHAHAL

We survived. Let that seep in. I took a huge breath when the news came. Of fresh air. A breath that reminded me of what I used to experience as a boy at dawn in my childhood home of Atlanta. I missed that feeling of a brand new start, a new beginning to the day. This is what this moment feels like. An extra bounce to my step, extra juice in my kickboxing workout and run. A sigh of relief and yet a smile, a joy, that we got on the other side of this. Light manages to do this—always.

I clearly remember the day I first met Kamala Harris. It was at a charity fundraising dinner in San Francisco where I was recruiting people to serve as co-chairs for a fundraiser I was co-hosting for Harold Ford Jr., during his 2006 run for U.S. Senate in Tennessee. Several people mentioned I should ask Kamala to serve as a co-chair, telling me she was a superstar but also warm and very gracious. "You've got to meet her," Malia Cohen, who would go on to win a seat on the San Francisco Board of Supervisors, implored me.

Everything they said about Kamala was true. What really struck me, the first time I sat down with her, was how smart she was. At the time in criminal justice the prevailing mantra nationally was get tough on crime. Kamala said a better approach would be to get smart on crime. She took bold initiatives to provide solutions to the root causes of a problem in order to fix it. She also got serious about upgrading her office via technology to provide her staff with the best tools to succeed. I was impressed. Being a capital-markets guy, solution-based thinking really appealed to me. Sitting there listening to her explain her vision, I felt the gears turning. Kamala was always a visionary, strategic in her thinking, and she always stood out for the way she treated everyone in her orbit. If you were on her team, you were treated with respect and dignity, no matter your role or title or background.

I am so happy for all the kids out there, especially the kids of color. Seeing their excitement about Kamala Harris as vice president-elect brings a smile to my face. Kindness and empathy matter. To see someone of Indian-American descent like myself in an unprecedented position of national leadership was truly transformative, especially since Kamala's first name reminds me of my mother's name, Kamlesh, and both of them are of South Indian descent.

This moment is going to carry many generations, young and old, to a new determination to get involved, many for the first time, and work for a more harmonious world. From the time I first met Kamala, I was struck by the diverse group she brought together, a group that transcended race, color, creed and socioeconomic background. I will never forget the expressions of pure joy I saw firsthand from candidates she endorsed, many of them running for the first time, knowing that Kamala had their back, which gave them a surge of confidence and purpose.

I celebrated the news along with everyone else, but the highlight for me was personally congratulating the vice president-elect. When asked by others how best to describe her, I have always said the special trait that jumped out to me was that she made it a point to lift others, a trait I have witnessed time and time again. She lifted me and now she has a platform to lift the whole country.

Getting here has been quite a roller coaster of a journey, especially after the gut punch I personally experienced, as did so many others, the day after the 2016 election. How did I get through the past four years? I was helped by lessons I learned via the grace of so many others: President Obama, Hillary Clinton, Shirley Chisholm, Reverend Michael Beckwith and Robert Kennedy circa 1964-1968; an ability to have an inner calm that I leaned on these past four years to get me to the other side.

Now at this historic moment, I feel grateful for the time to reflect, to learn, and to re-engineer my inner core in order to fully appreciate getting to this moment. Now this inner calm has morphed into a steely resolve of hope for the future combined with a firm resolve and determination that we can't allow what happened to happen again on our watch. Which means I am going to listen harder and do my best to walk a mile in the shoes of my brothers and sisters to best understand their hurt and their hopes. I find myself again and again coming back to these words from Bobby Kennedy:

> What we need in the United States is not division; what we need in the United States is not hatred; what we need in the United States is not violence and lawlessness, but is love and wisdom, and compassion toward one another, and a feeling of justice toward those who still suffer within our country, whether they be white or whether they be black. ... Few will have the greatness to bend history itself, but each of us can work to change a small portion of events. It is from numberless diverse acts of courage and belief that human history is shaped. Each time a man stands up for an ideal, or acts to improve the lot of others, or strikes out against injustice, he sends forth a tiny ripple of hope, and crossing each other from a million different centers of energy and daring those ripples build a current which can sweep down the mightiest walls of oppression and resistance.

We have a lot of work ahead of us. All I could think about is shifting this economy from a shareholder to a stakeholder one. We sorely need to reintegrate our rural and urban communities. My desire is to see government figure out how to provide easier and less cumbersome access to capital for entrepreneurs, especially women and people of color, to build their own business. I am going to personally push for government to get more creative and innovative to facilitate an entrepreneurship economy by showing all people how to realize financial, time, and health freedom for themselves and family.

We need to feel a sense of urgency. I am blessed to be an integral part of Plexo Capital, a 100 percent minority-owned firm founded by Lo Toney. Plexo provides institutional capital to fund managers and companies owned by people of color and women within the early stage venture universe in order to have a full flywheel effect to impact the entire startup ecosystem. It is imperative we all collectively come together to figure out how best to incorporate technology and forward-looking solutions to create jobs to bridge the urban-rural divide. Far too many of our citizens are really hurting and in pain right now, and quite frankly have been in pain for far too long. We need to restore the dignity of many of our fellow citizens and rekindle their deepest dreams.

BROOKLYN, NY

MICHAEL POWELL —A New Yorker born and raised, Michael Powell writes on free speech and intellectual debate for *The New York Times*. He previously wrote the Sports of the Times column and the Gotham column for Metro. He has covered national politics and poverty and the economy, and won a Pulitzer and a Polk Prize. He lives in Brooklyn with his wife, Evelyn Intondi, and a dog named Monk.

JOY IN FLUSHING

BY MICHAEL POWELL

First came the all-points beeping, a mad cacophony as dozens of hands pressed on car horns, then came the firecrackers and cow bells and horns, then the screams and joyous yells. Curious as to what madness was descending on my neighborhood, I stepped onto our front porch on that balmy November Saturday. I spotted a stocky young woman running down the block, arms akimbo, grinning and yelling:

"AYIIII. He's gone! AYIII. The sucker's gone!"

No need to ask: Which sucker be that?

Word had arrived in Brooklyn that Donald Trump was about to pass into history as the 45th president of the United States. The electoral counting in Pennsylvania had reached its terminus. For days after the Election Day, as new vote counts landed like roundhouse punches, Trump had clung to the ropes, a Mar-a-Lago bleeder. Now the Associated Press and the networks acted like boxing refs and stepped into the ring to call the fight. It was an electoral TKO of the one-term wonder.

In Flatbush, my corner of Brooklyn, all was joy; there was not a funereal soul to be heard or seen. I heard a bass thumping, the reverberations felt in my solar plexus. I peered down the block where a white Chevrolet Tahoe glided to a stop. The driver, a young Black man, was methodical. He put down all the windows. He swung the doors open. Then he turned up a sweet stereo system, with a booming back-beat and those lyrics spitting:

This is the activation of the emergency broadcast system
Fuck Donald Trump
Fuck Donald Trump

Good old Nipsey Hussle, poet laureate of bile. Little children bounced and danced so happy.

The mood had been different on Election Day, almost solemn. I had climbed out of bed and walked out to vote at 5:40 a.m., passing in the darkness beneath overarching beech and oak trees. I turned the corner and as I reached the vestry house of the 19th-century Flatbush-Tompkins Congregational Church, my polling site, I found a line snaking around the corner and down the block, nurses, orderlies, bus drivers, skateboarders and retirees waiting beneath a near full moon.

There is something deeply moving about a democracy and its secular high holy day. As a little kid, I had accompanied my mother on the voting line inside P.S. 87 and stepped with her into those old voting booths in Manhattan. She directed me how to flip the little pins for the candidates—Democrats, always Democrats, we Upper West Siders were as one-party oriented as any Moscow apparatchik—and then she let me pull on that big clanky lever. We laughed as the curtain flung open like something out of *The Wizard of Oz*.

Voting seemed a great lark—an idyll that now seems a distant memory. The days following Election Day 2020 offered a sweat-palmed ride, staying up late and later still to listen to the yack-yack of the CNN, MSNBC, NBC analysts, those state vote totals, Arizona-Georgia-Nevada-Pennsylvania, refresh-refresh-refresh. There was John King, the CNN stat guru with his methodical funeral director style, and on MSNBC the crystal meth bug-eyed look of Steve Kornacki, the data guru for MSNBC. Is it possible he did not change his shirt and tie for four days running?

Four years ago, when it became sorrowfully apparent that this joke of a fraud of a New York so-called developer Donald Trump was about to be elected president of the United States, my sons and their wife and girlfriend dragged themselves off our couch and silently walked away. I rose the next morning and wrote an email to them, urging us all to cling to hope like a man to a life preserver in roiling seas. Perhaps the only advantage to being older, I wrote to them, is that I've lived through '68 and the assassinations of MLK and RFK and the coming to power of

Nixon, and years later Reagan and his nuclear war jokes. Those were days of fear and loathing and we survived.

"Joe Hill, about to be executed, had it right," I wrote to them. "Don't waste time mourning. Organize."

In retrospect I would concede that ending on the last words of an about-to-be-executed labor organizer was perhaps not my most hopeful note.

This Election Night Evelyn and I walked downstairs to our basement to see if old Uncle Joe Biden could knock off this orange-haired pox. Biden rarely made my heart leap, and so what? He was an honorable aging man and he would not defile the White House with racist language and tropes.

Our boys are gone now, Nick and his wife, Caitlin, and their daughter, Penelope, moved to Galveston, Texas, and Aidan and his fiancée, Addy, gone to Los Angeles to pursue music dreams. They will be on and off the phone with us all night.

The early returns began to roll in. Florida went to Trump, then Indiana, then Texas and ... it felt like a rerun from hell. I felt like an old foxhole GI with the PTSD kicking in. We stayed up late enough to go to sleep with a touch of hope. Still I worried: Far more than last time, it felt like this election would offer a mirror onto our national soul. We knew what he was about this time and yet ...

In truth, we Democrats brought some of this upon ourselves. We kept electing candidates who looked happier with Wall Street financiers than the working people who Democrats claimed as "their voters." We had grown accustomed as a matter of course that former presidents and vice presidents would rapidly accumulate great riches upon leaving public service. None of these newly minted plutocrats had the grace to appear sheepish.

Trump may be—no, let me amend that: Trump *is*—a fraud, but Trumpism arguably speaks to the not so sneaking sense of many American workers that the casino that is the American economy is rigged in favor of the house. Free trade agreements, tax breaks, bank bailouts, not to mention wars in Iraq, Syria, Libya: If you lived in Beaver County, Pennsylvania, or Brownsville, Texas, or East New York, Brooklyn, you might be forgiven for feeling uncertain about how, precisely, the Democrats had your back.

Racism and nativism and misogyny did not offer a universal explanation for Trump's election in 2016. Hillary Clinton reduced many of his voters to a basket of deplorables but estimates are that upwards of 12 percent of those who voted Trump voted for Barrack Hussein Obama in 2012. Surely these Americans are not beyond hope or reaching.

Melancholy attends to these ruminations. My Flatbush neighborhood is terrifically diverse, white and Black gentry in their Victorian homes beneath giant sycamores that rise like a green Gothic abbey over the streets, and working-class West Indian, Tibetan, Bangladeshi and Pakistani immigrants fill prewar apartment buildings. And Hasidic families wend their way to synagogue on Saturdays and Palestinians spin pizza pies and two Bosnian brothers make a mean taco.

But Trump voters? Here?

Politically, ideologically, we are a city, a state, a nation near perfectly cleaved. Some Republicans can be found in South Brooklyn, in Staten Island, but no one goes there to talk politics. Nor are they much interested in talking to us. It's extraordinary how rarely we cross, as if we were Himalayan hikers tromping separate paths up a mountain.

In the 1970s and 1980s, it was typical for a presidential candidate to win a state even as its senators hailed from the opposing parties. No more. Twenty states voted against Trump in both 2016 and 2020. Democrats hold 39 of the 40 Senate seats in those states.

We are living inside hermetically sealed silos. The day before the national election was called, I talked with my friend Michael Gecan, who spent a lifetime as a leader with the Industrial Areas Foundation, perhaps the best collection of community organizers in the nation. A child of working-class Chicago gone to Yale to study literature with Robert Penn Warren, he fought with courageous East New York homeowners to stare down gangbangers and to build thousands of single family homes that rose like a phoenix on the rubble of the abandonment of the 1970s. He and his community leaders banged heads with the toughest mayors in America. Of late he's taken to working with ministers and folks in the rural hollows of southern Ohio to get broadband service and drug treatment for the opiate scourge.

No doubt most there are Trump voters and so what? I asked about the Democratic strategists who have written off people in these reaches as race-infected and deplorable. The phone line goes silent and he asks:

How many of these people do they know? Have they met 100? No? Two, maybe. We're down to zero real fast.

Those Americans are no less ignorant of us than we are of them. We hoot and holler and celebrate the defeat of Trump in Flatbush and the Upper West Side and Park Slope and Astoria and Williamsburg and Bedford Stuyvesant. And in rural south Ohio and central Oklahoma, residents listen to Fox and Republican politicians rehearse conspiracy lines about stolen elections.

Basta. I hop on my bicycle and push off into a balmy November weekend. At Grand Army Plaza in Brooklyn it's VE Day redux, several thousands dancing and kissing and playing trumpets and saxes and steel drums, celebrating Trump's imminent departure. (Only later will we learn that Donald Trump, whose adherence to democracy flickers like the picture on an old black and white television set, said that the vote result is foul, that Democratic cities are corrupt, and in a triumph of hallucination over fact he claims victory. I've covered this man in New York and he is a bully and a coward; I cannot claim to worry too much about his bluster. But talk in my city turns to worries of a coup).

I glide downhill to East Flatbush, a West Indian neighborhood where I once worked as a tenant organizer, helping immigrant tenants fight for heat and hot water in the prewar buildings that stand like so many dusty dowagers. Those were hardscrabble times: Rastafarian weed dealers walked me out of an apartment building they had colonized. At night, heading for the bus, I heard the high-pitched whine as, behind closed metal gates, Utica Avenue chop shops rendered stolen cars into marketable parts. It was a neighborhood perched on chasm's edge.

Now it thrives thanks to the same immigrants who Trump never fails to run down. Homes are freshly painted with rebuilt stoops and shiny brass fences. In summer, hydrangeas and crotons and roses explode in front yards. The buses that barely ran, the cops that rarely responded to calls for help, the feral children of the early 1980s are near forgotten memories.

West Indians take politics seriously, and this sprawling neighborhood delivered a grand margin of votes to Biden. As I biked Avenue I, I heard behind me a whirl of beeping. Two SUVs pulled abreast of me, the women drivers rocking back and forth to calypso and waving Biden flags. I raise my fist in solidarity and the beeping redoubles.

I curl out through Howard Beach, a largely Italian enclave on the north lip of Jamaica Bay. No celebrating; here purple "Trump 2020" and "Make America Great Again" banners billow in the wind. The election is over and the streets are empty.

I cut along Rockaway Beach, sand and ocean glinting in a soft autumnal light. Here and there "Biden 2020" signs are stuck in the sand. An hour later I arrive back home and hear my neighbors, fine jazz musicians, practicing in a nearby backyard. All spring and summer, this pick-up team of jazz musicians played every day at 5 p.m., in rain and chill and heat, the audience growing, young and not so young, African Americans and whites and Pakistanis and Mexicans, masked and occupying spaces between cars. It was like this the world round, Italians and Argentines, French and Greeks and New Yorkers, singing and playing in rebellion against the darkness.

I could not place this new song—I figured it for classic American songbook. A few minutes later these musicians took to the streets, wailing on saxes and melodicas and trumpets, playing drums, marching through like so many Pied Pipers, a hundred or more neighbors following behind, waving flags and clapping.

We joined in. What song is this, I asked my wife, Evelyn. She smiled and advised me to think of *The Wizard of Oz.*

Right.

Ding-Dong, the witch is dead!
Which old witch? The wicked witch.
Ding-dong, the wicked witch is dead.

So it was that dusk turned to night in Flatbush on the beginning of the end for Donald Trump.

LOS ANGELES, CA

ANTONIA HITCHENS has written for *The New Yorker, The New York Times, The Wall Street Journal, The New Republic, Wired* magazine and the *Los Angeles Review of Books*, among other publications. She teaches at Columbia University.

BEVERLY HILLS
FREEDOM RALLY

BY ANTONIA HITCHENS

The night before Election Day in Los Angeles had the almost contrived feeling of suspense before a plot's resolution, with its sense of anticipation for what the morning would bring—the luxury shops boarded up, the jewelry taken offsite from the jewelry district, tactical police teams on call throughout the city. I saw a lone figure in red leggings walking Rodeo Drive with his Trump flag folded up, as private security forces and Los Angeles County Property Preservations barricaded Saint Laurent and Gucci. The idea was to protect expensive things after some of them had been damaged by protests over the summer. Like many others, I was on the hook the next day to write an Election Night dispatch on the precarious conditional of "if people take to the streets/the world is on fire," making the promise of visual unrest seem reassuring in at least certain specific ways.

The day before the election was a university holiday, so the hours of Zoom I usually owed my workplace were cancelled, contributing to the lingering sense of constant lead-up to the event of Nov. 3. I decided to take part of the day to drive around L.A. County on the eve of the election. These sorts of wafting car trips to "see things and get a sense of the mood," readily available in California in a fuel-efficient vehicle, are admittedly not only usually a fool's errand, but can give a sense of a narrator unabashedly at a loose end, entirely without a motive even when the earnest—even grand—purpose is to "take the pulse of the world" at an exact moment before it is alleged to change, before the morning after. If you're a girl in your 20s, taking to the freeway can sound like a vapid rip-off of Didion's Maria in *Play It As It Lays*, up early to get in the car, full of dread and momentum, cracking a hard-boiled egg on the steering wheel to rush nowhere and then back. You don't see any action from the window of a car, and if, like me, you don't want to get out and bother a voter in Lancaster to confirm, without assignment, that they might like Trump, or at least that they might feel alienated, the main event of the trip ends up being cultivating a personal memory of a general tone that will later be hard to remember. I'd read stories about California voters in the weekend *Los Angeles Times* as I sat in my garden in Eagle Rock looking over an empty street; the world felt far away. I wondered if anything would come of going to see the aberrational swatches of L.A., the precincts daubed red on the largely blue electoral map: This comes down mostly to East Hollywood, where the Scientologists are, Beverly Hills, and the area around the high-desert town of Lancaster.

The only time I'd gone to Lancaster before was in the spring, earlier on in the pandemic and election season, when I went first to a neighborhood called Porter Ranch, a "master-planned development community" in the San Fernando Valley, to get a grill bought off Craigslist. The seller was in the pool with two young children, little girls in floating swimmer wings, and I followed the sound of their voices and trail of chalk hearts they'd drawn on the walking path. From there I drove the Antelope Valley Freeway to see the famous poppy bloom. The poppy reserve as an attraction was technically closed, because of the virus shutting down state parks, but the poppies themselves spanned empty decrepit public fields off of farm roads. A few Instagram-influencer types in flowery caftans were taking photos of nothing. I pulled off the road in an area where someone had flung a ton of trash, even what looked like an old desktop computer, and after walking a few minutes found the carcass of a dead animal with a few flowers blooming through its skeleton. The poppies were mostly closed, as flowers, because the sun was setting. I took a few seedlings and put them in a cardboard espresso cup I had on the floor of my car, then went to one of the five Walmarts around Lancaster to get propane for the grill. Bright police lights were up in the

Walmart parking lot and a long line of masked people waited to go in and get Mother's Day stuffed animals, ammunition for guns, baby formula.

The day before the election, after my second jaunt up to Lancaster—where I saw a few painted Trump signs and then the parking lot of the Dollar Store, in a complex of other big-box stores where I used the bathroom in a Starbucks—I told a newspaper editor friend I'd gone up there. He was home working on an opinion column. "The *Times* is always writing about Palmdale," he said. "I should go up there and see it at some point." For work and for myself, I'd done a certain amount of this resolute meandering, where most people—and this is heightened during Covid-time visits to red states—ask why you went there in the first place. I thought about James Fenton's piece on trying to see the fall of Saigon:

"I wanted to see a war and the fall of a city because—because I wanted to see what such things were like. I had once seen a man dying, from natural causes, and my first reaction, as I realized what was taking place, was that I was glad to be there. This is what happens, I thought, so watch it carefully, don't miss a detail. The first time I saw a surgical operation (it was in Cambodia) I experienced the same sensation, and no doubt when I see a child born it will be even more powerful. The point is simply in being there and seeing it. The experience has no essential value beyond itself."

I always liked this straightforward justification, and found it sort of propulsive, particularly during an election year in the U.S. I spent the last moments of crowded normalcy before the pandemic seeing Trump at a Keep America Great Again rally in Milwaukee, going to a car race in Daytona, Florida, to the New Hampshire primary, where the 12 residents of Dixville Notch cast their votes just after midnight, and then the Nevada caucus, which took place on the Las Vegas Strip in the ballroom of the Bellagio casino, where ties are broken by a card draw.

The immediacy of a Trump rally feels almost like being at a Rolling Stones concert or a 24-hour auto race. People come hours early to stand in the rafters, sometimes spontaneously breaking into song or dance, after giddily waiting in line all night to be there in person. The multicolored semicircle of 100,000 stadium seats at the Daytona International Speedway, where I'd covered the auto race, conjured a similar image—a diptych of crowds traipsing in and out of a large area to see something mesmerizing. NASCAR had the idea to implement a trade-in program where if you brought a Confederate flag you could swap it for an American one, no charge. Since Daytona's 24-hour race wasn't run by NASCAR, rebel flags were allowed. I spent the weekend in a sprawling outfield of trailers, many of which had Trump and rebel flags. The group I watched the race with offered me oysters and jello shots and jovially called me a member of the lying fake news media.

On the Fourth of July, I was under a tarp in Belgrade, Montana, where people smilingly welcomed everyone to an event called Rage Against the State, a picnic for Independence Day. I'd come there via standstill traffic over the I-15 into Vegas, where a room at the Mandalay Bay casino was $48. A man entered a full elevator wearing an N95 mask and remarked to everyone, "Six months ago we never imagined we'd be living like this."

"It's like Chernobyl," another passenger responded.

"What a good HBO series," said the original man.

As I arrived at the picnic in Montana, organized by anti-government types, a speaker advertised DVDs about the Constitution, before asking for a show of hands re: who researched the truth about 9/11— most people—and then advertising his bookstore of sacred texts in Livingston, Montana. The real American slavery, he said, is the country asking people to wear slave masks. The crowd nodded approvingly. The tenor of the event was that one should be scared of the government, not of the coronavirus. Speakers came up to say things like, "Do not wear the slave mask," and, "Be angry and sin not." The most-used joke was when someone paused or faltered for a moment in their remarks, they'd say, "Oh, I'm having a Biden moment." It always got a laugh. The family hosting the picnic didn't have Social Security numbers.

I'd come there with my boyfriend and a man he'd met reporting on the Bundy standoff in eastern Oregon—a lapsed Mormon farm boy who'd become a friend in some ways, though I knew his evenings were spent mostly watching right-wing YouTube videos in his trailer with his new puppy. He presented the trip with a Dantean schematic, wherein he was a sort of self-aware "redneck Virgil" who took us to see people he knew. He brought a handful of pocket Constitutions and gave us radios so that we could communicate between his car and ours while on the road. Because of Covid we'd asked to drive separately. As we drove up towards Montana that night, through the sand dunes of Idaho, he walkie-talkied incessantly back and forth between the two cars to weigh in about freedom and America: I kept trying to fall asleep and he'd crackle back in on the radio saying the country had to be separated into urban and rural, divided officially, the promise of one country finally done away with. Occasionally our radio would pick up signals from other cars; at one point a woman's voice blasted into the car asking for two hydrocodone pills.

And then this fall for the first half of October, I was in Idaho, visiting a sagebrush restoration project in the southern part of the state; because life is no longer localized and all my work could happen remotely, I was glad for a reason to spend the lead-up to the election in the banana belt of Idaho. The project was to swing a hoedad all day for 50 cents a plant and revamp a landscape blasted by fires. "It's heaven here, but they made it hell," a friend said matter-of-factly about the dusty Big Ag landscape. In Hagerman, Idaho, the place to get coffee, Bullets 'N Brew, doubled as a gun shop where there was a handwritten sign-up waiting list to buy an AR-15; people specified the color they wanted, and easily a third requested "rose." They also sold trucker hats that said Covid on them with a middle finger through the lettering. One day on the job site I tried to make small talk with a man who was drinking a can of Starbucks nitro cold brew—I wanted one—and he said, "I've never had Starbucks before. I thought this was a beer."

On the drive up through Nevada to Idaho, we ran out of gas and a one-legged veteran came and helped us get a gas can. I'd called ahead to the Sinclair station to say we were probably going to run out of gas two miles from their gas pump and could they help, then my phone cut out and it seemed like they just dispatched a customer who was in the process of badgering the store owner. He was living in a local motel—"Room 2, that's where I hang out, I painted it myself"—and had moved up from Vegas. "I got tired of the people in the city looking at me like I had coronavirus," he said. He told us he'd got $3.6 million in the settlement for his lost leg; he had a gun in the car and said he'd voted for Trump, who was at that moment hospitalized with Covid, twice.

* * *

I'd spent time peripherally in these circles not really knowing what it would amount to, unsure how Election Day itself would crystallize anything. The palpable feeling of the world of Trump—or just quotidian life in a red state—recedes in some obvious ways when I get back to Los Angeles from Idaho. As it happened, on Saturdays for the past few months, people had gathered in Beverly Hills for "freedom rallies" started by local dog walker, fitness trainer, and dance teacher Shiva Bagheri. "Beverly Hills is an unlikely outpost for Trump fans," read the *L.A. Times* headline. At the final rally before the election, 4,000 people attended; an alleged skirmish between Antifa and a pro-Trump protester made international news; Cardi B's husband got arrested. Small spinoffs of the gatherings began to take place almost every day along Santa Monica Boulevard, right by the Beverly Hills sign—sometimes groups congregated with "No More Bullshit" flags while passersby honked from SUVs shouting "four more years," or marched down Rodeo Drive in Trump paraphernalia.

I'd applied and was not selected to be an L.A. County poll worker on Election Day, so as a backup plan and out of curiosity, I signed up for the Army for Trump "Election Day operation." I texted back and forth with a friend who covers the far right to ask whether I could ethically click the Army-for-Trump-required box saying you promised under perjury that you would vote for Trump. In the end, I called Bagheri and asked what her group was doing for Election Day. She suggested that I come to Beverly Hills, where she'd be in a park with a dog named Blue, a 170-pound Great Dane, and then she told me Trump has made animal abuse a felony. You don't see the media reporting on that, she said. I drove across town, past the polling place at the Magic Castle on Franklin, where I got trapped behind an Uber dropping someone off to vote.

I met Bagheri in Holmby Park, a rectangle of green space in Beverly Hills, down the street from Playboy Mansion, and beneath the Manor, the largest and most expensive home in Los Angeles. It's one of several rogue patches of red in L.A. County: in 2016, Hillary Clinton easily won the West Side of Los Angeles, except for this one Beverly Hills neighborhood, which spans the Beverly Hills Hotel to the L.A. Country Club, and where President Trump owns a home. Bagheri had on a pink racerback tank top with the American flag on it and a pair of defensive boxing gloves a fan had given her. "For if I have to protect myself," she said. She encourages attendees at the Beverly Hills rallies to start organizing massive militias against the government.

Before we could walk far, Bagheri was approached by a personal trainer. "He's a big fan," said the trainer, gesturing to a man on a yoga mat. His client put down his barbell and thanked Bagheri for organizing the freedom rallies, which he attended each week. He recounted taking a video of an Antifa supporter who he says tried to provoke a skirmish with him at one of their rallies. The man showed her a cell phone video of the altercation. "Fighters are taught to respect. They only fight for self-defense," she said. She showed him her boxing gloves. She gets recognized all over the west side of Los Angeles. "They're people like me, who were intimidated because of our support for our president. I've got a block of liberals trying to get me evicted from my apartment for my support for Trump—trying to get me to take down my sign." Bagheri looped back towards the house where the Great Dane lived so that she could drop the dog off. She left a voice memo telling the client that the dog was back, then read me part of the Black Lives Matter website, which she had bookmarked on her phone. Bagheri was certain about the election results that evening. "I know Trump will win. I don't think he will—I know he will. Nothing the left says makes sense. They wear their Nikes while they talk about capitalism and oppression."

A mile down the road, Trump supporters congregated behind police blocks on Santa Monica Boulevard opposite a black mural that read PEACE. A few feet behind a sign mandating mask-wearing in Beverly Hills stood a man holding a sign that said "Enemies of the People: Corporate press, academia, Hollywood, deep-state, big tech." Underneath a tree, a man in black slacks and a black Don't Tread on Me T-shirt balanced his MAGA hat as he practiced handstands; others waved California Republic flags. A group sat in lawn chairs around a Blue Lives Matter flag; another circled with a sign that said LGBTQ Latinos for Trump. An elderly man stood alone waving a flag with the Roman numeral III, which indicates the three-percenter group, an anti-government paramilitary. Pickup trucks, convertibles and Range Rovers drove by with Trump flags.

"I'm not going to leave this state," said Bagheri, who is from Iran. "I'm going to fight for it. We can really fix California." Of the election results, she said, "If Trump doesn't win, I don't think our group is going to believe that result. We'll know it's cheating. There's no way he's not going to win." She went on, "I think there's going to be a civil war. People are fed up with the lies, the deception. You wouldn't believe how many gun sales there have been in Beverly Hills. People are armed and ready. If any of these people think they're going to come into our city, they've got another think coming." As we circled the park, children played in socially distanced setups, and people worked out in small groups outside. Masked couples walked their dogs.

"We will protect ourselves," said Bagheri. "We believe in self-defense. It's not about accepting the election results. We know that they lie. We don't want to live in a banana republic. What's happening now is a coup d'etat against our president. We're fed up with this."

Bagheri was out of time; she had to teach two dance classes. We finished our loop of the park, and she hopped into an idling white Lexus. "I gotta go," she told me. "I love you. Stay safe here."

On Friday, a Wilhelmina model in the freedom rally Facebook group posted that the Beverly Hills Freedom Rally would be meeting to pray and to peacefully protest the election results. I was curious about what the freedom rally people would do in the aftermath of a Biden victory; the election was far from over for them, and in some ways their particular type of interest in freedom had never had much to do with electoral politics at all. I told Shiva I'd come see her in the crowd. She showed up in front of the Beverly Hills sign in a blue onesie with a megaphone and her MAGA hat, dragging her daughter by the hand. People brandished #Stop the Steal signs and tacked "Trump: Do Not Concede" and "Hold the Line" posters onto police barricades, as men in hoodies stopped a blue Ford pickup truck with Trump 2020 signs in the middle of Santa Monica Boulevard to give a fascist salute through the sunroof. Most L.A. neighborhoods were in the midst of revelry after Biden's win was announced, skaters spraying Champagne onto passerby in Silver Lake, but in Beverly Hills, hundreds of Trump's supporters filled the streets shouting, "We're not done." Shiva told me she'd switched from Fox to NewsMax because Fox had turned on Trump. I talked to a woman in Louboutin boots standing alone in a leopard skirt, and asked her what she thought about Bagheri's sense of imminent civil war.

"The future of Trumpism is just going to get bigger and bigger—if they deny us our president, this movement is going to turn into something far larger."

The gathering was not so much a protest against the idea that Biden had won that morning, but a jubilant celebration of Trump and his future, election or not. For those gathered on Santa Monica Boulevard, the past four years had been just the beginning of Trumpism.

* * *

Over Christmastime in Los Angeles, the house across the street burned down and a charred page of a burnt dictionary floated into our driveway. Nobody was home for the fire, but the paper was there when we got back. It looks like a novelty item, manufactured to mimic paper that caught fire. It reminds me of when kids for a school project have to make a scroll, so they bake paper in the oven to give it the appearance of ancientness. It's the sort of succinct visual image that, when it appears in the real world, feels too on-the-nose during times that are described as apocalyptic for a number of different reasons. You wouldn't believe it in a novel, my boyfriend says of the dictionary paper scrap's appearance. It turns up in various places in our apartment for the next year.

By September, the air was gray and dull with wildfire smoke from the Angeles National Forest, blowing ash towards where we live. The West is on fire; more than a million acres have burned. Rolling blackouts mean the garage won't open and electric cars don't charge. You can't leave when the fire arrives. The TV goes black from outages in the middle of the Zoomed Democratic Convention and again during the live-from-D.C. Republican Convention. Twitter speculates conspiracy theories about each. The Santa Anas are allegedly on the way and everyone is quoting some version of the Raymond Chandler story where the winds make the wife reach for a knife as she eyes her husband's neck.

I left the California fires for the fires in Portland, Oregon. Armed civilian checkpoints stop cars full of evacuees to question them. Residents of Oregon towns, ordered to evacuate, have seen disinformation campaigns online and accuse journalists of being looters, shouting at them to leave. A friend insists that Interstate 5—which runs from teal-watered San Diego through the armpit of California's Central Valley, then up through Oregon—won't shut down unless China invades the

U.S. You can read headlines about a 13-year-old burning to death with his dog on his lap going to rescue his grandfather, who also burned alive, but these events take place in brackets on either side of the big main road. Asphalt won't burn.

In Oregon, the air is dense with smoke, thicker than fog, and makes my eyes water and swell up. I wanted to walk to the center of Portland, which had just had its 100th night of Black Lives Matter protests; the Patriot Prayer, a group of far-right extremist Trump supporters, come into town on Saturdays to clash with BLM protestors. I layered two masks and went to the Justice Center, the main square in the plaza of federal buildings, to see if the most diehard of the lot were congregating or marching. Early evening felt like two in the morning. The streets were empty and all businesses had closed because of the air. One group of teenagers rode by on Bird scooters. I got to the epicenter of where the "riots" that illustrated the urban-rural divide in Oregon had been playing out. It looked as desolate as the rest of the city, with a few homeless people asleep, and a small group of transients sitting in a group on the grass. In the middle of the square was a statue of an elk covered in chalk slogans, like "take the power back." People had left Prosecco and toilet paper at the elk's hooves, like an altar. One tent had a maskless woman grilling ribs to give out to protesters. I paused to look around for a minute, then walked back home. The air ended the protests. I texted a British journalist who joked that the American narrative was stopped by smoke.

I went back the next day to see it in the light. A guy was there with a tripod, obviously also looking for something to see. It was an area of residue and mild detritus, with a few more scattered encampments, people with masks around their nose back selling ribs in the tent, still to no customers. I noticed a basketball hoop and an old floral couch with a pair of teens canoodling on it. I thought of this vacant, empty—yet totally climactic and ongoing—American moment in Portland as we drove home through a silent, boarded-up Los Angeles on Election Night, and as I cased the neighborhood again the day after. Shiva had told me that Antifa, dressed as Trump supporters, were going to loot the shops. She'd also promised a civil war.

Driving to out to the beach early one morning this summer, I heard a foreign radio correspondent reporting on the American election, describing the possible forthcoming Biden years as "a presidency you can keep on in the background." But I wonder about a triumphant return to plodding normalcy and reassuringly tedious white noise—or a breath exhaled in relief at a blue wave—after spending time around people who already saw the country as being against their freedom and divorced from their lives, with Trump as the only possible salve, and who would now see Biden and his mask mandates as something to rebel against. I thought about the woman who told me a family asked her to leave their store because her face mask scared their children—and the more obvious images of armed maskless men outside statehouses. The Trump presidency was a fugue-like moment where what felt at first like fringe politics became visible, where what had always been lurking here became something you could easily just go look at and see. The nation's rifts remain, *The New York Times* headline reads today, every day—an existential hangover. This election, nearly half of the country voted for Trump, a portion of which now thinks the election was stolen from them. A Biden victory doesn't mean they'll recede or that the underpinnings will. I wonder what will happen in the 75 days Trump has left in the White House.

When the Dodgers won the World Series last month, you'd have known even if you weren't watching the game, because my neighborhood exploded in fireworks and people took to the streets. I wondered if a similar outpouring would be how I found out Biden won, or whether his victory would be a quiet Friday night. In Maricopa County, Arizona— which still hadn't officially been called for Biden—civil servants were surrounded by sheriff's deputies in riot gear to protect them from Trump's defenders gathered outside. I thought about driving to Phoenix or Las Vegas to see these armed protestors who wanted to try to stop the votes from being counted, but in the end I stayed home. I had no immediate sense of urgency to travel and be near history. The chance to see these scenes isn't going anywhere.

Storm Lake, Ia

ART CULLEN is editor and publisher of *The Storm Lake Times* in Northwest Iowa, where he won the Pulitzer Prize for editorial writing on agriculture and the environment. He is a columnist for *The Guardian US* and is author of the book, *Storm Lake: Change, Resilience, and Hope in America's Heartland.*

WE CAN BIND THE NATION'S WOUNDS THROUGH FOOD

BY ART CULLEN

STORM LAKE, IOWA, NOV. 6, 2020

The day set out fine. Temperature: 50 degrees with a forecast high of 79, a wisp of Indian Summer following last month's hard freeze. Clear skies with a three-quarter moon. No wind, a rarity in a prairie town called Storm Lake surrounded by North America's largest wind turbine complex.

At 5:30 a.m. Iowa time Joe Biden crept over the top by 1,097 votes in Georgia.

By 8 a.m. the son of Scranton marched into positive territory in Pennsylvania. Without Pennsylvania, Trump would be denied victory.

Through the morning the Biden advantage grew. He would deliver a victory speech tonight.

Our long national nightmare of Donald Trump in the White House is over.

Why, then, am I so numb or glum?

The map might be blue on those dots of metro counties that count for Biden, but there's a whole lotta red washing over our rural reaches.

Especially in Iowa, which launched Barack Obama's presidential bid with its first-in-the-nation caucuses in 2008, and voted for him twice. Donald Trump took Iowa handily in 2016, and won the Tall Corn State again on Tuesday along with incumbent Senator Joni Ernst, who stood by Trump through thick and thin.

What happened to the state that routinely split its vote the past half-century, that time after time sent both uber-liberal Tom Harkin and uber-conservative Chuck Grassley to the Senate? I understand so little anymore. I thought Ernst cooked her own goose when she could not cite the price of soybeans during a statewide TV debate with Democratic challenger Theresa Greenfield a few weeks ago. Nearly all the polls showed Trump and Biden, and Ernst and Greenfield, to be in dead heats. In the end, I figured, our disastrous trade wars with our best ag export customers—China, Mexico and Canada—plus Ernst's debate fumble, made worse by a raging viral pandemic, would put Iowa in the blue again.

Wrong. Wrong. Wrong.

On the weekend before the election, the highly respected *Des Moines Register*-Mediacom Iowa Poll found Trump and Ernst each with comfortable leads. It had to be wrong, the Democrats declared. Just a month before, the Iowa Poll had them in a dead heat like the other surveys. But pollster Ann Selzer found a huge swing to the right among independent voters who, betting on a Trump defeat nationally, wanted to keep the Senate under GOP control as a check on the "socialists." The false advertising, the Facebook disinformation (Democrats eat babies—really, that's what they were saying), the preachers in the pulpit damning liberal judges and politicians, and a relentless ground game that saw Iowa Republicans register 20,000 more voters than Democrats put a seemingly indelible red lock on what used to be a purple state.

Republicans gained seats in the Iowa House and Senate, which they already controlled. The governor, Kim Reynolds, is Republican. Dubuque, where union jobs drained south of the border steadily through the decades, used to be a blue bulwark on the banks of the Mighty Mississippi. Dubuque County voted for Trump at 51 percent. Incumbent Representative Abby Finkenauer, a Democratic daughter of a Dubuque union household, was defeated by TV news anchor Ashley Hinson, a Republican who supported Trump. The Finkenauer defeat and Ernst victory were devastating blows to a Democratic Party that has lost its way along the country blacktop roads.

The urban-rural divide is as vivid as ever. There is a palpable resentment among those flown over and left behind that finds its expression in terrorist rubes from the sticks dressed in Hawaiian shirts planning to kidnap the governor of Michigan and execute her to start a civil war. Believe it. Most of us are not ready to pick up a gun. But it keeps racism bubbling just below the surface. It erodes trust in institutions, like our courts. And it prevents us from solving existential crises like the pandemic or, even more threatening, global heating.

This November day marked the close of a two-year political orgy in Iowa, for which I had a ringside seat as editor of *The Storm Lake Times*. It started with the 2018 midterm elections as the first of a field of 25 Democratic candidates invaded our 99 counties on the long road to the nomination. On the Fourth of July I sat down with Pete Buttigieg in our newspaper office, where he said race will be our nation's undoing if we don't figure it out. He mused in the wake of the shooting of a Black man with a knife by South Bend police when Buttigieg was mayor. He got up from our interview to march in a parade where every nationality flies its flag in a meatpacking town that attracts workers from around the globe. About half our town of 15,000 people is immigrant, primarily from rural Mexico. We get along pretty well. We have to. Most of rural Iowa loses population every year, Storm Lake grows while speaking 30 languages.

One of the first campaign operatives I met was John Russell, Iowa rural coordinator for the Elizabeth Warren campaign. I called him up this morning after seeing the Pennsylvania results. He and I shared the same funk. Russell, a young man with an endearing smile and a dirty pickup full of yard signs, gave up his Ohio stump-grinding business and produce farm to campaign to save rural places. He gave it everything he had, first for Warren and then for an outfit called RuralVote.org, where he was in charge of getting yard signs out when the campaigns couldn't.

Russell was reared around Wellsville, Ohio, population 3,500, nestled in the corner of Appalachia that touches Pennsylvania and West Virginia. Like Dubuque, the Ohio River Valley used to be union country—steel, autos, kilns, dirty hands. Those jobs are lost and the unions busted by President Ronald Reagan, not by any poor Mexican immigrant. Eight years ago, the Democratic state legislator from Russell's county got 51 percent of the vote. This year, the Democrat got 26 percent. In Buena Vista County, Iowa, where I live, the Democratic legislative candidate got beat by the same margin on Tuesday. Turnout among Democrats in Storm Lake, the county seat, was half that of the rural precincts. Hence, Trump won my county and Russell's with more than 60 percent of the vote, largely ignored again by the Democratic infrastructure.

While in Iowa, Russell lived upstairs from a biker bar in Webster City, a typical county seat town about the size of Storm Lake that never really recovered from the Farm Crisis that snuffed out a generation of vitality in the 1980s. The Electrolux vacuum cleaner factory was moved to a maquiladora in Mexico. Retail trade bleeds to Amazon.com. Meantime, a new pork plant opened up nearby where the workforce is overwhelmingly Latino. Starting pay: $16 per hour, just enough to get by if you scrimp. Half the pork is bound for China.

Russell became friends in the bar with a foreman at the pork plant married to a teacher. Their household income would be well north of $100,000, big money in a small town. "He believes shit that would make your jaw drop," Russell said. "White folks are buying what Fox and Sinclair Broadcasting are selling—it's worldwide wrestling entertainment. Strong opinions loosely held."

They like to hunt and value clean water. Trump? Hell yes. Macho dude. They know that their towns are losing people, but they voted 20 years for a race-baiting, anti-immigrant congressman, Republican Steve King, who wants to deport all those undocumented people working in the meatpacking industry. King and Donald Jr. shot guns together. Good stuff.

Back home in Wellsville the TV station is owned by right-wing Sinclair. There is no newspaper. The *Youngstown Vindicator* folded. Ogden Newspapers of Wheeling, W.V., is the only newspaper publisher to speak of in the region, and they all bleed red. Ogden also owns the newspaper in Webster City and nearby Fort Dodge, which are served by a Sinclair TV station and where the bar has Fox News on. The primary news source in each place is Facebook—certainly not *The New York Times* or *The Atlantic*.

Hating on immigrants has lost some of its cachet since the border really did get locked down, especially during the pandemic. Still, people have been told by the right-wing bullhorn first held by Rush Limbaugh that Pedro is here to steal your job. Except, not many people want that job of cutting the bunghole out of a hog (and there really is a bunghole cutter on the packinghouse roster). Truth be told, it's a way to turn poor rural white people against poor rural Black people, who both take aim at the poor rural brown person. This has been going on since 1619. The Know Nothings hated on the Chinese and Irish, who hated on the Blacks. My dad, an Irish Catholic New Dealer, ran for state legislature on the Kennedy ticket in 1960. They burned a cross in his honor in Sioux Rapids, in the north end of the county. Neither Kennedy nor Dad won BV County. But we did briefly elect Democrats from Northwest Iowa in the post-Watergate wave of 1974. That is: Rural voters can be wooed, if you try and don't ignore them for three decades while NAFTA shut down Ohio.

Russell's buddy supervising the Mexican workers brought one of them to the bar. Carlos was said to be legal. But nobody saw his papers. Carlos was cool. It was the illegals who aren't. When you know a Latino, it's harder to hate him. So he must be legal. If you think there's an invasion going on, you are inclined to lock them in a cage at the border, except for the bunghole cutter if he doesn't raise a ruckus and talk up a union. It keeps everyone with their head down. And that's not how you build a rural community.

The police in Storm Lake say that their eyes and ears on the street among the immigrant community faded into the shadows over the Trump years. On Friday, their quieted voices started to emerge on Facebook— after the election, thinking they might now be safe from deportation with Trump finally emasculated. Yet much of the chatter in Wellsville and Storm Lake and Webster City dwelt on a stolen franchise, as Trump declared on TV the night before. The white guy scooping manure from a hog confinement building for $16 per hour just knows he got screwed like he always has. Two generations ago, he would have owned the hogs. Today, Wall Street or China Inc. does. We get the manure. It doesn't smell like money anymore. And the government is not here to help.

Everyone smells what is going on. Our rivers are thick with ag chemical pollution. Women know it gives them breast cancer, and farmers know it causes neurological disorders. We are losing our topsoil four to 10 times faster in the flat, black corn paradise of Iowa than nature can replenish it. Most of that black gold ends up in the Gulf of Mexico, where it is suffocating the fishing industry with a dead zone from ag fertilizer hypoxia the size of New Jersey. Extreme weather is our new normal. In 2019, tens of thousands of acres in southwest Iowa were scoured of soil by record flooding in the Missouri River. That land is lost forever to crop production. In 2020, western Iowa burned up with drought. Also, last summer a wind they called a derecho with speeds of more than 100 miles per hour ripped up at least 14 million acres of crops in Iowa. Nobody had seen anything like it. Then California and Colorado lit up with wildfires. They say we are in the beginning of a decades-long mega-drought unseen in the last millennium that will parch the Great Plains and Southwest. Phoenix and Las Vegas will have a hard time finding water. So will half the nation's cattle supply in huge feedlots spanning from Texas to Nebraska that will drink the Ogallala Aquifer dry within 20 years. Rural people, Democrat or Republican, are acutely aware of it. Yet they voted overwhelmingly for a man who thinks climate change is a hoax.

How to break through to the disaffected, disenchanted rural white voter who wants to "own the libs" and thinks Democrats are just out to pick his pocket with higher taxes and welfare? Buy them. It's what FDR did with the New Deal during times as trying as these.

That's what Trump did too. He saved his hide in Iowa, ultimately, and nearly in Wisconsin by pouring more than $100 billion into ag disaster subsidies over the past four years (disasters of his making). Trump flags flew proudly from the harvesters that swept up our corn crop last month. Socialism? Government payments now account for about half of farm income. What if we used that money to save soil rather than giant food conglomerates that control almost every acre of production in this nation?

What if President-elect Biden foiled his foes by going big—moonshot big—on making agriculture more resilient through massively increased conservation payments already built into the farm bill? And, what if he joined it with a renewable energy revolution that offered $75,000-per-year wind or solar technician jobs alongside fracking? David Wilhelm, a major Democratic player, is trying to sprout solar in Appalachian Ohio.

What if his efforts were massively ramped up by a bipartisan coalition led by Biden?

Iowa and Texas produce more wind energy than any state. Senator Grassley claims himself to be the "father of wind energy." These two notoriously red rural states also lead the country in renewable fuels production. How can Senate Majority Leader Mitch McConnell oppose increased hemp production in Kentucky, which he has championed, going into an entirely new renewable fuel industry that can supplant coal jobs in Harlan County while restoring income lost to tobacco farmers?

Both the conservative Farm Bureau and the progressive Farmers Union support paying farmers for environmental services. Planting grass on grazed pasture can sequester carbon and improve food production, while cutting down on agricultural pollution. We are growing so much corn we have to beg foreigners to buy it just to keep the chemical companies flush—why not plant grass in its place? Despite this year's drought, my farmer friend Ron Rosmann in southwest Iowa brought in an organic corn yield of 175 bushels per acre—right in line with his neighbors who farm with chemicals, except Ron fetches twice as much for his chemical-free crop than an agri-chemical grower does. Why doesn't everyone? "Propaganda," Rosmann said Thursday during a dour election postmortem somehow instilled with hope. Composting his hog and cattle manure eliminates dangerous methane emissions. He has two sons farming with him. They sell a lot of organic popcorn. They make money, though Ron is loath to admit it. He is a Democrat. His Republican farmer friend Ray Gaessner, who ran for state secretary of agriculture, is in common cause for a more sustainable agriculture. They can agree. Could their party leaders for the sake of rural areas, for the sake of national unity, for the sake of the planet?

Biden told me nearly a year ago during a pre-caucus interview that really muscling up ag conservation and renewable energy investments can bring the sort of high-paying jobs that keep rural sons and daughters from their otherwise inevitable exodus to the Twin Cities or Chicago. (We call it our brain drain.) Smaller, more diverse livestock operations can support smaller, more diverse food processing operations that are not so susceptible to collapse as the big packers were last spring. (Three packers control 80 percent of our nation's beef supply, and one of them, JBS, is domiciled in Brazil. The nation's largest pork company, Smithfield

Foods, is owned by a Chinese agribusiness giant.) Grassley has been a vocal supporter of anti-trust enforcement against ag conglomerates. He chairs the Senate Finance Committee and sits on the Agriculture Committee.

Several surveys of rural voters, liberal and conservative, show support for increased water quality and for natural resource conservation. It all depends on how you frame the question. If you ask: "Shall we eliminate oil production and make diesel for your pickup more expensive?" you have already put yourself out of the conversation. If you ask: "Should we incentivize ag conservation?" nearly every rural voter will agree, including Grassley and Ernst and Ohio's Democratic Senantor Sherrod Brown. Or, "Can we build a better electric car in Ohio than you can in China?" and everyone will answer in stereo: "Hell yes."

Joe Biden is positioned to ask those questions and pose those moon-shot challenges. He emphasized unity in a speech in Gettysburg a month before the election. "We can do anything if we put our minds to it," Biden said.

Our civic society depends on bringing everyone along, rural and urban, Black and Anglo and Latino and Asian, men and women, Republican and Democrat. How to break through the noise that shrouds the hate? How do we bring along those people left behind by the great coastal economic juggernaut, from Iowa to Ohio? It's an important question for Democrats to answer, but it is more important for a nation that hopes to heal its wounds left gaping since the Civil War.

The wildfires, droughts and derechos have no regard for our division except to flourish in it. We can save the Gulf of Mexico. We can feed a burgeoning world population. We can restore hope off the beaten path through new jobs built around clean water, clean air and prosperous rural communities from Appalachia to the Great Plains. Making America Great Again was a powerful appeal. So is: "We can do anything if we set our minds to it." Biden has two years at the outside to begin to heal the rift by proving that government can solve big problems. None is bigger. The question is whether Rural America will listen anymore, the noise is so loud. That's why the relief of Trump not being in my face is not enough.

Los Angeles, CA

SOPHIA LEAR is a television writer.

I KNOW NOTHING

BY SOPHIA LEAR

I grew up in an age when history had plausibly ended. Story was done. Events would happen—but they wouldn't count as story. World history as Shakespearean comedy—fading into domestic squabbles after the curtain drops. That theory didn't pan out, but it points at something I think about as a TV writer all the time—what is the difference between event and story? We are living in a national narrative crisis. The same events are different stories.

We have all found our echo chambers in this time. My mom's is *The New York Times* and she doesn't know it. Mine is my boyfriend, and the "Red Scare" podcast, two Russian-immigrant girls who shit on neoliberal hypocrisy. It was recommended to me by a writers' assistant on a show I worked on, who told me about it in hushed tones after I voiced some dissent to what I found a stifling rote liberal political discussion.

(I remember a co-worker, not looking up from Twitter, casually remarking that anyone who is religious is an idiot; and all Trump voters are dumb, racist idiots. The crudeness of the argument didn't bother me—it was that there was no argument at all—these statements were assumptions, beliefs taken for granted as shared. I will indulge in the Republican "I have a daughter" trope, to say: My step-dad is a practicing Catholic. My step-mom's parents are Trump voters. They are kind, serious people. They are not stupid.)

For the past few months, my boyfriend and I often drive to Malibu to go fishing. We did not fish before. But now we do. Malibu beaches are technically public, but the residents would prefer they weren't, so the entrances are made as inconspicuous as possible. Part of the fun is finding the secret passageways, hidden in plain sight. Fishing off the beach in Malibu is an odd thing to do. The early-morning dog walkers and joggers, emerging from their multimillion-dollar properties, eyes still crusty from sleep, do not know what to make of us. Nor do the hottest people I have ever seen, playing beach volleyball. They are bemused at the sight of us. When we catch a fish, they are shocked: What was a passive setting suddenly jolts to life—hinting at a world pulsing with needs and action other than their own. We recognize our privilege—the Filipino fishermen who are our compatriots at other spots, digging up live sand crabs to use as bait, would probably get a different reaction.

The drive to Malibu takes about 30 minutes, and our echo chamber is never louder or more enjoyable than on these rides. We rail against the left's endless ability to be outraged. We gasp at the insanity of whatever Trump did that day. We commend his innate showmanship. We bemoan the distortion of all political debate. We imitate the odd pauses and grunts of the host of "The Daily" podcast. We marvel at how no one has ever really gotten to the bottom of how Trump achieves his orange glow. Seriously, how has this not leaked? Who are his makeup people? And then we land on Charlottesville, or some other atrocity, and touch on the stakes of what we were living through. And then we would fish, on a beach in Malibu where no one fishes, as dolphins leaped and pelicans swooped and the sun set wildly.

No one on Zoom understands. Do you keep the fish? No. We ate a perch once and it was mushy. So you throw them back? Yep. Oh.

In New Haven, Connecticut, my mom put up her Black Lives Matter sign, her Biden sign. It mattered to her to do so, but everyone around agreed with her, so it wasn't very exciting. But in Branford, Connecticut, on the shoreline of the Long Island Sound, my mom has a little cottage. It is a source of great peace and comfort, the cottage. And on her walks around the neighborhood she noticed two Trump signs. She started to monitor the signs, as if someone had assigned her to keep a meticulous daily log. Wednesday: Both signs still present. No additional signs spotted. She weighed carefully how to respond, and landed on a sign with an abstract image of Trump's head—basically an orange circle, with a slick of yellow hair—and the word "Nope" beneath it. My mother was pleased with this. But still, she monitored. The house with the largest Trump sign was up on a hill, set among a dramatic display of vintage tractors and hay bales. My mom fantasized about sneaking up there, under the cover of night, and covering this huge Trump sign with Biden stickers. A week before the election, a new sign appeared at the tractor house: "The price on ammo is up, so I don't do warning shots." My mom was very upset by this sign: Why? Who was this sign for? What was it trying to do? I offered that if it was trying to deter liberal busybodies from trespassing, it seemed to be doing its job perfectly. She laughed. She researched the owner of the property—an 89-year-old retiree who once ran an excavating company. My mom was somewhat comforted by the knowledge he wouldn't be with us for long.

The day of the election, I was on Zoom, writing for a network sitcom in which neither Covid nor Trump exist. When work ended, I left the garage-slash-office and joined my boyfriend and his two young sons in the house. We all moved in together in August, and in doing so I became in effect a step-mom to a four-year-old and an eight-year-old.

We had watched the NBA championship, the World Series, the elder boy determined to parse all the stats on the screen—shot clocks, RBIs, pitch counts—so when I turned on CNN at 4:30 p.m. he gamely took on the CNN scoreboard: 97 percent for Biden! Wooo! I had to point to the other numbers on the screen—3 percent reporting, a county of only a few thousand. We had to pace ourselves, I told him. But he kept on cheering, giddy with excitement.

As we went through our evening routine, a bleakness slowly descended. The eight-year-old had given up on cheering. My text thread of friends were ... worried. CNN talking heads seemed to be entering a boggy twilight zone, unsure of what was happening, yammering away over a creeping existential dread. My friend—who would know these things—said Trump was going to win. I tried to maintain my cheer until the boys went to bed.

And then they went to bed and my boyfriend and I looked at each other. This was happening. Trump was going to win the election. We paced, full of adrenaline. What do we do? How do we tell the boys? We were horrified, but slowly another feeling bubbled up—like in the aftermath of a bad earthquake. Everything is destroyed, everything is in rubble, but you are alive, your family is alive, and you feel a primal pulse from deep within—we will survive this. Here's what we do, I said, with unearned clarity: Everyone is talking about moving out of the country, but what we do is, we move *in*. Nebraska, Montana, wherever, the point is, everyone else is going out, we go in. For some reason this idea comforted us. We fell asleep for a few fitful hours.

By the morning, the fever-dream had broken, the world was precarious but perhaps righted. We were the couple who mistook fireworks for gunshots and dropped to the floor in terror. We were a bit embarrassed. We dusted ourselves off.

In popular culture, kids are portrayed as making life a chaotic mess. Harried moms in commercials leaning on a newfangled mop, taking a moment to blow the hair out of her eyes, resigned but charmed as kids blow past her, tracking in mud and spilling chocolate milk.

In my limited experience, yes, there are Cheerios smushed in the couch. Tiny pajamas strewn everywhere, conveying the energy of the little body that hurled them off. But in general I find living with kids to be actually a very civilizing force. On Wednesday, after the boys left for their mom's house, I quickly descended into a whiskey-fueled CNN/MSNBC/Fox fugue state. I showered too little. I ate too much, or not enough. I thought about John King's home life. It is not a long stretch to say I went mad.

I was raised in a home with no TVs, and my boyfriend was raised in a home with TVs in every room that were never turned off, and this difference in upbringing showed. I found him standing inches away from the TV, watching talking heads on mute, a comforted smile on his face. I felt physically tortured by the experience of watching it, and I could not bear to turn it off.

So I was relieved when the boys returned on Friday. I showered. I decided to stop drinking for the weekend. I turned off the churning Key Race Alerts of Nothing from Nowhere. Biden was going to win. I put my phone down. My boyfriend made pork ribs for dinner. I asked the eight-year-old how he felt about the election. He said, "I feel fortunate and excited that Biden is going to win the presidency."

On Saturday morning I didn't look at my phone right away, so it was only after I had made my tea, and cuddled with the boys, that I discovered the race had been called for Biden. It was a text from my mom: "Are you up, sweet face? BIDEN IS THE PRESIDENT-ELECT! We can start again. I feel such a heavy weight sloughing off me." Later, I got a text from my dad, "Rather good news!" And later, my boyfriend told me his 95-year-old Nana was "literally throwing up" she was so upset about Biden's win.

On hearing the news, the eight-year-old wanted to bang pots and pans, so I fetched them for him. Outside, it was unusually cold and windy, and despite our diehard liberal neighborhood, eerily silent. I watched as he banged away into the quiet morning of Mar Vista, California, while across the country, in New Jersey, his great-grandmother, distraught, retched. And I felt a wave of sadness come over me.

My friends, who I leapfrogged into parenthood, sent pictures of themselves in Washington Square Park, screaming in joy, a Champagne bottle duct-taped to one hand. I couldn't access that joy. If I had been there, I probably would have felt joy—the collective outpouring would have stirred me, and that made me sad, too. That my reaction could be so contingent.

In the days between Election Night and the race being called, my mom put up an American flag on her lawn. The next day, she added a homemade sign, the lettering carefully alternating in red and blue: "One Nation. Indivisible. With Liberty and Justice for all!"

I drove to get a haircut, in Beverly Hills, which was boarded up, and cruised past a Trump rally. I felt lost.

But there was one moment I did not feel lost. Pacing our bedroom on Tuesday night, wild-eyed and frantic. Almost half the country wanted Donald Trump to be president. Again. We had almost digested 2016—people were upset, fine, they wanted to give a middle finger to the government, okay, if Trump is a toddler his voters were teenagers—petulant and acting out. But this was different—this was almost half the country saying they made no mistake, they liked what they saw, they wanted it again. It stunned me. I think most of the people who voted for Trump are not idiots, and they are not, at least consciously, interested in hurting others. For one moment it smacked me in the face—I know nothing. I know nothing of what is happening in this country. Everything I thought I knew fell away—and I was left humbled and curious. We have to go in. There is something big we don't understand. And we need to go in.

The liberal mistake is the certainty our story is true—that the others will come to see our story as theirs, too, and the rest are just beyond salvation. There is another story. I don't know what it is. I do not know where we go from here, because I have no idea where "here" is. And that, perhaps, is a place to start.

ABOUT WELLSTONE BOOKS

Wellstone Books is the publishing arm of the Wellstone Center in the Redwoods — **www.wellstoneredwoods.org** – a small writers' retreat center in Northern California founded in 2012 by Sarah Ringler and Steve Kettmann. WCR offers writing residencies, fellowships and three-month resident internships for aspiring writers, and hosts periodic Author Talk events with writers like Mary Roach, Cara Black, Jonathan Franzen and Viet Thanh Nguyen. Wellstone Books does not accept unsolicited manuscripts, but we are always looking for writers who are familiar with our publishing philosophy and want to work with us to develop future projects. Interested writers, or journalists in search of review copies or author availability, write to: **steve@wellstoneredwoods.org.**

ALSO AVAILABLE FROM WELLSTONE BOOKS

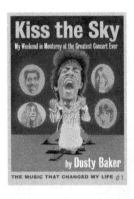

Kiss the Sky: My Weekend in Monterey at the Greatest Concert Ever

BY **DUSTY BAKER**

For his eighteenth birthday, Dusty Baker's mother gave him a great present: Two tickets to the Monterey Pop Festival of June 1967, a three-day event featuring more than thirty bands, and use of the family station wagon for the weekend so young Dusty could drive down from Sacramento to the Monterey Bay. He was another young person, trying to take it all in, sleeping on the beach with his buddy, having the time of his life soaking up the vibe and every different musical style represented there. Baker's lifelong love of music was set in motion, his wide-ranging, eclectic tastes, everything from country to hip-hop. He also caught the Jimi Hendrix Experience, who put on such a show that to this day Baker calls Hendrix the most exciting performer he's ever seen. He went on to years of friendship with musicians from B.B. King and John Lee Hooker to Elvin Bishop. This account grabs a reader from page one and never lets up.

"At its best, the book evokes not only the pleasure of music, but the connection between that experience and the joy of sports," NewYorker.com writes.

"Reading *Kiss the Sky* is like having a deep conversation with Dusty Baker – about baseball, fathers and sons, race, culture, family, religion, politics – and always music," says Joan Walsh of MSNBC. "He doesn't sugarcoat anything, but he makes you feel good about being alive nonetheless."

#1 in Wellstone Books' "Music That Changed My Life" series.

ACKNOWLEDGEMENTS

We'd like to thank the networks for eventually getting around to calling the 2020 presidential race for Joe Biden and Kamala Harris, only days late. This project was already well along at that stage and the in-built drama, we hope, adds to the sense of these essays offering a valuable kaleidoscope portrait of a strange and inscrutable moment in U.S. history. We want to thank all 38 contributors, from established authors and commentators who leaned into the challenge with evident glee and panache, to younger writers who offered surprising forays deep into the why and how of now, to public figures who lent their voices and took us unexpected places. (And if we can get Hillary Clinton and J-L Cauvin's mom on a Skype call, so much the better.)

Huge thanks to the power duo of Alicia Feltman of Lala Design and Pete Danko of the *Portland Business Journal*, the backbone of this project in so many ways. Alicia helped us through a brutal publishing schedule with good cheer and upwelling creativity; Pete stayed sharp and thoughtful, doing his best to speed-copy-edit even on days when he'd already reported and written four—yes, *four*—PBJ stories. Thanks also to Aaron Hobbs and Angela Maclean and the whole team at Ingram/PGW, who were quick to embrace the concept for this book and scrambled to make it happen. Special thanks as well to Mark Ulriksen, for gamely writing an essay as well as providing our cover, and to contributors (and would-be contributors) who also proofed pages and made valuable suggestions: Jacob Heilbrunn, Bronwen Hruska, Michael Shapiro, Elaine Luria, Christopher Buckley, Mary C. Curtis, Hussein Ibish, Pedro Gomez, Kuji Chahal and Antonia Hitchens.

CPSIA information can be obtained
at www.ICGtesting.com
Printed in the USA
LVHW021701101220
673828LV00002B/2